WORLD WAR 4

Nine Scenarios

CAPTAIN DOUGLAS ALAN COHN, USA (RET.)

Guilford, Connecticut

An imprint of Rowman & Littlefield

Distributed by NATIONAL BOOK NETWORK

British Library Cataloguing in Publication Information available

Library of Congress Cataloging-in-Publication Data
Names: Cohn, Douglas, author.
Title: World War 4 / Douglas Alan Cohn.
Description: Guilford, Connecticut : Lyons Press, [2016] | Includes bibliographical references and index.
Identifiers: LCCN 2016007521 (print) | LCCN 2016007794 (ebook) | ISBN 9781493018772 (hardcover) | ISBN 9781493023738 (e-book)
Subjects: LCSH: War—Forecasting. | Twenty-first century—Forecasts.
Classification: LCC U21.2 .C63 2016 (print) | LCC U21.2 (ebook) | DDC 355.0201/12—dc23
LC record available at http://lccn.loc.gov/2016007521

♾™ The paper used in this publication meets the minimum requirements of American National Standard for Information Sciences—Permanence of Paper for Printed Library Materials, ANSI/NISO Z39.48-1992.

CONTENTS

I. INTRODUCTION

    War planners must envision the unexpected and plan for
    the improbable.

II. SCENARIOS

    It began between allies, not enemies, in seemingly
    unconnected events.

    Much of the expansionist work of both communist and
    tsarist Russia disappeared with the demise of the Soviet
    Union. That Russians and their leaders would seek to
    reverse this situation should not come as a surprise, and in
    many respects the parallel with early American history is
    not lost on them.

    No nation has risen as far as fast as early twenty-first-
    century China, an accomplishment it achieved by
    embracing capitalism in an authoritarian command-control
    economy, supplanting, in the process, communism with a
    form of fascism that far outpaced its predecessor example:
    Germany in the 1930s.

Notes on the Text

1. British spellings are not altered.
2. Quotes retain original spelling and grammar; sources are in the endnotes.

FOREWORD

WE CANNOT PREDICT THE FUTURE, BUT WE MUST ANTICIPATE IT. THIS is what political and military leaders, ably supported by the expertise of war planners, regularly do. This is what I did as the commanding general of the US Army Intelligence and Security Command and as the director of the Defense Intelligence Agency. And this is what Captain Douglas Cohn has masterfully accomplished with his multiscenario analysis of potential threats and consequences.

The meticulous weaving together of history, politics, geography, and military knowledge takes the reader through logical progressions of the possible. It is a push-pull endeavor. Initiated and devised by the writer, events are allowed to take on their own realities, drawing each conflict to a plausible conclusion.

Yet, hope prevails. During his out-of-office Wilderness Years, Winston Churchill warned of the threats posed by fascism in the 1930s, and his dire concerns proved to be devastatingly prescient. However, had his ominous blueprints of the coming conflagration been believed, all might have been prevented.

We defend the nation by divining the future. This is a multidiscipline endeavor, and it is rare to see them encompassed in one work as they are here. Threats are exposed and outcomes are described, but implicit in each is the knowledge that anticipatory scenarios contain within them the seeds of countermeasure solutions.

Lt. Gen. Harry E. Soyster, USA (Ret.)
Former Director of the Defense Intelligence Agency

PART I

INTRODUCTION

Introduction

IF IN 1921 A PROGNOSTICATOR HAD PREDICTED JAPAN WOULD WITHIN two decades attack the US Pacific Fleet at Pearl Harbor and a racist Austrian corporal would rise to become Germany's chancellor, shunting aside President Paul von Hindenburg, the country's renowned World War I field marshal, and thereafter commence a suicidal war and religious holocaust, who would have believed such scenarios possible?

Indeed, many conflicts in human history defied prediction by more than a few years. At what point were the American and French Revolutions considered possible, let alone probable? When were the Cold War (World War III), the Korean and Vietnam Wars anticipated if at all? Were Iraq and Afghanistan even considered spheres of sufficient national interest to commit American armed forces years before they first consumed American blood and treasure?

For these reasons war planners envision the unexpected and plan for the improbable. The political and religious institutions of mankind are not static and often not even cumulative because learned lessons tend to diminish in direct relationship to the number of generations that pass, there being no foolproof safeguards to protect people from the follies of their ignorance.

Because big events often spring from small or obscure occurrences and at other times from barely noticeable glacial evolutions, each scenario here should be viewed in these contexts and accordingly judged upon their logical—or illogical in the case of irrational enemies—progression of possibilities flowing not only from initial premises, but in particular from the overriding premise of this book: mutually assured survival (MAS), a concept running counter to the prevailing thoughts and theories notably advanced in 1921 by Italian Gen. Giulio Douhet in *The Command of the Air*:

> *No longer can areas exist in which life can be lived in safety. . . . On the contrary, the battlefield will be limited only by the boundaries of the nations at war, and all of their citizens will become combatants, since all of them will be exposed to the aerial offensives of the enemy. There will be no distinction any longer between soldiers and civilians.*

World War I and World War II shook and shaped the first half of the twentieth century, but in the span of four midsummer days, atomic bombs reconfigured the future, deterring major conflagrations while simultaneously making the world safe for limited wars, regional and worldwide. "Chapter III, Historical Perspective: The Atomic Bomb— Weapon of War, Deterrent of War, or Limiter of War" provides a review and analysis of the debates leading up to those world-changing nuclear attacks of August 6 and 9, 1945, events that would impact leadership decision making around the globe ever after. Those discussions, rooted in Douhet's concept of strategic bombing, were taken up by many of World War II's air-arm generals, and the concept remains a euphemism for the bombing of cities to destroy militarily important industries while undermining civilian morale. It was the failure of this theory that made succeeding limited war scenarios possible.

Those twentieth century theories of total war are being rendered obsolete by the twenty-first century's nuclear-enforced concept of limited war. As the two centuries were turning, limited wars fought by great-power surrogates had already been conducted under the nuclear umbrella of mutually assured destruction (MAD), but, in the future, with mutual acceptance of national survival in place, mutually assured survival wars could be waged directly between nuclear powers without introducing nuclear weapons. Of course, as in the Cold War, this presupposes rationality on the part of nuclear-nation leaders.

This should not be confused with MAS scenarios predicated on missile defenses such as Israel's Iron Dome, Arrow 2 and 3, Iron Beam, and David's Sling systems, the difference being that manmade defenses may only protect one side in a conflict and are always subject to failure or circumvention, whereas mutual guarantees of national survival are grounded in self-interest. As a result, anti-missile systems should be viewed as secondary lines of defense, with first-line reliance being placed upon MAS.

In sum, belligerents' mutual assurances of survival will forestall the use of nuclear weapons and make the world safe for limited world wars, horrible though they may be.

In a 2010 speech, Admiral Giampaolo di Paola, chairman of the NATO Military Committee, addressed the evolving nature and variety of twenty-first-century geopolitical challenges facing the world's great powers, and with prescient fatalism, he anticipated the 2015–16 terrorist attacks in Paris and Brussels:

> *The efforts of terrorist networks to recruit and train individuals to carry out attacks in NATO or partners' countries show no signs of abating. . . . In the future NATO will have to deal with asymmetric threats often aimed at NATO's populations or economic communications and infrastructure assets rather than territory as such. . . .*
>
> *Globalization has made irreversible the flow of goods, services, people, technology and ideas but also of crime and weapons to which open democratic societies will remain vulnerable. Such threats may be directed at the territory of Allies or at their citizens, economic systems, energy supplies, infrastructure or troops in operations. In the longer term, climate change could exacerbate long standing global problems such as poverty, hunger, illegal immigration and pandemic disease.*
>
> *Cyber-attacks are among the challenges that require special attention and effort, as these attacks have become more organized and costly in that they can cause severe damage to national administrations, businesses, economies and infrastructures.*

This and more are contemplated in the nine scenarios of World War 4.

PART II
SCENARIOS

World War 4: The Post-NATO War

In Europe, we remain steadfast in our commitment to our NATO allies. NATO provides vital collective security guarantees and is strategically important for deterring conflict, particularly in light of recent Russian aggression on its periphery. U.S. Operation ATLANTIC RESOLVE [see Appendix B], our European Reassurance Initiative, NATO's Readiness Action Plan . . . serve to underline our dedication to alliance solidarity, unity, and security. . . .

Denying an adversary's goals . . . puts emphasis on maintaining highly-ready, forward-deployed forces . . .

—The United States Military's Contribution to
National Security, June 2015
Courtesy US Department of Defense
(See Appendix A for the complete transcript)

Scenario 1 Acronyms
Financial Acronyms
ECB: European Central Bank
EZ: Euro Zone (nations that replaced their currencies with the euro)
Fed: US Federal Reserve System of regional Federal Reserve Banks
GDP: Gross Domestic Product (a nation's output of goods and services)
NCB: National Central Bank

Military Acronyms
AWACS: Airborne Warning and Control System
NATO: North Atlantic Treaty Organization
OODA Loop: Observe, Orient, Decide, Act

National Acronyms
CEU: Central European Union (predicted entity)
EU: European Union
UK: The United Kingdom of England, Scotland, Wales, and Northern Ireland
USSR: The Union of Soviet Socialist Republics (the Soviet Union—the Communist Russian Empire)

Map 1: Member countries in gray (United States and Canada off map)
MAP AND DEPLOYMENTS COURTESY OF NATO

Treaty Acronyms
CFE: Treaty on Conventional Armed Forces in Europe
UNCLOS: The 1994 United Nations Convention on the Law of the Sea

> *At its origin, the organization's goal, as famously stated by Lord Ismay, the first NATO Secretary General, was "to keep the Russians out, the Americans in, and the Germans down."*
> —ADMIRAL GIAMPAOLO DI PAOLA

NATO FINANCES
In 2015 Steven Erlanger reported in the *New York Times*:

> *There will be pressure from the United States for NATO members to live up to their pledge to spend 2 percent of gross domestic product*

Chart 1: NATO Deployments

Region	Deployment
Iceland	NATO fighter aircraft
Latvia, Estonia, and Lithuania	NATO aircraft
Albania and Slovenia	NATO aircraft
Germany	E-3A "Sentry" Airborne Warning and Control System (AWACS) aircraft deployed over Poland and Romania
Kosovo	NATO-led Kosovo Force
Turkey	Patriot anti-missile batteries
Mediterranean Sea	NATO's Operation Active Endeavour vessels patrol shipping lanes
Ethiopia	NATO strategic air and sea-lift support for the African Union
Arabian Sea	NATO's Operation Ocean Shield combats piracy
Afghanistan	NATO's Operation Resolute Support provides training and support

on defense, as Britain finally agreed to do this year [2015]. "I hope that will be welcomed in Washington," said British Defense Secretary Michael Fallon. . . .

But the United States still accounts for some 75 percent of all NATO military spending; Germany, for example, spends only about 1.3 percent of GDP [gross domestic product] on defense.

Mr. Fallon noted that while only five members [the United States, the United Kindgom, Poland, Greece, Estonia] currently spend 2 percent, seven more have increased their military spending since the events

Chart 2: NATO (in bold), European Union (EU), and Non-EU Countries

Euro (€) EU Countries	Non-Euro (€) EU Countries	Non-EU European Countries	Non-European NATO Countries
Austria	**Bulgaria**	**Albania**	**Canada**
Belgium	**Croatia**	Belarus	**United States**
Cyprus	**Czech Republic**	Bosnia	
Estonia	**Denmark**	**Iceland**	
Finland	**Hungary**	Kosovo	
France	**Poland**	Macedonia	
Germany	**Romania**	Moldova	
Greece	Sweden*	**Montenegro****	
Ireland	**United Kingdom**	**Norway**	
Italy		Serbia	
Latvia		Switzerland	
Lithuania		**Turkey**	
Luxembourg		Ukraine	
Malta			
Netherlands			
Portugal			
Slovakia			
Slovenia			
Spain			

* Russian provocations in the Baltic Sea have given Sweden cause to consider NATO membership.
** Despite Russian objections, Montenegro was invited to join NATO in December 2015. Although not an EU member, the country uses the euro without EU authorization.

in Ukraine and the last summit meeting in 2014, citing France, Poland, Norway, the Czech Republic, Lithuania, Latvia and Romania.

The war will begin between allies, not enemies, in seemingly unconnected events. The trends have long been there, encapsulated in the words and phrases of dissension: disunion, devolution, national identity, ethnicity, currency, culture, popular sovereignty, secession, religion, language, and more. It will be a war of mind-numbing complexity.

2010–2017

As an uncomprehending world watches Europeans play Grexit—their quaint acronym for a peer-over-the-precipice game of money, wills, and odds that sooner or later is expected to force a Greek exit (Grexit) from the European Union (EU) and/or from the Euro Zone (EZ), its currency union—the war will begin in Belgium, one of those contrived countries carved out of other countries without regard for ethnicities or languages. The Dutch-speaking Flemish in the prosperous northern region of Flanders and the less affluent French-speaking Walloons in Wallonia to the south have never bridged their differences, while many Arabic-speaking North African immigrants live apart in enclaves such as the Molenbeek-Saint-Jean district in Brussels. Eventually, events elsewhere in Europe and the Middle East are going to finally force a separation between them. All this was ominously apparent during the 2010 government crisis when secessionist cries erupted in the Belgian Parliament: "Long live free Flanders, may Belgium die."

Chams Eddine Zaouguin of the Flemish newspaper *De Standaard* wrote:

Dutch-speaking Flemings and the French-speaking Walloons . . . live completely apart.

This also leads to administrative dysfunction: Belgium has no less than six governments: a federal government, a Flemish government for the Flanders region, a government of the French community, a government of the German-speaking community, a government of the Walloon region and a government of the Brussels-Capital Region. . . .

> *Brussels . . . is governed like a small city-state—with 19 dis-*
> *tricts, each with its own mayor, and six police authorities, which only*
> *reluctantly work together, and sometimes not at all. Political distrust*
> *between mayors from different parties or between rich and poor city*
> *districts sometimes translates into a total lack of communication and*
> *coordination.*

"The country operates on the basis of linguistic apartheid," wrote Ian Traynor for the *Guardian*. "Brussels is French-speaking, surrounded by Dutch-speaking municipalities. . . . This makes suburban Brussels the battleground, for the capital is the only officially bilingual bit of Belgium. . . . There are no national political parties, no national newspaper, no national TV channel, no common school curriculum or higher education. If push came to shove, the preferred option would be velvet divorce as in Czechoslovakia, rather than Yugoslav violence."

But preferences are not reality. The sides are too drawn. And home-grown, ISIS-directed terrorist attacks made matters worse as faith in the government deteriorated with each side concluding that the country's inherent disunity was leading to official disarray. Unlike the peaceful breakup of Czechoslovakia in 1993, Belgium is going to come apart in low-level conflict.

Void will play upon void, beginning with the collapse of the euro, a currency built upon the erroneous concept that the nations of Europe could manage their own fiscal policies of taxation, borrowing, and spending without controlling their own monetary policies, especially the expansion and contraction of money supply. An equivalent scenario would have the world witness the United States' Federal Reserve surrendering control of its monetary policy to the Frankfurt-based European Central Bank (ECB), the Governing Council of which is comprised of the ECB's Executive Board and one member each from the EZ countries' national central banks (NCBs). In such an arrangement, the United States, like Greece and the other NCBs, would be relegated to one inconsequential vote.

When the Great Recession of 2007–08 struck, halving the stock market and driving real estate values below mortgage balances, US

Federal Reserve Chairman Ben Bernanke convinced a majority of the Reserve members to flood the market with electronic money in what was called quantitative easing. That action plus congressional legislation prevented a depression. However, if the ECB had been in control and instituted the opposite policy of money tightening—as it has to the chagrin of member nations with weak economies—there is no telling what financial disasters might have ensued.

Just such tightening has created turmoil in Europe, especially with Greece. On the other hand, believing the EU would never let a member nation spiral into the chasm of financial collapse, Greece failed to clamp down on its citizens' widespread practice of tax evasion, and the country spent without restraints that could have been imposed by its own central bank, the Bank of Greece, had it been independent of the ECB. So, on July 5, 2015, the EU and ECB demands were put to the ballot, and an overwhelming number of Greek voters said όχι (no) to austerity and belt-tightening. In particular, they said, όχι to Germany, the EU's financial behemoth. It has become increasingly apparent that when the EU or ECB speaks it is Germany speaking, and World War II and German militarism are not so distant in time that old animosities do not resurface with each new assertive dictate from Berlin.

In truth, neither Germany nor Greece is correct, hence the unwinnable game of Grexit continues to lure Europe into the abyss, though the Greeks were convinced to reverse their όχι vote—for the time being. However, both nations will discover this is not a simple-solutions game.

The EU's attempt to operate in a functionally inoperable system characterized by separate fiscal and monetary policies contrasts with the flexible and complex US system, where a constitutionally and congressionally coerced balance between the fiscal policies of Congress and the monetary policies of the Fed interact to create a structural solution capable of lessening the depth, breadth, and duration of financial depressions, deep recessions, and panics.

Greece, the EU, the ECB, and their game of Grexit also roiled the world's financial markets, causing the wide swings uncertainty engenders.

In response and with voices transcending political suasions, Nobel Prize–winning progressive economist Paul Krugman and conservative columnist George Will weighed in.

Krugman:

"Suppose that there were a way to end this depression. Then Greece's fiscal problems would melt away, with no need for further cuts. But is there any way to do that?

"The answer is, not as long as Greece remains in the euro. . . .

"On the other hand, Grexit would produce a rapid improvement in competitiveness, at the cost of possible financial chaos. This is not a route anyone has been willing to go down, but one does have to say that as the crisis worsens it becomes a more plausible outcome."

Will:

"Greece, with just 11 million people and 2 percent of the euro zone's GDP, is unlikely to cause a contagion by leaving the zone. If it also leaves the misbegotten European Union, this evidence of the EU's mutability might encourage Britain's 'euro-skeptics' when that nation has a referendum on reclaiming national sovereignty by withdrawing from the EU."

It is in this context that Greece or some other financially strapped nation, unable to meet its EU and ECB financial commitments, will first drop the euro as its currency and soon after drop out of the EU altogether, having realized that monetary and political sovereignty are too intertwined to do otherwise. True, the United Kingdom never did adopt the euro, and just as true, the United Kingdom has been a tepid member of the EU.

These events are certain to expose the underlying weakness of a common currency governed by a central multinational monetary body, the ECB, prompting other nations such as Spain and Portugal to follow the Grexit pathway, reverting to their old currencies while concurrently recreating national identities and economies of prior decades.

NATO, on the other hand, predated both the EU and the euro, but the United States–dominated alliance can only fail as it attempts to adapt to the new dynamic. The world has turned over many times since the end of World War II and the subsequent creation of NATO, an alliance perpetuated by its ability to recognize and counter new external and internal threats. This time, however, the NATO nations are going to be blindsided by Belgium as the move to divide that crucial country occurs simultaneously with the breakup of the EU and the demise of the euro. Indeed, as the European-wide turmoil feeds upon itself, Belgian dismantling is going to encourage other secessions from the EU just as those EU secessions circularly give impetus to Belgium's breakup into affluent, conservative Flanders and struggling, liberal Wallonia.

When the first crack in the EU does happen, the underlying conceptual weakness in the organization and its currency are going to become starkly apparent. And as goes the euro, so goes the EU. Currently nine of the twenty-eight EU nations do not use the euro (see chart on page 12 and the note regarding Montenegro), and the nineteen others are sure to follow. Overnight, economic nationalism is going to be followed by political nationalism. Abandoned border checkpoints were once again being manned by border guards in the wake of terrorist attacks in Paris and an influx of refugees from Syria and elsewhere. And the vanishing dream of a united Europe will impact nations and equally affect unassimilated ethnic groups whose movements press for devolution or secession in Spain and elsewhere.

Harvard professor Richard N. Rosencrance, who served on the State Department's Policy Planning Council, lamented: "The European Union strode forward with leaders such as [EU founding father] Jean Monnet, [former prime minister of France] Robert Schuman, [former president of the European Commission] Jacques Delors, and [former chancellor of West Germany] Helmut Schmidt, but the European coalition has suffered

"That Byzantine bureaucracy posturing as a confederacy."

under hesitant leadership since. There is no obvious cohort of future leaders that can manage existing institutions in the detail needed to avoid negative contingencies."

George Will succinctly described the disunity inherent in the EU, that Byzantine bureaucracy posturing as a confederacy: "The EU has a flag no one salutes, an anthem no one sings, a president no one can name, a parliament whose powers subtract from those of national legislatures, a bureaucracy no one admires or controls and rules of fiscal rectitude that no member is penalized for ignoring."

THE NEAR FUTURE

Year 1

The world and NATO are going to suddenly awaken to the disruption in Belgium, which they should have long anticipated. With NATO headquarters located there, and its capital, Brussels, being the de facto capital of the EU, the NATO nations have a vested interest in keeping the nation whole, although the effort could have the opposite effect. Despite pressures and incentives to the contrary, the central Belgian government will collapse, causing the Belgian presence in NATO and the EU to vanish, although the euro will be retained for lack of a viable government-minted alternative. As with Montenegro, this will transpire without the ECB's approval.

The populace, having no allegiance to a central Belgian government, is likely to have even less allegiance to NATO, an alliance dominated by foreign politicians, statesmen, and military officers. And the longer NATO attempts to maintain its headquarters in Brussels, the more estranged the local population may become from an organization pretending to deal with a country no longer in existence—or which many residents believe never existed in the first place.

Brussels is the largest diverse city in Belgium, a place where Flemish and Walloon citizens could have met and merged, but never did. Instead, for the most part they remained separated, and when the breakup begins and fighting starts, first in small-scale cross-neighborhood conflicts, and then in increasingly larger, coordinated actions, all could spin out of control for this nation that never should have been.

As fighting spreads in Belgium, undermining NATO and the EU, the fight to save the euro as a European-wide currency is certain to fail.

First Greece, then Spain and Portugal, followed by Italy, lacking any other choices, must revert to their old currencies followed by a fragmentation into a Southern Europe vs. Northern Europe split.

The Socialist Greek government, having reached a breaking point with its EU and euro partners over loan repayments, is likely to tilt the only other direction available, a direction signaled in 2015: toward Russia. This turn of events could prove to be far more significant than its departure from the EU, although strangely enough, Greece might attempt to also retain its NATO membership, if for no other reason than the financial benefits such an affiliation can bring through weaponry and the potential stationing of ground and air units and fleets. But NATO was formed as a counterweight to the Soviet Union and evolved into a bulwark against noncommunist, yet equally aggressive, Russia. Clearly, Greece will be unable to continue with one foot in each camp, though as events play out, the issue will become moot.

The impact of dramatic Southern European currency devaluations is going to leave the region's newly independent central banks no choice but to feed further devaluations through the increasingly larger issuances of Greek drachmas, Spanish pesetas, Portuguese escudos, and Italian lira, undermining the ability of those countries to meet their euro debt obligations to Northern European creditors.

Continuing their intransigent approach, it is conceivable that the EU president and the EU Parliament might actually debate the possibility of resorting to gunboat diplomacy to seize certain Southern European territory and assets as a means of forcing debt repayments. Although such a maneuver would be neither rational nor feasible, the mere fact of its consideration could only further alienate the region. In fact, in a 2015 move falling short of gunboat coercion, but provocative nonetheless, the German finance minister drafted a proposal calling for Greece to give the EU collateral and/or sell assets such as unspecified Greek islands, and part of this concept was actually adopted through the forced privatization of various properties. France and Italy objected, their leaders claiming it was humiliating Greece, and pedantically noting how, historically, national humiliations have not ended well.

As North-South animosities heat up and Southern European nations drop out of the EU, their attempt to form a separate union out of a financially weak coalition is going to be facing the stronger German-dominated union of the North as well as unaligned France in the middle (see Year 2, Week 8), even though that nation has been the strongest advocate of debt solution leniency.

Meanwhile, NATO's search for a new home must accelerate as Belgium divides and the EU dissolves. It will not be a simple search. France long ago forced NATO out of its headquarters near Paris, and a resurgent German military continues to concern Europe and the world, a fact guaranteed to undermine that nation's bid to host Europe's preeminent defense establishment. Italy and Spain are unstable and will not be considered.

Then, in the midst of this search, internal dissensions caused by the euro's upheaval as well as ethnic devolution demands will begin to infect other nations in NATO, and they, too, can be expected to begin withdrawing troops from the coalition. Before long, NATO is going to become a near-empty shell, a US-led alliance comprised almost entirely of US forces, which had already accounted for nearly three-fourths of NATO's military personnel and equipment.

When NATO does come apart, like the EU, it may be expected to fragment into new coalitions, new unions, reluctant allies, nonparticipating allies, and individual nations along the following lines:

Chart 3: NATO Breakup

NATO Remnant	Germany's Central European Union	NATO-Disenfranchised Southern European Coalition
Canada	Czech Republic	Greece
United Kingdom	Germany	Italy
United States	Hungary	Portugal
	Luxembourg	Spain
	Netherlands	
	Slovakia	

Ex-NATO Nations	Eastern European	Ex-NATO
Belgium	**NATO Remnant**	**Chinese-Balkan Alliance**
France	Estonia	Albania
Turkey	Latvia	Bulgaria
	Lithuania	Croatia
Nonparticipating	Poland	Montenegro
Nordic NATO Remnant		Romania
Denmark		Slovenia
Iceland		
Norway		

(Note: Non-NATO Austria is likely to join the Central European Union.)

NATO was the great military alliance keeping the Cold War cold. But, with lightning speed it is going to all but disappear, creating a void greater than anyone anticipated, a void reverberating around the globe, generating unforeseen consequences, which taken together, will lure the world to war.

Year 2, Week 1

After Belgium comes apart and drops out of both the EU and NATO, the coalition's headquarters will move off the continent to the United Kingdom, leaving European unraveling to accelerate. Because NATO was primarily formed to safeguard continental Western Europe, the move will be far from ideal, the United Kingdom itself having long since left the EU, but it will be the only reliable choice for NATO headquarters as the EU dissolves and the euro disappears. Dissension and uncertainty shall rule the day.

Meanwhile, this steadfast American ally had been facing its own problems with the countries comprising the United Kingdom seeking greater autonomy through devolution. Not only were these movements active in varying degrees for Scotland, Wales, and Northern Ireland, but there was even a devolution movement in England. Further, the UK Army has been steadily declining toward a mere 80,000 or possibly 50,000 troops, making it one of the smaller armies in the world, let alone among the great powers, and its NATO commitments correspondingly dwindled. This appears to be in keeping with the post–World War I theories of Captain B. H. Liddell Hart, whose opinions, like those of so many others, had been molded by the shocking losses suffered in trench warfare. An early proponent of massed armor in fluid combat, he also advocated a return to Britain's eighteenth- and nineteenth-century naval-centric peripheral strategy with its reliance upon sea power to support small-army incursions on the peripheries of primary theaters of war.

In the midst of all this, Article 5 of the NATO Charter, the cornerstone of the alliance—an attack on one is an attack on all—will come into question. It has only been invoked once, following the terrorist attacks against the United States on September 11, 2001.

Article 5 of the NATO Charter

> *The Parties agree that an armed attack against one or more of them in Europe or North America shall be considered an attack against them all and consequently they agree that, if such an armed attack occurs, each of them, in exercise of the right of individual or collective self-defence recognised by Article 51 of the Charter of the United Nations, will assist the Party or Parties so attacked by taking forthwith, individually and in concert with the other Parties, such action as it deems necessary, including the use of armed force, to restore and maintain the security of the North Atlantic area.*

NATO's Eastern Europe remnant—Estonia, Latvia, Lithuania, and Poland—threatened externally by Russia and internally by Russian-supplied and Russian-incited dissidents, is certain to invoke the article, an event that can only hasten the breakup of NATO as one member nation after another hesitates or refuses to come to its aid, claiming the nations of that remnant were never full NATO members. Their arguments will not be without merit. According to the terms of NATO's May 27, 1997, agreement with Russia, no permanent NATO forces were to be stationed in those countries. It was a stunning concession, undermining the founding basis of NATO, an organization that had kept the Soviet Union at bay by doing just the opposite, notably in Germany, where the US Berlin Brigade acted as a trip-wire deterrent guaranteed to trigger US and NATO armed intervention if that city were attacked.

Specifically, the 1997 agreement stated: "[T]he member States of NATO and Russia will, together with other States Parties, seek to strengthen stability by further developing measures to prevent any potentially threatening build-up of conventional forces in agreed regions of Europe, to include Central and Eastern Europe."

With the Cold War ending and the Soviet Union collapsing, this agreement referenced the reduction-in-forces Treaty on Conventional Armed Forces in Europe (CFE), signed November 19, 1990. Russia abrogated that treaty in 2015 after NATO circumvented the 1997 agreement by rotating temporary units into the Baltics and Poland through Operation Atlantic Resolve (see Map 1 and Appendix B), a ploy Russia found to be disingenuous and provocative. The United States then went farther, stationing heavy weaponry in the Baltics against the wishes of other NATO members, especially Germany, and, as could be expected, the strong objections of Russia. The Russians reacted by beefing up their forces and commencing threatening air missions in the region despite the fact that Russian provocations in Ukraine had alarmed these nations in the first place.

Steven Erlanger wrote for the *New York Times* in December 2015:

One [Russian] exercise in March [2015] practiced an invasion of the Baltic States including the seizure of nearby territory from Finland, Denmark, Sweden and Norway, intended to show NATO how hard it would be to retake the Baltic nations, even under Article 5. . . .

Poland's new right-wing government is pushing for permanent deployments of NATO troops, preferably American, on Polish soil. But Washington and Britain still prefer what officials call "a persistent and continuous presence" of NATO troops under various national commands to a "permanent presence."

And Washington is not happy with loud calls by the Poles for nuclear weapons to be based in Poland, even if President Vladimir V. Putin of Russia talks more often than Soviet leaders used to about the possible use of tactical nuclear weapons.

Meanwhile, Ukraine, in the process of fending off Russian military incursions while seeking NATO membership, is going to be left out on a limb, Russia's for the taking unless the United States or another great power steps into the void created by NATO's developing implosion. Previously, the United States had delivered limited assistance under Operation Atlantic Shield, so limited it was not even addressed by Russia.

"The Law of Inverse Construction: An essential building block's benefit is asymmetrically outweighed by the repercussions from its failure or loss."

When the EU and, later, the EZ were created, it was thought these events would strengthen NATO by further unifying Europe, and, initially, this appeared to be the case. No one dreamed these very building blocks would one day be the instruments of NATO's demise, the EU and EZ founding fathers apparently not considering that the unraveling of those entities would create a sense of disunity that could spill over, infect, and undermine the alliance. But that is precisely what will happen. It is a phenomenon of what I will call the Law of Inverse Construction: An essential building block's benefit is asymmetrically outweighed by the repercussions from its failure or loss.

Year 2, Week 4

With Southern Europe falling into a depression caused by currency devaluations, the nations of the region are going to be unable to meet their NATO commitments, and NATO will threaten to expel them, with Germany being especially insistent. No official action is likely to be taken, but neither are those southern nations going to be briefed on or included in NATO operations, a stance creating de facto expulsion. Disenfranchised, and forced to look inward, they can be expected to form a Southern European Coalition, consisting of Greece (tentatively), Italy, Portugal, and Spain.

In the north, Denmark, Iceland, and Norway are going to remain as a Nordic NATO remnant, but, also in an act amounting to nothing less than de facto self-expulsion, they are not about to commit military forces to what they correctly perceive as a crumbling alliance.

Year 2, Week 8

Back in Belgium, where fighting between French-speaking Walloons and Dutch-speaking Flemish continues to heat up, the French will naturally support their linguistic soulmates just across the Franco-Belgian border, causing the Flemish in turn to seek aid from the Netherlands just over the Dutch-Belgian border. And the Flemish will go beyond, to Germany, for even greater, more dangerous war-escalating assistance. This then, will mark the end of the EU and European-wide NATO in one blow. Although France, the Netherlands, and Germany will not send troop units into Belgium, opting instead to feed in equipment and advisors, the continent's major powers will be allies no more.

Such surrogate fighting only serves to inflame animosities, and France, unwilling to continue in an alliance with a now-hostile Germany, will become the first major nation to abrogate its NATO treaty commitments and invoke Article 13 of the alliance's founding document, the 1949 North Atlantic Treaty: "After the Treaty has been in force for twenty years, any Party may cease to be a Party one year after its notice of denunciation has been given to the Government of the United States of America, which will inform the Governments of the other Parties of the deposit of each notice of denunciation."

France, like Russia, can rely upon its nuclear deterrent to ensure survival as an independent nation. And in that vein of military self-sufficiency, France will insist upon a waiver of Article 13's "one year" clause, but it is not going to be forthcoming. Instead, France will simply walk away, refusing to participate in NATO meetings or contribute troops and matériel to NATO operations as it comes to see itself as the India of the West: large, strong, nuclear, independent, and nonaligned.

Year 2, Week 12

Into this mix, the second-largest economy in the world, the People's Republic of China (Communist China), will suddenly make an appearance alongside a reestablished friend, Albania. They had been allies throughout most of the Cold War, having in common their break with the Soviet Union. Albania had continually pressed for UN recognition of the People's Republic of China in lieu of the Taiwan-based Republic of China, and their Resolution 2758 was finally passed in 1971, primarily due to US support following two secret missions to Beijing that year by Henry Kissinger, President Richard Nixon's national security advisor. Pakistan, another China friend, had laid the groundwork. When this was followed by Nixon's trip the next year to solidify the US-China rapprochement, the ardently doctrinaire Albanian communist government was so offended that its China relationship soured.

However, Sino-Albanian reconciliation counterintuitively improved following the collapse of Albania's communist government in 1992. The Soviet Union had broken apart, and both China and Albania were embracing capitalism.

In 2001 China financed Hydro Central, a major hydroelectric project in northern Albania, which was followed by other large infrastructure projects. And on July 28, 2015, the defense attaché of the Chinese Embassy, Senior Colonel Luo Tiefeng, speaking in Tirana, Albania, announced: "The Chinese-Albanian relations are developing rapidly, like our Ambassador Yu has declared. China is the third largest trade partner [of Albania] while more and more Chinese companies are coming here. Even Chinese-Albanian military relations are developing steady well."

This phenomenon was not unusual because the assumption that nations throwing off the yoke of communism would also discard their Cold War alliances proved not to be universal. Some of them did, and in the case of several Eastern European nations, including Albania, they even joined NATO. But others held fast to their old friends. In addition to the Albania-China relationship, post-communist Russia's inexplicable support of Syria's dictator, Bashar al-Assad, comes to mind.

In the current disarray, China will be able to exploit and expand its bond with Albania, initially by flooding the Albanian economy with desperately needed aid and investments, while the world's most ubiquitous currency next to the dollar, the Chinese renminbi, effectively replaces the disappearing euro and the devalued local currencies of the Balkan region.

This apparently stabilizing event is sure to impact the economic thinking of other Balkan nations as Chinese influence rapidly expands throughout the peninsula, creating in its wake an ex-NATO Chinese-Balkan Alliance—Greece being the exception as it finally makes the jump to the Russian sphere.

To facilitate this alliance, China will need to have open sea lanes to transport commercial equipment and personnel, to which the Chinese will add military equipment and troops in increasing numbers, all requiring an expanding Chinese naval presence (see Year 2, Week 20).

Year 2, Week 14

The Greek tilt to the East could not possibly be well received in Turkey, an ancient enemy of both Russia and Greece, particularly in light of Russian-Turkish estrangement following Turkey's downing of an intruding Russian warplane flying in support of Syria in 2016 and as a result of other encounters thereafter. Indeed, Greece and Turkey had only been NATO allies of convenience, and such alliances easily fall prey to old antagonisms of which there were many in the Greco-Turkish history, from ancient times up to actual fighting over Cyprus during the 1960s and 1970s.

Turkey will take the "null set" option, coyly playing all sides. Already isolated like France, Turkey is simply going to walk away from faltering NATO. However, unlike France, a nuclear power, and Greece, now aligned with Russia and its nuclear shield, Turkey is likely to insert itself into what the British called "the Great Game," its nineteenth-century geopolitical rivalry with Russia over Central Asia. Turkey will enter the game" by courting Pakistan, a fellow Muslim country, as a new nuclear patron to replace NATO and the United States. Then, in a major realignment of post–Cold War alliances comparable to Eastern Europe's earlier abandonment of Russia in favor of NATO, Turkey will take the strategy a step farther, opening a dialogue with China as an even more reliable nuclear ally than Pakistan. Although neither potential partner would be immediately essential as the current escalating conflict bypasses Turkey, this could quickly change, depending upon the attitudes and actions of Russia and Greece.

The primary NATO remnant, consisting exclusively of English-speaking nations, the United States, Canada, and the UK, is going to be ensconced in NATO's new London headquarters, reeling from its literal expulsion from the Continent. From Dover their leaders can peer across the English Channel at a Europe dissolving into medieval chaos, compressing those centuries and their actors as if both Russia's Ivan the Terrible and the Golden Horde of Mongolia were simultaneously descending on Eastern Europe while Western Europe self-destructs in internecine warfare. It would only remain for Turks and Moors to pour in from the southeast and south to complete the analogy.

In fact, the large Arabic population in France and the rising Turkish population in Germany, which at first glance appear to have no stake in Europe's unfolding events, are going to be an increasing factor. Driven in part by religion and in part by opportunity, these Muslim enclaves, fueled by immigration, are going to demand greater autonomy and political representation.

Almost any spark could ignite a worldwide conflagration with the collapse of the euro and subsequent depression in Southern Europe; with France, the Netherlands, and Germany at odds over Belgium; with Russia looming ever larger over Ukraine, Poland, and the Baltic States; with China opening a sphere of influence in the Balkans; with Turkey and Greece slipping back into old antagonisms; with Arab and Turkish immigration to Europe expanding and alternately being stunted; and with the United States, Canada, and the UK sitting on the sidelines in London atop what is left of NATO.

There may be opportunity in complexity, in this case a negative opportunity for aggressive opportunism.

Year 2, Week 15

As these events unfold, a settled solution for Belgium is sure to be sought by Germany as its attention focuses on Russia's increasingly threatening actions toward Poland and the Baltic States, entailing, in turn, a full-blown resurgence of the German defense establishment. This is the very event all Europe had long dreaded. Furthering the fear, and partially reminiscent of the hegemony of its pre–World War II era,

Europe's German powerhouse will attract adjacent nations in a new Central European Union (CEU), effectively replacing NATO, the EU, and the EZ in a continental European financial/military alliance reminiscent of Imperial Germany's pre–World War I aspirations to create Mitteleuropa, a term that acquired a sinister meaning with the rise of Nazism.

Notably excluded from the CEU will be Poland, that nation finding its dominant role in a Baltic States alliance to be a more attractive option than continuing in a subordinate and second-class position in NATO and in an increasingly resented membership in the EU. Ivan Krastev, the chairman of the Center for Liberal Strategies in Sofia, Bulgaria, and a permanent fellow at the Institute for Human Sciences in Vienna, wrote in December 2015:

> *Why has Poland, the poster child of post-Communist success and Europe's best economic performer of the last decade, suddenly taken an illiberal turn? . . .*
>
> *The [Viktor] Orban model of rebuking the European Union while accepting billions in aid money has worked [for Hungary]. . . .*
>
> *At some point there will be no European Union to blame. Indeed, Poland's drift may result in a backlash by Western Europe; already, one hears rumblings in Paris and Berlin that it was a mistake to give the new, Eastern entrants the same power within the European Union as the established members of the eurozone. . . .*
>
> *These populist and radical parties . . . promise voters what liberal democracy cannot: a sense of victory where majorities—not just political majorities, but ethnic and religious ones, too—can do what they please.*
>
> *The rise of these parties is symptomatic of the explosion of threatened majorities as a force in European politics. They blame the loss of control over their lives, real or imagined, on a conspiracy between cosmopolitan-minded elites and tribal-minded immigrants. They blame liberal ideas and institutions for weakening the national will and eroding national unity. They tend to see compromise as corruption and zealousness as conviction.*

Year 2, Week 20

China's continued expansion of its Balkan role can somewhat offset Germany's unwelcome resurgence. The region's residents certainly remember the spark igniting World War I came when Germany backed Austria's ultimatums against Serbia, and Russia came to the aid of their fellow Slavs. Now, with Sino-Slav cooperation becoming influential in the Balkans, even Serbia could rationalize its way into China's generous orbit. From there, it is only a short distance to Ukraine. Only Romania stands in the way, and the Romanians, fearing Russia as much as the Ukrainians do, are certain to welcome Chinese support. With NATO collapsing and Russia taking larger and larger slices of its territory, Ukraine itself will have little choice but to accept assistance wherever it can be found, whether from the US-led NATO remnant, the German-led CEU, or the Chinese-Balkan Alliance. Already having failed to obtain sufficient US support, and remembering its World War II experience with Germany, Ukraine will be inclined to choose China. However, the proximity of CEU forces will combine with Ukraine's long-standing orientation toward Western Europe to instead convince Ukrainians to instead tilt away from the Chinese and their Balkan allies.

Meanwhile, the US-dominated, London-based NATO remnant may be expected to remain on the sidelines and await events, much as America did at the beginning of both World War I and World War II, as no other compelling or viable options at first appear. Russia's new ally, Greece, and long-time antagonist, Turkey, will also opt out, choosing the course of neutrality, but only after Turkey allows a major Chinese fleet unobstructed passage through the Dardanelles and Bosporus Straits into the Black Sea.

This will require deviations from the 1936 Montreux Convention Regarding the Regime of the Straits that severely limits non–Black Sea nations' right to free transit of military vessels because Turkey is not a signatory to the less restrictive 1994 United Nations Convention on the Law of the Sea (UNCLOS) (see Scenario 5 for an in-depth discussion of UNCLOS). The Montreux Treaty provisions were largely ignored for NATO nations once Turkey joined the alliance in 1952, but making an exception for China would be tantamount to the abrogation of the treaty altogether. And since the dominant Black Sea nation, Russia, and its Black Sea Fleet had long been the primary beneficiaries of the treaty, the Russians will vehemently object, but to no avail, though they will not want to add Turkey to their growing list of soon-to-be hostile states. In any event, when the secret Sino-Turkish agreement becomes known once the Chinese fleet's route and objective are discerned, it will be too late for Russia to mount a campaign against Turkey and close the straits.

Year 2, Week 22

Chinese rumblings notwithstanding, Russia can only perceive the simultaneous fall of NATO, the EU, and the EZ as a once-in-a-century opportunity to retrace and surpass the imperial ambitions of Catherine the Great, Peter the Great, and Stalin. Belarus, both incapable and unwilling to stand in the way, will immediately sign a pact with Russia in which it in effect surrenders autonomy, opening the door to Poland as Russian forces continue pressing forward in Ukraine and probing Estonia, Latvia, and Lithuania (see Map 2 in this scenario and Ukraine maps in Scenario 2).

Kaliningrad, Russia's enclave between Poland and Lithuania, as well as Transnistria, the pro-Russian unrecognized breakaway territory belonging to Moldova, were previously regarded as isolated and untenable positions. However, in the face of European disarray, those outposts are going to become focal points and bridgeheads for Russian expansion, their strategic value considered so important that Russia must undoubtedly move with unexpected speed to link up with them. If successful, the Russian corridor from Belarus to Kaliningrad will isolate the Baltic States, while a rapid drive from Russian-occupied Crimea to Transnistria, and therefore, Moldova, completely cuts off Ukraine from the Black Sea. The Russians will have mistakenly assumed the Chinese fleet was headed for the Mediterranean Sea to augment its forces in Albania. As a result, the Russian offensive to drive the Ukrainians away from the Black Sea will look prescient, though their self-congratulatory period will be brief.

Year 2, Week 24

Russia is going to attempt its Ukrainian strategy in the Baltics—launching hostile moves without resorting to general war—by continuing to claim the fighting is being carried on under the banner of Baltic dissidents rather than Russian armed forces. Naturally, no one would normally be expected to believe such a canard, but Russia, realizing this, is certain to count upon the collapse of NATO and consequent weakening of European resolve to generate an inclination toward self-delusion. Russia will be banking on such a collaborative lie to convince the remaining NATO and pseudo-NATO countries to circumvent their Article 5 obligations.

As in the 1930s, such blatant blind-eye actions sooner or later are brought to account, after which open hostilities can no longer be avoided. In the latest iteration of European strife, it will fall to the German-led CEU to stop the Russian linkup with Kaliningrad, but the CEU will hesitate, and by the time it awakens to the threat, the linkup will have been achieved almost overnight.

These initial moves will strengthen the Russians' position, placing most of Ukraine, all of Belarus, and the Kaliningrad corridor firmly in their hands. That corridor along with the Russian Baltic Fleet will reduce Baltic State assistance from the West strictly to airborne resupply missions. The previous US/NATO prepositioning of military equipment there is going to prove to have been nothing more than a weak gesture, and Estonia, Latvia, and Lithuania will soon fall to Russian and dissident arms.

Instead, the first Europeans to fully confront the Russians after they overrun the Baltic States and most of Ukraine will be from the Balkan countries, primarily due to Chinese support. This will bring about the first major big-power clash when the Chinese-Balkan Alliance begins to press eastward into Ukraine and comes up against both Russia and the German-led CEU to the north.

Year 2, Week 26

At this point Russia will seek peace, claiming it has merely regained territories historically belonging in the Russian sphere, its Manifest Destiny (see Scenario 2) territories. Clearly, to proceed farther could risk a big-power nuclear confrontation at worst or a spread of the fighting to Asia and the Pacific at least.

Here, then, comes the critical moment, and the Chinese should opt out. They will not. Russia's leaders will have overplayed their hand, not

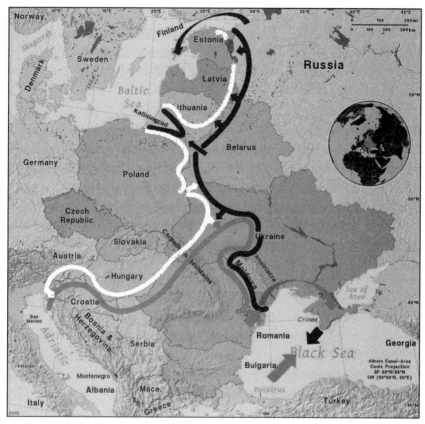

Map 2: World War 4: The Post-NATO War

© 2010, 2013 BY IAN MACKY, WITH MILITARY OPERATIONS BY DOUGLAS COHN

LEGEND: BLACK = RUSSIA, GRAY = CHINESE-BALKAN ALLIANCE, WHITE = CEU

realizing that by then China is certain to view itself as all-powerful. Having completely eclipsed the Russian economy and defense spending, and firmly established its superiority in Asia, where it cowed all other powers by successfully asserting sovereignty over most of the East China and South China Seas, China views itself as ascendant. Now, having gained a foothold in the Balkans and introduced a major fleet into the Black Sea, China is not about to back down in the face of Russian aggression or miss an opportunity to end the Russian threat once and for all, even though the region being menaced for the moment is Europe, not Asia.

Year 2, Week 28

Assessing the risk of nuclear war to be low, China and its Balkan allies will launch their counteroffensives, reasoning that no nation is going to resort to nuclear weapons unless its survivability is at risk. And China will make clear from the outset that it is seeking only to remove the offensive claws from the Russian Bear, not the bear itself—a clear application of the theory of mutually assured survival.

The Chinese Black Sea Fleet is going to quickly dominate the northwestern shore in support of its land-based Chinese-Balkan Alliance campaign moving east just south of Moldova against Russian-occupied Ukraine. A secondary Chinese-Balkan offensive will proceed as planned against northwest Ukraine only to become enmeshed in a double battle with Russia and the CEU (see Year 2, Week 30). Meanwhile, when the Russian Black Sea Fleet ventures forth from Crimea, the largest sea battle since World War II is certain to take place. Russia, having already committed so much in power and prestige to the war, cannot back down, and its fleet is going to pay the price.

Year 2, Week 29

The Battle of the Black Sea will be unlike any other naval action in history. World War I had witnessed the Battle of Jutland, the large surface fleet action between the UK and Germany when battleships reigned supreme. With aircraft carriers dominant in World War II, the Battle of the Coral Sea and the Battle of Midway were fought from the air without the US or Japanese fleets ever coming within visual contact of one another. Now, in the Black Sea, missiles and drones are going to dominate. The Chinese and Russian navies alike have neither combat experience nor successful naval legacies, but China's technologically superior fleet will prevail in this battle between untested vessels, armaments, and personnel.

Year 2, Week 30

The Chinese victory in the Battle of the Black Sea is certain to directly impact the land campaign as the Chinese-Balkan Alliance drives toward Crimea. The Russian Army that had so successfully pushed the Ukrainians away from the Black Sea will merely have opened the door for the

Chinese-Balkan armies to replace the southern wing of the Ukrainian Army and catch the Russians in a hammer-and-anvil battle—the Chinese fleet being the anvil to the Chinese-Balkan armies' hammer. In short order Crimea will fall to this irrepressible land-sea combination. What remains of the Ukrainian Army, opposing both the Russians and the Chinese-Balkan Alliance, will have retreated into the Carpathian Mountains, hoping for relief from the CEU.

In the north, Germany and the CEU will have cause for celebration and concern as Russia begins to reel under Chinese pressure, though that very pressure is likely to create uncertainty, lest China simply replace Russia as the new threat to Europe. At last grasping the magnitude of this dilemma, the CEU is going to finally commit its forces along with the remnants of the Ukrainian Army against Russia, China, and China's Balkan allies in central Ukraine, the objectives being to restore balance and ensure Ukraine's continued independence as an unaffiliated, neutral buffer state. Of course, Russia will not believe this limited-war motive.

Year 2, Week 32

These events are sure to interest Italy and the Southern European Coalition (SEC) when they discern an opportunity to regain prestige and take land in Slovenia and Croatia. Italy's partners, Portugal and Spain, might commit limited assistance, but only as a means of positioning themselves to be in on the spoils of a successful war, while risking little in the event of defeat. Abandoning its new Russian ally, Greece, surrounded by enemies, is not about to enter the fray and neither is Turkey. It will have been enough that Turkey opened the door for a Chinese fleet to enter the Black Sea, a crucial concession Ukraine, the CEU, and the Chinese-Balkan Alliance were certain to remember in victory, and not so overt that Russia would overreact in the unlikely event of the opposite result.

Neither are the Nordic nations going to intervene. With the breakup of NATO, they are certain to stand by their refusal to honor Article 5. Further, there would be no point in their involvement, it being unnecessary once self-interest spurred other nations and coalitions to confront and defeat the Russians, which had been the long-standing goal of NATO in the first place.

Confronted with a different motivation, France, the other stand-aside power, is not about to align itself with enemies or antagonists, which is how it will come to view Russia, China, and Germany, the major belligerents in the war. It is the same position France took in the 1930s when its neighbor, Spain, erupted in a bloody civil war that drew fascist Germany and communist Russia in on opposing sides. Opposed to both, France stood aside. And, now, France will once again do likewise.

Year 2, Week 34

As three belligerents—the CEU, the Chinese-Balkan Alliance, and Russia—engage in triangular fighting along Eastern Europe's eastern edge, in faraway London, the NATO remnant sits. A quandary holds them there, for like France, the United States, the United Kingdom, and Canada regard Russia and China at the least as antagonists and often as enemies, and, like most of the nations of the world, the remnant members are sincerely concerned about a remilitarized Germany, which is already dominating the CEU. On the other hand, in concert with the CEU, the remnant looks upon China as the greater threat, having taken Russia at its word that it has no further territorial ambitions, and knowing that word is being ensured by Russia's military, economic, and technological limitations. Further, having catastrophically lost the Battle of the Black Sea, the Russian threat can no longer pose the same level of concern. Therefore, the NATO remnant can only conclude that China is the enemy to thwart. This will not come as welcome news to former NATO member Turkey.

Having made this determination, the question on the table is where best to inject US-led power. With the three-way fighting trisecting Eastern Europe, there would be little point in joining that confused front. Instead, realizing that China had accomplished through bullying and bluffing in the East China and South China Seas the peaceful expansion Russia was attempting to do through war in Eastern Europe, and further realizing that China was employing its best forces in Europe, the United States will determine that the most logical place to strike a responsive blow would in the Pacific. The US "Pivot to Asia" strategy had already enhanced land, air, and sea forces in the region, especially through the strengthening of the already powerful US Seventh Fleet. Backed up by allies, including Japan, South Korea, the Philippines, Australia, and New Zealand, along with the nations of Southeast Asia, the proposed Pacific strategy would become increasingly obvious when compared to a European campaign relying upon the weakened strength of the London-based NATO remnant. Lacking strength, land, or allies, an argument in favor of the remnant joining the Eastern European fighting could not compare in scope, whether assessing land, military capabilities, or militarily reliable allies.

As if playing a master chess tournament, the place to intervene would be determined by selecting the target offering the greatest benefit for the least risk, which clearly would be somewhere in the western Pacific. As sites are considered and evaluated, only one would finally emerge as optimal. The unanimous recommendation of military planners and political advisers alike will be none other than China's ally, North Korea. After all, except for China, what nation could object to eliminating such a rogue regime? And since North Korea had never signed a peace treaty with its Korean War enemies, the United States and UN, a state of war continued there even if open hostilities had abated. No declaration of war would be necessary, and the attack could be thoroughly planned and executed without warning, an absolute necessity because the massive concentration of North Korean artillery on the border poses a near-nuclear equivalent threat to the South Korean capital, Seoul. Further, the uncertainty surrounding North Korea's nuclear capabilities had cast a pall over the peninsula for years.

In 2003 Barbara Demick wrote in the *Los Angeles Times*:

> *When the U.S. military tries to explain the difficulty of using force to stop North Korea's development of nuclear weapons, the oddly poetic phrase it turns to is the "tyranny of proximity."*
>
> *The phrase, which has been in the lexicon of the U.S. forces in South Korea for years, stems from the imposing array of conventional artillery that the North Koreans have dug into the hills just north of the demilitarized zone, a mere 30 miles from this capital city of 12 million [Seoul]. The nightmare scenario is that if the United*

States opts for a more forceful approach to curb North Korea's nuclear ambitions, the communist regime would retaliate not only against the 38,000 American troops stationed in South Korea, but also against South Korea itself.

Year 2, Week 36

With most of the US-led alliance's military assets already prepositioned for the North Korean Campaign, the balance of the attack formations could be marshalled while the campaign was being planned and reconnaissance missions were collecting data. This is a classic example of military theorist Col. John Boyd's OODA Loop (Observe, Orient, Decide, Act) by which plans are constantly revised and updated in real time while information and decision making are continually fed back (looped) to the Observe element before being forwarded to the succeeding Orient, Decide, and Act elements.

As a result, the operation would soon be planned, updated, and revised again and again until it is launched, beginning with the simultaneous elimination of the threatening artillery batteries and North Korea's nuclear weapons facilities, though intelligence reports indicated such weapons were probably operational but far from deliverable. However, intelligence reports have been wrong before, necessitating the deployment of a large Special Operations force to attack the facilities, knowing that casualties would be high.

The unexpected lightening campaign will catch the Chinese and North Koreans by surprise. With its Seoul-targeted artillery and nuclear facilities neutralized faster than enemy commanders thought possible, a defanged North Korea will collapse, the North Korean Army simply vanishing under land, sea, and air pressure. A stunned China, realizing its eastern (western Pacific) flank is in trouble, will begin disengaging in Europe. It will be too late. And, in case the point is missed, the US-led coalition will demand that China pull back from the resource-rich islands it unlawfully annexed in the South China and East China Seas. Naturally, China's suddenly desperate leadership is going to object, threaten, and even position military assets in response, but in the end, there can be no choice in the face of the Allies' overwhelming power amassed and amassing in the region while China is overcommitted in Europe.

The elimination of North Korea will prove to have been precisely the right strategy on the right pressure point to restore the balance of power with the United States in control. The United States will have won the war without ever having engaged either of its primary antagonists, Russia or China, and it will have done so with the least possible cost in casualties and fortune.

Year 2, Week 40

A chastened China is practically guaranteed to replace its leadership and accept the concept of economic competition in lieu of military confrontation. The Balkan nations, having suffered substantial losses fighting Russia for what they came to understand was for China's benefit, are going to politely ask the Chinese to take their forces home. New leadership in Russia, under continued pressure from the CEU and its overt and covert Ukrainian allies, is going to have no choice but to evacuate its forces from the Baltic States and Ukraine, including Crimea, as well as cede Kaliningrad to its proper parent, Poland. Meanwhile Russia's destroyed Black Sea Fleet will be replaced by a new US Black Sea Fleet, which will take place with Turkey's blessings, that nation finally being relieved of centuries of ominous Russian threats and actions while sidestepping retribution for its China-leaning role leading up to the Battle of the Black Sea.

Only Germany's newly acquired military strength could be in question, but faced with the strength of a megapower such as the United States, the Germans are going to see that their future lies in economic quests, not in any resurrected idea of resurgent military power.

The fighting in Europe, having been costly and severe, in the end it will have achieved almost nothing other than the status quo ante, whereas the fighting in Asia, having cost little in blood and treasure, will have accomplished much. And neither battlefront will have witnessed the introduction of nuclear weapons because no nation except North Korea was threatened with extinction, and the people of that nation will soon discover the advantages of citizenship in a newly free and united Korea.

Having previously fought World War I, World War II, and the Cold War (World War III), the United States and its closest allies will have learned not only how to win a war, but the peace as well, unless a modern wave of isolationism reminiscent of the 1930s grips the nation and paves the way for resurgent rivalries around the globe. NATO will be reconstituted. European unity will be restructured along America's fiscal and monetary lines. China's new leadership will begin moving their country on a path toward freedom and democracy. Russia will have been declawed, and the world will wait and watch as that nation hopefully recaptures the democratic spirit it so temporarily found and lost after the fall of the Soviet Union—"hopefully" being the operative word.

Scenario 2

World War 4: The Great Russian War

While Russia has contributed in select security areas, such as counter-narcotics and counterterrorism, it also has repeatedly demonstrated that it does not respect the sovereignty of its neighbors and it is willing to use force to achieve its goals. Russia's military actions are undermining regional security directly and through proxy forces. These actions violate numerous agreements that Russia has signed in which it committed to act in accordance with international norms, including the UN Charter, Helsinki Accords, Russia-NATO Founding Act, Budapest Memorandum, and the Intermediate-Range Nuclear Forces Treaty.

—The United States Military's Contribution to
National Security, June 2015
Courtesy US Department of Defense
(See Appendix A for the complete transcript)

Western nation citizens have a difficult time understanding the motivations behind Russian expansionism, generally skewing comprehension with an ethnocentric view, although one prescient leader, a writer and maker of history, came close to making sense of that inscrutable nation. On October 1, 1939, a month after the onset of World War II and nearly two years before Germany turned against and invaded its Russian ally, Britain's First Lord of the Admiralty Winston Churchill—still more than seven months away from becoming prime minister—grappled with the conundrum and an inconceivable future: "I cannot forecast to

41

Map 3: The Russian War area of operations
© 2010, 2013 BY IAN MACKY, WITH ENHANCEMENTS BY DOUGLAS COHN

you the action of Russia. It is a riddle wrapped in a mystery inside an enigma; but perhaps there is a key. That key is Russian national interest. It cannot be in accordance with the interest of the safety of Russia that Germany should plant itself upon the shores of the Black Sea, or that it should overrun the Balkan States and subjugate the Slavonic peoples of south eastern [sic] Europe. That would be contrary to the historic life-interests of Russia."

Yet, the inconceivable did happen on June 22, 1941. Germany launched Operation Barbarossa, the invasion of Russia, and within a year its armies had reached the gates of Moscow, the shores of the Black Sea, and the Volga River before being turned back. The counteroffensive eventually brought Russia's armies not only into the adjacent lands of its fellow Slavs, but across all of Eastern Europe, marking the historic zenith of Russian expansion, conquest, and hegemony. It would be a short-lived empire.

With the collapse of the Soviet Union in 1991, all this and more was lost, and the newly constituted Russia found itself smaller than it had been in 1941, having given up Latvia, Estonia, Lithuania, Belarus, Ukraine, and Moldova in Europe as well as Armenia, Azerbaijan, Georgia, Kazakhstan, Kyrgyzstan, Tajikistan, Turkmenistan, and Uzbekistan in Central Asia. With these land losses came commensurate losses of approximately 50 percent of the Soviet Union's population. The empire had vanished.

Much of the work of both communist and tsarist Russia had vanished overnight. That Russians and their leaders would seek to reverse this situation should not come as a surprise, and in many respects the parallel with early American history was not lost on them. So a brief digression into America's past is in order, be it a rationalization or justification in Russian minds.

All this leads to a long-history, short-history phenomenon. Long-history Russians view the events in short-history America as almost recent, whereas Americans tend to look upon activities occurring prior to World War II as belonging to a different era, a long-ago past for which they cannot be expected to bear responsibility. These polar-opposite outlooks cause Americans to view Russia's aggressive expansionism as nothing less than an illegal land grab, whereas many Russians describe it as their version of Manifest Destiny. It is even conceivable that they dismiss America's rejection of imperialism following the Spanish-American War and its subsequent tilt toward the concept of might for right in two world wars as sanctimonious moralizing made possible by a two-ocean moat. Russians, surrounded by erstwhile enemies, understand they are geopolitically inhibited from matching this "sea to shining sea" description of America's Atlantic-to-Pacific

America's Manifest Destiny

Even before America became a nation, the thirst for land caused settlers to spill over the Appalachian Mountains despite King George III's 1763 decree to the contrary.

Twelve years later, the American Revolution began and culminated with the creation of a new nation whose western border soon reached the shores of the Mississippi River, and there it might have stopped had it not been for the Louisiana Purchase, the largest single peaceful land transfer in history. This dramatic expansion led to the messianic concept of Manifest Destiny, the idea that the United States had a divine mandate to create a continental nation. Although Britain prevented the northward push to annex Canada during the War of 1812, the midcentury victory in the Mexican-American War did succeed in creating a coast-to-coast country.

This combination of land-motivated conquest and religious fervor was further fueled by the discovery of gold in newly acquired California, an unexpected dynamic that precipitated a massive population migration and solidified the young nation's westward expansion.

The acquisition of Alaska and Hawaii came later in the century, the first because Russia was willing to sell it (gold was also later discovered there), the second due to sugar planter machinations

Manifest Destiny. Nonetheless, they are perpetually attempting to emulate America's geographic dream through the substitution of a set of complex objectives that could simultaneously provide secure borders and warm-water, sea-based commercial and military outlets, beginning with the reconquest of Ukraine.

World War II, known in Russia as the Great Patriotic War, is estimated to have claimed more than twenty million lives, half of them civilians, and most of those Ukrainians. Nine years before Germany's invasion, Soviet dictator Joseph Stalin's brutal policies had caused a massive famine in Ukraine, killing millions of people. That along with other arbitrary and senseless actions so alienated the Ukrainian populace that many of them initially greeted invading Germans as liberators and even

and the advent of steam-powered ships and their need for coaling stations and distant harbors.

Throughout these various expansions, indigenous natives were simultaneously and systematically displaced, civilized, evangelized, or attacked, which was justified and immortalized in Rudyard Kipling's racist poem "The White Man's Burden: The United States & The Philippine Islands, 1899":

> Take up the White Man's burden—
> And reap his old reward:
> The blame of those ye better
> The hate of those ye guard . . .

The Philippines had been acquired during the Spanish-American War in what was America's flirtation with empire building, an endeavor then in full swing by Great Britain, Germany, and other nations. However, the opposite happened. Major US expansions ceased after the American public rejected the idea, not even holding on to Cuba (but keeping Puerto Rico, Guam, and, until 1946, the Philippines), over which the war was fought.

Here then, encapsulated in one country were several rationales for national expansion: land, religion, natural resources (gold), ocean trade routes, civilizing duty, racism, and, as in the case of Alaska, availability and opportunity.

formed a Ukrainian division in the Wehrmacht, the German Army. Then Lebensraum (depopulation programs to create living space for Germans) and the Holocaust came to Ukraine. Nazis viewed Slavs and Jews as inferior beings in control of fertile lands, the Russian breadbasket, and they began to systematically engage in ethnic cleansing through deportations, imprisonment, and mass murder.

Eventually, despite mixed motivations, most Ukrainians turned against Germany and joined the Red Army in large numbers, suffering high casualties as a result. Several of the epic battles on the war's Eastern Front were fought on Ukrainian soil, and this fact, combined with divided loyalties and Jewish genocide, resulted in more than half of the Soviet deaths in the war.

Nikita Khrushchev, who came to power in 1953, had a long history with Ukraine, having worked in the Donbas region—which would become a battleground between ethnic Russians and Ukrainians in 2014—and becoming head of Ukraine following World War II, when pro-Russian eastern Ukraine and independent-minded western Ukraine fought one another. Upon reaching the pinnacle of power in the USSR, he transferred Crimea to Ukraine, which had already become a semi-autonomous region inexplicably recognized by the UN as an independent nation. With the breakup of the Soviet Union in 1991, the fiction became fact when Ukraine truly did achieve independence.

In Russia, whether it was tsarist authoritarianism, post-tsarist democracy, the communist dictatorship of the proletariat, or post-communist democracy, a strongman took hold. The last failed attempt at democracy came with Boris Yeltsin's presidency spanning the years 1991 to 1999, after which his chosen successor, then–Prime Minister Vladimir Putin, a former lieutenant colonel in the KGB (the Soviet Union's spy and state security agency, Komitet Gosudarstvennoi Bezopanosti), came to power. No democrat, Putin held power directly or indirectly from 1999 forward, and in many respects his rule resembled that of tsars whose perpetual mission was to complete the expansion of Russia to what they deemed to be its proper borders, whatever those might be. To them, and apparently to Putin, it was a matter of Russia's Manifest Destiny to consolidate, by force if necessary, the Slavic people under one banner, to obtain warm-water ports, to secure defensible borders, to encompass fertile fields, and something more: to recapture the glory and prestige of Mother Russia or what some Russians falsely romanticize as the intoxicating days of Imperial Russia or of the Soviet Union era when the Soviet Empire was a superpower capable of challenging the United States.

The United States had been able to do all this in North America and one thing more: provide freedom from fear for the homeland. During World War II all of the other major belligerents suffered terribly on and off the battlefield, and in the case of the USSR, civilian casualties outnumbered military losses. Not so for the continental United States, where virtually no civilian casualties were sustained (clearly there may have been a small number attributable to sabotage or attacks on coastal shipping, but nothing like the millions of dead suffered by the Soviets).

Both nations had their reasons and rationalizations for expansion, but whereas the United States succeeded and did so more than one hundred years ago, Russia is once again in the process of reinventing and rebuilding a nation, or, in the minds of some, an empire without regard for the altered geopolitical realities nearly two centuries have created. This resurgent Russian expansion followed a Cold War period of suppressed antagonism marked by surrogate warfare, threats, brinksmanship, and occasional lethal mishaps, but also by an absence of superpower warfare. In the end, the Soviet Union, and later Russia, got the worst of it, especially in the realm of hegemony when most of its former Eastern European satellite nations joined NATO and Ukraine began looking to Western Europe for new allies and realignments.

Its West-leaning government would like to join the European Union and NATO, but Russia adamantly opposes such alliances for its neighbor. When, for example, NATO invited Montenegro to join the alliance the response from Russia, as reported in the *New York Times* on December 2, 2015, was immediate and hostile:

> *"The continuing expansion of NATO and NATO's military infrastructure to the East, of course, cannot but lead to response actions from the East, namely the Russian side," [Kremlin spokesman Dmitri] Peskov said. . . .*
>
> *NATO no longer regards Russia as a "strategic partner" but as a country seeking to undermine the post–Cold War order and restore its sway over the old Soviet empire, prompting a degree of confrontation that is reminiscent of the Cold War in tone.*
>
> *Adm. Vladimir Komoyedov, chairman of the Duma's defense committee, said, "They are ready to admit even the North Pole to NATO just for the sake of encircling Russia." The invitation to Montenegro, he said, means that NATO "was and remains an adversary of Russia."*

Rutgers political science professor Alexander John Motyl wrote, "Putin's Russia, in contrast, has reverted to 20th-century Soviet Russian behavior, both insisting on its manifest destiny in the former Soviet space and refusing to countenance any degree of responsibility for its criminal acts vis-à-vis Ukraine and the other non-Russian states."

In this context Putin and his successors, like their predecessors from tsarist days, may view Russia in the mold, not of the twentieth-century USSR, but of nineteenth-century America, involved in the messy business of expansion. But any leader trying to emulate the hundred-year-old actions of another nation is on a self-delusional errand, especially in light of the rapidity of change in the invention-driven modern world. America and its allies may understand Russia's nineteenth-century motivations without condoning its twenty-first-century actions because Americans today do not accept responsibility for the sins of their ancestors, and they are not about to stand aside as Russia rationalizes and justifies encroachments into Western-aligned nations' lands. Conversely, Russia is not about to stop. In this conflict of concepts lay the seeds of war.

Russia will continue to gnaw away on its neighbors, especially those with significant Russian-speaking populations such as Ukraine, Transnistria, Belarus, and the Baltic States. And where conquest is not possible, hegemony might be as it once was in the Balkans. There, Serbs, who, like Russians, are mostly Slavs, provided the ethnic connection and excuse that ushered Russia into World War I.

However, the immediate Russian interest is Ukraine, where the intertwined history of languages, religions, and ethnicity creates natural allies and natural enemies alike. Further, Ukraine has traditionally served as Russia's granary, and, in modern times, the land through which pipelines deliver Russian natural gas to Western Europe.

Such was the state of affairs in 2014 when Vladimir Putin, in a move reminiscent of Hitler's 1936 occupation of the Rhineland (see Scenario 1), sent Russian troops into Ukraine's Crimea, annexed it, and invaded eastern Ukraine. All the while, the US-led NATO nations stood by, ostensibly because Ukraine was not a NATO member, ignoring the fact that the troubles began when Ukrainians ousted their Russian-leaning government and tilted West. Economic sanctions were then imposed against Russia,

Map 4: Ukraine area of operations

GNU FREE DOCUMENTATION LICENSE, WITH ENHANCEMENTS AND MILITARY OPERATIONS BY DOUGLAS COHN

an appropriate but partial response that proved to be partially effective, especially in their impact on the Russian ruble (see below). Like Germany in 1936, Russia was not militarily ready. Like Hitler, Putin was bluffing. Like France and Britain in 1936, NATO failed to call the autocrat's bluff.

During the Rhineland gamble, Hitler told his generals he was prepared to back down if France and Britain countered his move. And so would have Putin had NATO countered his aggression in Ukraine. He would have had no choice. The Russian economy was a basket case. It could not have begun to support a military establishment capable of confronting NATO, and the argument that NATO's military structure had been hollowed out was irrelevant because the massive economic engines funding it are its underlying source of strength, and Putin knew this. He also was aware that his source of strength was the bully's bluff.

With the bluff made, what has been NATO's response? Whereas Putin was acting provocative from a position of weakness, NATO eschewed counterprovocations from a position of strength. By earlier ill-advised agreements, major NATO forces were not initially deployed to Eastern European member nations from Poland to the Baltics (see Scenario 1), and they have been taken off the table for nonmember Ukraine.

The solution was as clear as in 1936. NATO should have immediately renounced its 1997 agreement with Russia (see Scenario 1) and moved "forward-deployed forces" to bases in the Baltics and Poland. Eventually, and without abrogating the treaty, limited forces were deployed, but not to non-NATO Ukraine.

But against substantial deployments, what could any Russian leader do? Launch a nuclear war? Send his inferior forces against NATO? No, he would do precisely what Hitler was going to do in 1936: back down because there could be no other choice. Containment was an appropriate policy in the Cold War; it remains appropriate today. But NATO, other than sending Ukraine outdated equipment, will not initially act there. Ukraine, lacking natural allies, will seemingly be left to stand alone.

Will NATO finally relent and go to Ukraine's aid in any event, just as it did in the Balkans when non-NATO Yugoslavia broke up in the 1990s? At first glance, not likely, but upon closer evaluation there will eventually be no choice.

To the north, Latvia, Estonia, and Lithuania—the Baltic States—are NATO allies protected by the organization's underpinning Article 5 guarantee (see Scenario 1) that an attack on one NATO nation is an attack on all NATO nations. Yet, if Europe turns its back on Ukraine, the Baltics are certain to be the next or even simultaneous Russian targets, and those countries will wonder why NATO went into Yugoslavia, but not Ukraine. They will begin to question the alliance's resolve, especially on the European mainland, and in response, they might even begin by ceding to Russia their Russian-speaking territories. Yet, to do so under the threat of invasion would be tantamount to surrender in the face of aggression, invoking a NATO response, a response that will not immediately come. The quibbling would contend that voluntary cessions are not NATO triggers, although such nonaction could undermine the alliance altogether, an event that would leave any number of nations at the mercy of the Russian Bear.

Therefore, Russia will continue its provocations in Ukraine, forcing NATO to finally intercede, but at first only with modern equipment and limited numbers of military advisors. Air cover followed by major ground forces will be in the offing, though not before doctrines are discussed and debated.

When Gen. Dwight D. Eisenhower became president in 1953, the concept of massive nuclear retaliation became the controlling defense theory, a theory advocated by Strategic Air Command (SAC) Commander Gen. Curtis LeMay. This was later challenged when Army Chief of Staff Gen. Maxwell Taylor advanced the strategic concept of flexible response, a doctrine reliant upon substantial conventional forces. As it turned out, Taylor was right. The nuclear age had made the world safe for limited and surrogate wars, one of which, the Korean War, had just ended. And before the decade was out, the United States found itself advising, then fighting in a double surrogate war when Soviet surrogate North Vietnam propped up South Vietnamese communist surrogates, the Viet Cong, followed by the introduction of its own regulars to the conflict. In the 1980s this surrogate strategy was reversed in Afghanistan, when US-backed Mujahideen insurgents fought and defeated the Soviet Army.

Throughout the Cold War, the question with the unknowable answer was: At what point does nuclear war intersect limited or surrogate war? Ukraine will become a case in point. Russia's leaders continue the fiction that Russian-speaking separatists, not Russian troops, are fighting the Ukrainian Army. This is in keeping with the concept of plausible—or in the Russian case, implausible—deniability so as not to allow a war amply sprinkled with various disingenuous cease-fire agreements to be viewed as a potential major-power confrontation. The Russian plan appears to be that such thinly veiled cloaking, if successful in Ukraine, might likewise be successful against the Baltic States.

As a result, just as the Balkans were the tinderbox for World War I, the Baltics could provide the spark to ignite World War 4. Already having been successful in Ukraine's Crimea and eastern provinces, Russia may decide that incursions into the Baltics are more feasible than previously thought. NATO has neither the immediate strength nor the will to confront Russian troops there, and this is where surrogate war could potentially creep up to the intersecting line of nuclear war, bringing the concept of mutually assured survival to the fore and the distinctions between presumptions and assumptions into the decision making.

Presumptions are informed judgments; assumptions are uninformed judgments. So, is it presumption or assumption to conclude that the Russian leadership will become increasingly rational as the stakes rise and successors will be more amenable to peaceful dialog with the United States and NATO? There being nothing substantive upon which to make such a determination, assumptions will carry the day, uncertainty will rule, and nuclear confrontation will become increasingly possible. Under the circumstances, the only responsible course will be to prepare for a continuity of Russian bullying or the accession of other, possibly more intransigent, hardliners until more information moves the decision-making needle into the presumption zone.

Of most importance are the Russian objectives. That nation never wielded more power than it did as the Soviet Union, which was actually a continuation and expansion of the tsarist Russian Empire, an expansion far outpacing the conquests of both Catherine the Great and Peter the Great. This came about as a result of the Russian Revolution and the Russian Civil War, followed by World War II. The first two conflicts created and expanded the Soviet Union, while the war increased its hegemony over the USSR's newly subverted Eastern Europe satellite states, which were then formed into a NATO counterweight, the Soviet-dominated Warsaw Pact.

End of the empire came with defeat in the Cold War and the breakup of both the Soviet Union and the Warsaw Pact. Is it that empire Russia wishes to reconstitute or is there more? Or is it less? Perhaps a consolidation of the Slavic people? Or is it control of natural resources?

As Russia's leaders scan the industrialized world, what do they see? Does power come from land? Large populations? Natural resources? Gross domestic product (GDP, the total output of goods and services)? Monetary strength? Military power? China has all of these. Except for a large population, the United States has even more, relatively speaking.

China has become a fascist nation; the United States is a republic. Which example is Russia seeking to emulate? Perhaps neither. Perhaps Russia is simply playing for power in a game devoid of philosophy or idealism. Russia's leaders have embraced neither communism nor democracy, capitalism nor socialism. Instead, they have apparently simply settled on control.

In October 2014 the Russian defense budget was set at 3.3 trillion rubles or $81 billion using an exchange rate of $.0245/ruble, but the plunge in the ruble to $.015 by May 2016 reduced that budget to $49.5 billion. Precipitously falling oil prices have prompted a further 5 percent cut in the defense budget, reducing it to 3.135 trillion rubles or $47 billion, which continues to consume an increasing percentage of Russia's GDP as not only falling oil prices, but NATO sanctions over Putin's military provocations in Ukraine continue to negatively impact the Russian economy. Certainly, these figures are subject to change as the price and discoveries of oil (see Scenario 9) and the ruble fluctuate, and despite these falling figures, Russian defense spending remains the third largest in the world, behind the United States and China.

Disarray creates opportunities, and the substantial disarray Putin's preliminary moves created in Eastern Europe will prove to be too enticing for him or his successor to ignore. Russian forces will make their move. Russian-supplied separatists will press forward in Ukraine and the Baltics from Russia and the Russian enclave of Kaliningrad, as well as from Russian allies Belarus and Transnistria, keeping the fighting as low key as possible. But this stage will rapidly give way to increased involvement from regular Russian land and sea formations as the Russian Baltic Fleet seals off the Balkan States.

Here, NATO's Article 5 will be put to the test. Latvia, Estonia, and Lithuania are going to desperately demand intervention under that clause, but reality will dictate otherwise. The region is small and time short, so short that a NATO response could not come even if NATO were of one mind to do so—a requirement because the NATO alliance requires unanimity, which, thanks to the ambiguity of the 1997 agreement with Russia, is not going to be forthcoming.

RUSSIA ATTACKS: UKRAINE CAMPAIGN

Having annexed Crimea and occupied Ukraine's Donetsk region, Russia will move to absorb what it refers to as Novorossiya (New Russia), an area of southeast Ukraine primarily populated with Russian speakers.

The objective will be the Black Sea port city of Odessa, Novorossiya's strategic key. The Russian-speaking and Russian-occupied regions of Transnistria in eastern Moldova as well as Crimea will be linked up with Russia if Novorossiya is quickly taken, occupied, and annexed.

Moldova, allied with NATO member Romania by ethnicity and language, is not a NATO member, and will prove powerless to contest the loss of Transnistria. On the other hand, Ukraine will continue to contest every inch of ground—unsuccessfully. Only NATO will be the question mark.

Russians have learned to operate in stages—virtually a national characteristic. Act, pause, and act again. At this point Russia will suddenly pause. It is a matter of strategic psychology, and as it worked in Crimea, Transnistria, and eastern Ukraine, it is going to work in Novorossiya, primarily due to the Russian ethnic makeup of the region and the fact that Ukraine is not a NATO member or a member of any other defense alliance. These facts alone are going to prove sufficient to keep NATO on the sidelines—for the moment. That is the purpose of the "pause." Having struck, but not too hard or too far, Russia will await a reaction, the absence of which will be regarded as a ticket to continued conquest.

In 1938, Czechoslovakia, also alone, first lost its German-speaking Sudetenland to Hitler, after which the whole nation was overrun by the German Wehrmacht. As then, so now. After awaiting a response from the West that fails to materialize, Russia will strike, but not from Russian territory. Its armored units will pour out of Belarus, its autocratic and subservient ally (dotted arrows on Map 5).

The Ukrainian Army remnant will retreat to the eastern slopes of the Carpathian Mountains along the Polish, Slovakian, Hungarian, and Romanian borders to await events.

Duly alarmed, NATO, at once ponderous, bureaucratic, and powerful, will begin to mass its forces, but not before Russia's Baltic Campaign kicks off.

Map 5: Ukraine campaign
GNU FREE DOCUMENTATION LICENSE, WITH ENHANCEMENTS AND MILITARY OPERATIONS BY
DOUGLAS COHN

RUSSIA ATTACKS: BALTIC CAMPAIGN

The Baltic capitals, Tallinn in Estonia, Riga in Latvia, and Vilnius in Lithuania, are the political, economic, and cultural hearts of each of those small countries, and, accordingly, Russia's targets. Only NATO membership can protect them, but only if NATO honors its Article 5 commitment, which, as explained, it will not, or, at least, cannot in a timely manner.

As in Ukraine, Russian-speaking surrogates in the eastern Baltics, aided by Russian weapons, advisors, and limited surreptitious units, having created dissension and disorder, will suddenly be joined by overwhelming Russian armored forces as well as the Russian Baltic Fleet.

The fleet will cut off any hope of outside assistance while Russian divisions overrun all three nations within days. In the process a Russian column will break through and link up with the Russian enclave of Kaliningrad, sealing the Baltics off from Poland, another NATO nation.

Map 6: Baltic area of operation
© 2010, 2013 BY IAN MACKY, WITH ENHANCEMENTS BY DOUGLAS COHN

Once again, Russia will pause, but ever so briefly because (a) its forces will need to complete the campaign to include defensible borders, and (b) NATO patience must be assumed to be nearing an end.

Therefore, in short order, springing out of Kaliningrad by land and sea against Poland (dotted arrows on Map 7), Russian forces will drive to the Vistula River and take Warsaw from the west while Belarusians attack from the east. Russia will immediately place a large covering force along the east bank of the Vistula to forestall any NATO move while Russian and Belarusian troops from this northern campaign move south along the Vistula to link up with their forces in Ukraine, then in the process of building a defensive line on the eastern bank of the Dniester River.

Concurrently, the Russian Baltic Fleet, having completed its Baltic mission, will move astride the narrow portion of the sea separating Poland and Sweden, closing the region to NATO interference as it effectively—if only temporarily—turns the Baltic Sea into a Russian lake, a stunning achievement no Russian imperialist or communist navy had ever realized. NATO's coalition fleet, lacking instructions to engage, will have dutifully moved west.

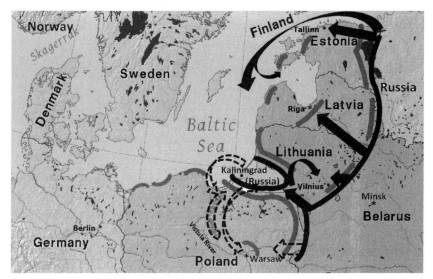

Map 7: Russian Baltic Campaign

© 2010, 2013 BY IAN MACKY, WITH ENHANCEMENTS AND MILITARY OPERATIONS BY DOUGLAS COHN

Russia will have in lightning fashion completed its intended conquests, its armies now stretching in a continuous line from the Baltic Sea to the Black Sea, protected by the twin natural barriers of the Vistula and Dniester Rivers. Here the Russians will not pause; they will halt and offer peace, claiming they have only sought their natural and defensible borders, their Manifest Destiny to govern regions populated in varying degrees by Russian-speaking Slavs. This plan, their gamble, will fail.

Unable to believe Russia's commitment to peace even if so inclined, NATO must react. Russia's strength is in its land forces, its navy having never fully recovered from the fall of the Soviet Union. The opposite is the case for NATO. The strong US Sixth Fleet dominates the Mediterranean Sea, and in June 2015 NATO also flexed its strength in the north, though in light of subsequent events, Russia proved not to be impressed. Operation BALTOPS, a forty-nine-vessel Baltic Sea exercise, was conducted with ships from the United States, the United Kingdom, France, Germany, the Netherlands, Norway, Turkey, Belgium, Canada, and notably, Latvia, Estonia, and Lithuania. NATO partners Finland, Georgia (where the May 2016 NATO joint exercise Noble Partner

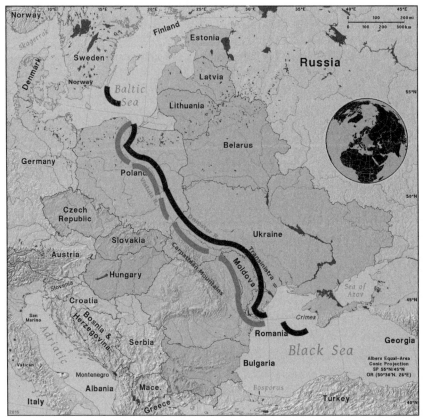

Map 8: Russia's Vistula-Dniester defense line
© 2010, 2013 BY IAN MACKY, WITH ENHANCEMENTS AND MILITARY OPERATIONS BY DOUGLAS COHN

sparked a Russian denunciation), and Sweden also participated in a substantial show of naval power unity in this annual operation. Whether those partner nations would continue that unity in war could neither be known nor expected.

The NATO plan is going to be nothing less than a strategic double envelopment (see Map 9)—the classic example of this on a tactical level being Hannibal's 216 BC victory over Rome at the Battle of Cannae. Just as Russia is using the Vistula-Dniester Rivers line for defense, NATO will do likewise from the rivers' western shores and continue the line into the Carpathian Mountains, where what remains of the Ukrainian Army

58

BALTIC SEA (June 9, 2014) Ships from various nations in the Baltic Region and the US Sixth Fleet command and control ship *Mount Whitney* begin the underway phase of Baltic Operations (BALTOPS) 2014. Initiated in 1971, BALTOPS is an annual, multinational exercise to enhance maritime capabilities and interoperability, and to support regional stability.
US NAVY PHOTO BY MASS COMMUNICATION SPECIALIST 3RD CLASS LUIS R. CHAVEZ JR./RELEASED

will have dug in. Accepting the fact that Russia probably did intend to at least take a breather on this line, even if it was not fully committed to stopping, NATO will have sufficient time to build up its own forces during the lull. In fact, while Russia is attacking, halting, and attacking again in Ukraine and the Baltics, NATO will have already begun to mass its armies.

Reasonably believing its forces to be a sufficient deterrent along the Rivers Line, NATO will be free to concentrate on its naval capabilities, beginning with the positioning of two armadas, the US Sixth Fleet to pass through NATO partner Turkey's Bosporus Strait into the Black Sea and the NATO fleet moving from the North Sea to the Baltic Sea through Germany's Kiel Canal south of Denmark, the same waterway Kaiser Wilhelm II had enlarged to accommodate dreadnaughts (battleships) in World War I.

But neither the allied fleets nor the Russian Black Sea Fleet and Russian Baltic Fleet are going to be focusing on battleships or even aircraft carriers. This is the missile age, and according to *Defense News*, "Russia's Baltic Fleet consists of some 50 different vessels, comprising diesel-powered submarines, one Sovremenny-class destroyer, about eight Steregushchy- and Nanuchka-class missile corvettes, two Neustrashimy-class guided missile frigates, six Paschim-class anti-submarine warfare vessels, and a few dozen smaller vessels and landing ships."

Another factor is the Russian Navy's more than one-hundred-year gap in combat experience. Its technology, untried in a hostile environ-

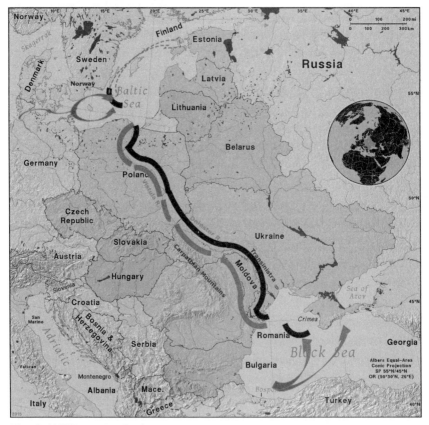

Map 9: NATO counterattacks

© 2010, 2013 BY IAN MACKY, WITH ENHANCEMENTS AND MILITARY OPERATIONS BY DOUGLAS COHN

ment, will not properly perform. As a result and as expected, the ensuing battles will be no contest. Both the Russian Baltic and Black Sea Fleets will quickly be dispatched by the US and NATO fleets, opening wide Russia's vulnerable land flanks. In the south, Crimea will fall to US Marine landings from the Sixth Fleet. In the north, the Estonian island of Saaremaa will be taken by landing troops from the NATO fleet, effectively bottling up the Gulf of Riga, turning the Russian lake into a NATO lake.

With both flanks turned and their rear areas laid wide open, Russia will be compelled to pull troops (dotted arrows on Map 10) off its Rivers Line as well as bring in reserves from east of the Ural Mountains. The eastern reinforcements would follow the pattern established in World War II when Germany's Axis partner, Japan, failed to open a Far East Front against the Soviet Union. Now as then, Russian forces that had been facing China instead of Japan will be freed up for the same reason: China will choose to sit out the conflict.

Even so, these Russian reinforcements will be unable to arrive in time to alter the outcome. NATO will have already launched Phase II of its offensive (see Map 10).

The US Sixth Fleet will finish off the Russian Black Sea Fleet in front of Odessa while a detached task force passes through the Strait of Kerch into the Sea of Azov and simultaneously establishes a beachhead on the Russian side of the strait.

In anticipation of Phase II, NATO will have massed additional forces in front of Russia's weak and unreliable ally, Belarus, and when Russia pulls its best units off that line in a rush to reinforce its faltering strategic flanks, NATO will be ready to launch a massive ground and air assault. The Russians will be stunned. Belarus will panic. With their Baltic and Black Sea Fleets destroyed and NATO forces in their rear, Russia's Belarus ally will suddenly sue for a separate peace.

This is the point where mutually assured survival enters the calculus. Just as Russia emphasized it had only sought limited territory, it would now be incumbent upon NATO to do likewise, clearly stating it is halting after freeing the Baltic States and Ukraine, though noting there will be a Russian price to pay. NATO will keep the Kerch Strait beachhead

Map 10: NATO counterattacks. Phase II, ground and final naval campaign

and, having replaced the autocratic Belarus government with a temporary NATO-controlled regency preparatory to holding democratic elections, Belarus will join NATO. NATO forces now there in occupation will remain there as allies just as they place permanent formations in the Baltic States. Ukraine will also join NATO, and NATO troops will be permanently established there. And finally, Kaliningrad will be ceded to Poland.

This is a small penalty for Russia, but it would virtually guarantee an end to Russian provocations in Europe. On the other hand, NATO will encourage the Russian leadership to redeploy major forces to the Far East as insurance to prevent China from taking advantage of Russia's weakened state. For, while Western Europe rejoices in its victory, NATO's leaders understand how Russia's defeat might provide an unintended opportunity for the People's Republic of China. All will turn on NATO's ability to overcome Russia's innate paranoia.

World War 4: The Great China War

We support China's rise and encourage it to become a partner for greater international security. However, China's actions are adding tension to the Asia–Pacific region. For example, its claims to nearly the entire South China Sea are inconsistent with international law. The international community continues to call on China to settle such issues cooperatively and without coercion. China has responded with aggressive land reclamation efforts that will allow it to position military forces astride vital international sea lanes.

—THE UNITED STATES MILITARY'S CONTRIBUTION TO
NATIONAL SECURITY, JUNE 2015
COURTESY US DEPARTMENT OF DEFENSE
(SEE APPENDIX A FOR THE COMPLETE TRANSCRIPT)

[Fascists] demand free enterprise, but are the spokesmen for monopoly and vested interest. Their final objective toward which all their deceit is directed is to capture political power so that, using the power of the state and the power of the market simultaneously, they may keep the common man in eternal subjection.

—VICE PRESIDENT HENRY A. WALLACE, 1944

These conditions gave rise to Fascism, the belief in a totalitarian dictatorship controlling nearly all aspects of the state: government, army, press, schools, etc. However, unlike the Soviet model of Communism, it allowed free enterprise and private property, thus appealing to the

business-oriented middle class since it gave them economic security.
Finally, Fascism was also intensely nationalistic and aggressive in its
foreign policy.

—CHRIS BUTLER, "THE FLOW OF HISTORY"

LEAD-UP TO WAR

Stephen Chen, writing in the *South China Morning Post*, explained:
"China really is the Middle Kingdom—literally, and for much longer
than we ever knew, scientists say. China, whose own name translates as
Middle Kingdom, was located in the centre of the world's first super-
continent, called Nuna, 1.8 billion years ago—cocooned by other ancient
plates that later broke off to North America, India, Australia and others."

"In modern Chinese, the term for China is Zhongguo [中國/中国],"
as described in *Empire to Nation*. It "often literally translated as 'Middle
Kingdom.' The term is of ancient origins, its earliest usage referring to
the 'central states' of the pre-unification period."

The ancient Chinese used the term in lieu of a national name, believing there were no other nations, only barbarian tribes. How engrained
this became in the modern Chinese psyche is unknown, but it does offer
a worldview unlike any other elsewhere among the major nations on
earth, creating an us-versus-them undercurrent at once xenophobic and
paranoiac, a volcanic combination.

No nation has risen as far as fast as China has in less than a decade,
a feat accomplished by embracing capitalism under the auspices of a
command-control economy in an authoritarian one-party system, which
is a definition of fascism, not communism. In this manner China is far
outpacing the economic example set by its fascist predecessor: Germany
in the 1930s.

In 2013 Chinese president Xi Jinping announced: "We all need
to work together to avoid the Thucydides Trap—destructive tensions
between an emerging power and an established power, or between established powers themselves. . . . We aim to double the 2010 level of GDP
per capita income and build a moderately prosperous society by 2021
when the Communist Party of China marks its one hundredth anniver-
sary. The second goal is to turn China into an all-around modern and

socially advanced country by the middle of the century when the People's Republic marks it centenary."

In *History of the Peloponnesian War*, Thucydides postulated that the threat an emerging state (Athens) posed for the dominant state (Sparta) is what led to war. For Xi Jinping, tensions, real and perceived, resulting from his nation's economic emergence are creating an avoidable trap, a stunning statement due to his omission of any reference to China's military emergence or geographic expansionist policies.

Countries may be expected to move in patternless undulating cycles, but China, like Germany of the 1930s, literally moved in a nearly straight line, with its economy and defense establishment increasing in tandem. By the time Adolf Hitler came to power in 1933, German Finance Minister Hjalmar Schacht had already been following famed British economist John Maynard Keynes's advice, employing massive deficit spending to avoid the Great Depression, which at the time was devouring the economies of the United States, the United Kingdom, and France. So as those nations' defense spending languished, Germany's was increasing. Is this what the Chinese leadership has in mind or are they seeking to emulate post–World War II Germany and Japan whose economies experienced rapid growth without commensurate military spending? China's actions bespeak the former, Xi's speech the latter. In remarks attributed to Arnold J. Toynbee, the renowned historian described this dilemma as "the perpetual alternation of a Yin state of quiescence with a Yang burst of activity."

The following chart from my book *The President's First Year* graphically displays Germany's rise to military dominance through the use of deficit spending. The finance ministers of Germany, Japan, and Italy listened to Keynes; the leaders of America, Great Britain, and France did not, and their military preparedness accordingly suffered.

Without a thriving economy, Adolf Hitler would have been just another megalomaniacal blowhard discarded to the trash heap of history. And even with Germany's emerging strength, Hitler jumped the gun in 1936, sending troops into the demilitarized Rhineland against his generals' advice. The German Army was not yet prepared to face its former World War I foes, but the gamble paid off when the French and British failed to assert their military advantage.

Blame Keynes—US vs. German Military Spending 1932–1945 (in billions of US$)

Year	United States	Germany	Comments
1929			Hoover becomes president; stock market crashes
1930			Great Depression begins
1931			
1932	$.702	$.250	US income taxes dramatically increase
1933	$.621	$.290	FDR succeeds Hoover; Hitler comes to power
1934	$.541	$.292	
1935	$.728	$2.415	
1936	$.916	$4.352	
1937	$.968	$4.704	
1938	$1.021	$6.908	
1939	$1.294	$12.048	World War II commences in Europe
1940	$1.567	$16.550	
1941	$5.875	$24.180	Hitler invades USSR; United States enters World War II
1942	$22.633	$31.120	
1943	$60.882	$36.590	
1944	$74.670	$44.500	
1945	$80.616	$25.780	World War II ends

Sources:
US Department of Commerce, Bureau of the Census, Historical Statistics of the United States, Colonial Times to 1970, Part 2.
Charles Maier, The Economics of Fascism and Nazism: In Search of Stability (Cambridge: Cambridge University Press, 1987).

A similar situation is playing out on the other side of the world. Fascist China has become the world's second-largest economic power, but that financial power has not yet created a comparable military machine, though the Chinese government behaves as if it has. In recognition of this growing threat, the United States initiated the "Pivot to Asia" of enhanced alliances and deployment of military forces. This is a beginning, but it only addresses defense of nations and seas not in dispute. The true test will come over the issue of unpopulated islands in the East China and South China Seas, the Rhinelands of the Pacific. China, Japan, South Korea, Vietnam, Malaysia, Brunei, and the Philippines all lay claims to several of these islands and the potential oil reserves in the waters surrounding them.

China has become increasingly aggressive, declaring sovereignty and a no-fly zone over the East China Sea islands and constructing a runway in the South China Sea's Paracel Islands while laying claim to the Spratly Islands there as well. The United States has already put the no-fly proposition to the test, and now it is time to take the next step. The unoccupied islands will be occupied by a consortium (the step being as economic as it is military in scope) of US and regional forces and defended by the Seventh Fleet. The consortium will then submit each member's competing claims along with those of China to a neutral international tribunal. In this way, Chinese aggression can be confronted, and the message made clear that the rule of law, not military bullying, will prevail in the region.

Whereas Russia cannot begin to match the West financially, China can, making China the greater threat. By changing the dates and names on the "Blame Keynes" chart above from the 1930s and Germany to the twenty-first century and China, the course for America and its allies becomes clear. China must be contained while trade and diplomatic dialogue continue, giving time for the Chinese people to continue pressing for increased political freedom.

CHINA ATTACKS

However, if China continues on the path of the 1930s German model, the East China and South China Seas moves will be calculated to test Western resolve just as the German move into the Rhineland tested the French and British. And when that resolve is not forthcoming, China will make its next and quite unexpected move. Just as Germany turned its attention away from the Rhineland and moved against Czechoslovakia and Austria, China will move against two friendless nations: North Korea and Burma (Myanmar).

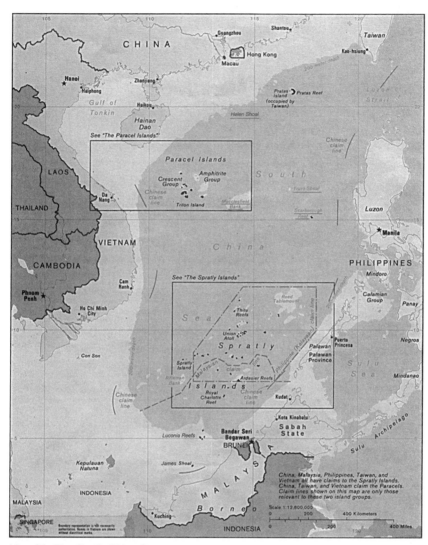

Map 11: The South China Sea
COURTESY OF CIA

Map 12: The East China Sea Air Defense Identification Zone (ADIZ) as shown in gray boundaries

Indeed, North Korea's only ally is China, which is why no nation will come to its aid. China is a nuclear power adjacent to nuclear powers, Russia, Pakistan, India, and to an emerging degree, North Korea. Although Pakistan is a China friend, if not an ally, Russia and India are not, and China has fought border conflicts with both of them. However, with its massive population centers, China cannot win a nuclear war, and its leaders have accordingly made a no-first-strike pledge. A reciprocal pledge can only be made by rational leaders of stable governments as exist in India and Russia, but North Korea is another matter. All the world knows that nuclear weapons in North Korea's irrational hands present a threat to mankind.

In this situation, the world would applaud, if only in private, a Chinese move against North Korea. Certainly, no nation is going to come to its aid. But besides eliminating a potential nuclear threat, albeit from an ally, what does China gain? It gains an easy conquest that confuses the West, opens a door to the Sea of Japan, brings its forces eye to eye with US forces in South Korea, and anchors its eastern flank while Chinese armies concentrate elsewhere. And, like Germany in the 1930s, China will have put both its power and its willingness to use it on display. When looked upon in conjunction with China's rolling takeover of the East China and South China Seas islands, the move will also force the US Seventh Fleet to spread itself thinner.

Then, with all eyes on those seas and Korea, China will make its move against Burma. Quickly driving down the Irrawaddy River against another easy mark, China will finally oust Burma's military rulers, a feat long wished for by most civilized nations. True, those rulers had been moderating their activities and theoretically acceded to civilian rule, but they still asserted substantial control, and their nation, like North Korea, lacks allies.

North Korea had a substantial army, but it was primarily deployed on the Demilitarized Zone (DMZ) facing South Korea, whereas Burma, with a negligible army, did have its limited forces facing China, its long-time adversary, but to no avail. In both cases the weaknesses in military strength, positioning, and defenses will offer invitations to invasion by the fire-breathing Red Dragon on its northern borders.

The conquest of Burma will open another door and a major coup: Singapore, the fourth-largest commercial center in the world, sitting astride the Strait of Malacca, one of the world's busiest waterways. That extraordinarily wealthy city-state's large majority is ethnic Chinese, and the Chinese government will offer them Hong Kong–like semiautonomy while providing all the benefits, military and economic, sufficient to entice

an irrepressible reality. Like the Anschluss when Germany peacefully marched into and annexed Austria in 1938, Chinese troops will swarm into Singapore and not a shot will be fired.

The benefits to China will be enormous. In a lightning move China will have gained a major presence in the Indian Ocean through Singapore and Yangon (Rangoon), Burma's largest city, port, and capital. At the same time, and in conjunction with its island expansions in the South China Sea, almost all of Southeast Asia—Malaysia, Thailand, Laos, Cambodia, and longtime foe Vietnam—will be encircled and the sea lanes dominated.

Presented as China's response to the Pivot to Asia, it had actually long been in the planning, and all will be accomplished within the span of a few weeks, long before the United States and its allies can formulate a countermove. Coming as a complete surprise to countries not already included in the Pivot, it would be a repeat of 1950, when the United States created a defensive ring to thwart communist expansion in Asia, but by openly excluding South Korea, unwittingly offered an opening for aggression that North Korea, and eventually China, accommodated in what became the Korean War.

As China's strategic goals suddenly become apparent, the result of all this—North Korea, the East and South China Seas islands, Burma, Singapore, and the isolation of Southeast Asia—would be more calamitous than the fall of Singapore to the Japanese in 1942. Suffering only negligible losses, China will have gained increased power, prestige, territory, trade routes, one of Asia's economic tigers (Singapore), and more. From Yangon to Singapore to North Korea, China will have established with minimal cost and effort an East Asia Empire and placed the nations of Southeast Asia on a path toward Chinese hegemony.

THE FAILURE OF AGGRESSOR'S GRACE

As in the Russian scenario (see Scenario 1), China will suddenly halt. It's the Aggressor's Grace. We have seen it before. Hitler conquered France and offered peace to Britain. Japan conquered most of the Pacific by 1942, creating its Greater Co-Prosperity Sphere, that nation's way of saying, "We have gone as far as we intend to go; it is a fait accompli the world must accept." The world did not, because the Aggressor's Grace is just that—a period of grace before continuing, an interlude, a momentary halt while it digests its conquests.

Yet, in this scenario, the United States would be unable to counter China on land without the transfer of major forces to a like-minded ally's soil just as occurred between the United States and Britain in World War II, a time-consuming endeavor. Contiguous Russia could certainly react to China, but to what purpose? China's moves are not threatening Russia. But one country would out of necessity react: India. India's nuclear arsenal, like China's, thwarts the risk of being overrun, and this will free India to engage China in a limited war while it seeks allies. China, which fought India in the past, will now pose an even greater threat by intruding upon India's deep-sea domain, the Indian Ocean, and that ocean's Bay of Bengal in particular. With a hostile Pakistan to the north and west and a hostile China to the east and now also to the southeast, India cannot stand idle. The nation will seek assistance, but go it alone if necessary. In any event, due to the rapid movements of China, the go-it-alone scenario would have to suffice for the immediate response.

Two routes of Indian attack would be possible. First, the possibility of engaging China in Tibet as it did in 1962 would seem to offer certain benefits, especially due to Tibetans' hostility toward the Chinese occupiers who have controlled their country since 1950. However, the mountainous terrain favors the Chinese defenders.

The other route would be to replicate the World War II Burma Road strategy, though this, too, would involve difficult terrain as well as dense jungles. Even so, this is the route leading to Yangon (Rangoon), which is the key to liberating Singapore. If Yangon falls to Indian forces, the Chinese supply line to Singapore will be cut. Keenly aware of this fact, China is certain to prepare defenses in depth along the India-Burma border, setting the stage for a bloody battle.

India maintained good relations with the Soviet Union throughout most of the Cold War and continued in that vein with its successor state, Russia. Now, with war looming, India will call upon Russia to at least commence military maneuvers on its border with northern China. This being a risk-free accommodation, Russia will comply. On the other hand,

Pakistan will take advantage of the situation and initiate military moves into Kashmir, a region long in dispute with India.

India will also implore Vietnam to open a second front against China, its longtime antagonist. But Vietnam will hesitate, preferring to first consult with its Southeast Asian neighbors as well as the United States, the only major sea power in the region.

With so many diplomatic missions in play and the buildup of Indian forces on the Chinese border proceeding with dispatch, the potential vulnerabilities facing China are going to become increasingly clear and must be confronted.

Rather than being surrounded by barbarians, the Middle Kingdom, aka the People's Republic of China, well realizes it is simply surrounded and that military success will come only if it keeps those surrounding nations apart, which is why China must defeat India before India can form any viable coalitions. This is why China, having first tried the Aggressor's Grace and failed, will immediately launch a new offensive, just as Germany did with the Battle of Britain in 1941 and Japan did at the Battle of Midway in 1942. In both instances those aggressor nations thought they had already delivered knockout blows only to find themselves faced with intractable foes. Neither country's prewar planning had included campaigns that would lead to the British Isles or Midway. Likewise, China will not have included an invasion of India in its prewar planning, a fact that is going to require significant ad hoc adjustments as assets and forces are rapidly repositioned.

THE SINO-INDIAN CAMPAIGN

India will prove to be as intractable as the United States and Britain, aided by time and terrain, which will work in concert against China— time because a defiant India might attract allies and terrain because that same mountainous jungle China counted on to dissuade Indian moves eastward must now be overcome as China goes westward with its own preemptive offensive. The problem is further complicated by the waterways, all of which run north-south, except the northeast-to-southwest Brahmaputra in eastern India, and that is where China will attack, down the river's valley using neutral Bhutan to the north and neutral Bangladesh to the south as flank protection, thereby avoiding Burma's jungles. The entire campaign will be predicated upon India concentrating its forces in the south for a direct thrust toward Yangon, in which event they will be trapped between Burma and Bangladesh while the Chinese offensive proceeds west. In keeping with the tenets of mutually assured survival (MAS), the Chinese objective will be limited to the conquest and annexation of Assam and the other isolated provinces of northeast India. It is a sound plan, provided assumptions about India's military dispositions are correct and the execution is properly conducted.

The Chinese will be wrong on both counts. Enemies rarely do what is expected, and India, taking note of the Chinese concentration along the Brahmaputra, will scrap its Burma-first strategy, and instead also concentrate astride that river, where it will retreat instead of stand, drawing the Chinese deeper into a trap. At a precisely timed moment, India will suddenly violate Bhutan and Bangladesh neutrality and strike the Chinese Army's flanks and supply line, surprising and confusing the Chinese generals in the first round of the Sino-Indian Campaign. To mollify China, Bhutan and Bangladesh will loudly object to India's violation of their neutrality, but fully aware of the threat posed by China, they will take no military actions.

Whether India's campaign succeeds will not be important. It will only be important for India to demonstrate to the world that it is a match for China, that it can resist and survive to buy the time necessary for other countries to awaken.

What will surprise the world even more will be the poor quality of Chinese military leadership. China has not fought a significant war since its brief conflict with Vietnam in 1979. Now, in the twenty-first century, the People's Liberation Army (PLA) is an army without veterans. Before World War II, Gen. George Marshall, who would become the US Army chief of staff, kept a little black book filled with the names of promising officers, most of whom were World War I veterans, and when war came he drew on that book when selecting his generals; even then he was forced to fire and replace a number of them. But the PLA has no general with a little black book of promising veterans, so its untested armies are led by untested leaders. The result should have been predictable. Strategic planning in Beijing and strategic execution at the front could not possibly coincide. In such an environment, tactical mistakes abound, especially instances of friendly fire as troops move through unreconnoitered terrain such as the Himalayan foothills adjacent to the Brahmaputra.

Opposing them, the West Point–trained Indian commanding general will take a page out of the 1939–40 Winter War, when a superbly trained and led Finnish Army fighting on its own familiar territory initially defeated a vastly larger Soviet Army. Often strung out in long road-bound columns, the Russians were susceptible to furious, ghost-like attacks by white-camouflaged, ski-equipped Finns who struck and cut them up front, flank, and rear. The Chinese reaction to the similar Indian attack will mirror the Russian response, with firings, executions, shattered

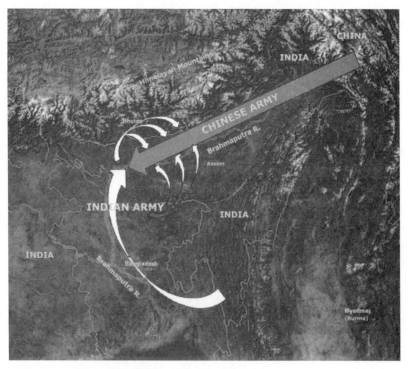

Map 13: Sino-Indian Campaign
© 2010 COURTESY OF NASA

nerves, and plummeting morale, first among the officer corps, followed quickly by the rank and file.

The PLA near-bloodless campaigns against North Korea (where Chinese troops poured across the undefended Yalu River, catching their erstwhile allies flatfooted) and Burma (a country that lacked the strength to even put up token resistance) will have provided false hope and unearned bravado for officers and troops who collapse when a modern, well-equipped Indian Army confronts them, an army kept finely tuned due to encounters with Pakistan and involvement with other neighboring nations. India also militarily benefits from being the largest contributor of forces to UN peacekeeping missions around the world, whereas China's UN peacekeeping roles have entailed far fewer troops and far fewer command positions.

Vulture Allies Join the Fray

With China suddenly struggling to hold its own with India, vulture allies will quickly join the fray, beginning with Russian incursions into China's Manchurian region and followed by the former Soviet Muslim "Stan" states on China's western border: Kyrgyzstan, Tajikistan, and Kazakhstan (which is dropping the "stan"). Particularly inviting to the Stans is the fact that they border China's Uyghur Autonomous Region, a hotbed of antigovernment Muslim separatists.

These Russian and Stan moves will unexpectedly stymie India's potential Southeast Asia allies and the Western Pacific nations of Japan, South Korea, Taiwan, and the Philippines, all nations that had been considered most likely—along with their mega-ally, the United States—to confront China over what they consider to be the illegal occupation of islands in the South China and East China Seas. Initially, the United States will increase its military footprint in South Korea, the purpose being to tie down the Chinese forces now occupying North Korea rather than engage them. The other Western Pacific "allies" will take the opportunity to occupy and divide the numerous unoccupied East and South China Seas islands among themselves. This will be a mistake, because India will look upon itself as being abandoned and forced to turn to and strengthen its ties with Russia and the Stans.

The wild card will be Pakistan, faced with the dilemma of following its faith or following its friend. With its fellow Muslim countries, the Stans, moving in an alliance of convenience on the side of Hindu India against its longtime friend, China, Pakistan cannot remain neutral, for to do so would be a betrayal to both the Stans and China. The situation would be enough to confuse a Confucian.

Faced with the unravelling of its war strategy, China will once again seek peace, though this time not the fake armistice of the Aggressor's Grace, but a real peace born of necessity. Too late. India cannot stop until China is out of its eastern provinces as well as Burma and Singapore; India's vulture allies, Russia and the Stans, will not stop until they have picked apart their pieces of China; and the United States and its Pacific Rim allies would be foolish to stop before they even began, lest they lie vulnerable to a future of Chinese provocations and aggressions.

China Under Siege

With its peace overtures rejected and its forces struggling against India and Russia and just holding its own against the Stans, China will find itself under siege, not knowing where the next blow will land. China will not have long to wait.

Past alliances notwithstanding, Pakistan can see which way the wind is blowing and will quickly come to terms with India over the disputed Kashmir region, preparatory to launching its own strike against China. To China it's the meanest cut of all, one its army only vaguely had contingency plans to confront, though it is certainly no meaner than China's betrayal of North Korea. There will be more.

The US Navy will flood friendly and desperate Malaysia with troops, a move designed to instantly cut China off from its recent prize: Singapore. The US forces will not have fired a shot, and Singapore will once again become independent as the Chinese occupation of that valuable city-state will no longer be tenable.

On the northeastern corner of Southeast Asia, Vietnam, China's historic foe, will remain idle, content with tying down a large Chinese Army merely with the threat of belligerence. This will be the case because Vietnam and its fellow Southeast Asian nations have nothing to gain by invading China, for to do so would bring large Chinese populated areas under their control, a population that would never be allowed Vietnamese citizenship and would always present the problems disenfranchised minorities typically present to occupiers.

This same reasoning should have dissuaded Russia from its invasion of Manchuria, but Russia will, in all probability, engage in ethnic cleansing by forcibly expelling the Chinese populace it conquers. This reasoning would not apply in the western theater, filled as it is with non-Chinese populations. In these regions, Muslim nations joined to invade the Muslim Uyghur region of China. Meanwhile, India will be liberating, not conquering, Burma and possibly Tibet. This leaves the issue of Chinese-occupied North Korea. Will it be resolved by acceptance, military confrontation, or peace-table negotiations?

CONGRESS OF VIENNA REDUX

From 1814 to 1815, great and small powers met in Vienna to redraw the map of Europe following Napoleon's defeat. What the Congress of Vienna mostly did was turn the clock back, but not completely. The freedoms inherent in French republicanism and the law and order of the Code Napoleon had infected the European populace. In any event, in the twenty-first century, Vienna once again—due in part to diplomats' sense of history and in part to a belief by all parties in the neutrality of the locale and its leaders—will look like an appropriate place for redrawing maps. So, as the campaigns in Burma, Uyghur, and Manchuria press on, the belligerents will begin peace talks in what will be dubbed the Second Congress of Vienna.

However, these campaigns represent separate wars fought for separate reasons, and as such, there will have been no coordination between the campaigns, and, unsurprisingly, no coordination in peace negotiations. Only one absolute will hover over the proceedings. If China's foes press too hard and too far, the risk of nuclear war could come into play. This, at least, will have a dampening effect on all of the various military operations.

China will press for the status quo ante, but that is almost always a nonstarter for the aggressor nation. India will demand the removal of

Chinese forces from Burma and Tibet. Pakistan and the other Stans will expect China to relinquish control of the Uyghur Autonomous Region. Russia will demand a piece of Manchuria. The United States, not having openly engaged in hostilities, will join South Korea and its Pacific Rim allies to insist upon China's cession of North Korea to create a unified Korean nation. And all of China's enemies will join together on one subject: independence for Hong Kong, the reason being that this one-time British possession had dramatically enhanced China's economy after Britain's ninety-nine-year lease ended and sovereignty was transferred to China in 1997. Rightly or wrongly, China will be perceived as having used Hong Kong's wealth to help fund its offensive military capabilities.

China's peace conference strategy will be predicated upon two pillars: the threat of nuclear conflagration and allied divisiveness. The first of these will force a halt to further intrusions of Chinese territory; the second could be fed through separate treaties with each of the belligerents.

When faced with a similar situation in 1815, Austria's clever conservative Prince Klemens von Metternich and France's slithery brilliant Charles Maurice de Talleyrand were able to overcome provincial claims of numerous disparate parties. Now, in the twenty-first century, will diplomats such as them appear once again to do likewise? If not, only power politics might prevail.

No country will have benefitted more than India. Following Chinese land cessions, India will replace that country as the most populous nation on earth and acquire hegemony over Burma and Tibet, the nations it liberated and will hereafter defend with troops on the Tibet-China and Burma-China borders. This will be a fait accompli and require no negotiations; India will walk away from the peace table.

China will easily—almost happily—cede the Uyghur region to the Stans, of which the most powerful, the Kazakhs, will take control.

Russia will be the problem. Just as it took a slice of Japan at the tail end of World War II, so it will attempt to replicate the procedure in China's Manchuria. This will provide an opening for the United States and its numerous allies. Not having directly opened hostilities with China, the United States will be somewhat free to claim the honest broker mantle. Backed by its powerful land, air, and sea forces, and actively supported by Japan, the Philippines, Taiwan, South Korea, Vietnam, Laos, Cambodia, Thailand, and Malaysia as well as Indonesia and Australia, the United States will make and receive three concessions: the unification of Korea by South Korea, Hong Kong independence, and China's renunciation of any claims over Taiwan. In exchange, the United States and its allies will become a Chinese ally against Russia, and a guarantor of China's newly drawn western boundaries. Russia could not begin to consider confronting such a coalition, and it will accept a greatly reduced slice of Manchuria instead of the great swath it was claiming.

Pakistan, having come late to the party, will leave empty-handed while facing a significantly enhanced India, a balance-of-power adjustment certain to end its provocations over Kashmir. Under the circumstances, Pakistan could have fared far worse.

In the end, China will have attempted much and lost much.

The big winner will be the nonbelligerent, the United States, which will see the results of its Pivot to Asia paying off beyond anyone's expectations. As the leader of a huge coalition of nonbelligerents, the United States will prove to be in the strongest position to push Russia back while forming a new and lasting relationship with a humbled China. Although the nuclear card will prevent the United States from demanding a change in China's fascist government, the United States and its allies will now be positioned to bring economics to the fore for that purpose. The world will wait—and hope.

World War 4:
The Chinese Civil War

The presence of U.S. military forces in key locations around the world underpins the international order and provides opportunities to engage with other countries while positioning forces to respond to crises. Therefore we will press forward with the rebalance to the Asia Pacific region, placing our most advanced capabilities and greater capacity in that vital theater. We will strengthen our alliances with Australia, Japan, the Republic of Korea, the Philippines, and Thailand. We also will deepen our security relationship with India and build upon our partnerships with New Zealand, Singapore, Indonesia, Malaysia, Vietnam, and Bangladesh. Such efforts are essential to maintaining regional peace and building capabilities to provide for missile defense, cyber security, maritime security, and disaster relief....

The ability to quickly aggregate and disaggregate forces anywhere in the world is the essence of global agility. We are striving to increase our agility by improving campaign planning, sustaining a resilient global posture, and implementing dynamic force management processes that adjust presence in anticipation of events, to better seize opportunities, deter adversaries, and assure allies and partners. We also are more fully sharing forces among Combatant Commands to address transregional threats. We are positioning

forces where they are most needed, exemplified by our rebalance to the Asia-Pacific region . . .
—THE UNITED STATES MILITARY'S CONTRIBUTION TO
NATIONAL SECURITY, JUNE 2015
COURTESY US DEPARTMENT OF DEFENSE
(SEE APPENDIX A FOR THE COMPLETE TRANSCRIPT)

Extend the sphere and you take in a greater variety of parties and interests; you make it less probable that a majority of the whole will have a common motive to invade the rights of other citizens; or if common motive exists, it will be more difficult for all who feel it to discover their own strength and act in unison with each other. . . . A religious sect may degenerate into a political faction in a part of the Confederacy; but the very sects dispersed over the entire face of it must secure the national councils against any danger from that source.
—JAMES MADISON'S FEDERALIST PAPER NO. 10

MADISON WAS THEORIZING HOW ETHNIC AND RELIGIOUS DIVERSITY spread across America's geographic expanse was a safeguard for the nation's form of self-government. It is not a theory China ever accepted, opting instead for homogeneity over diversity. But Madison warned how an absence of diversity allows a tyrannical and oppressive majority to take root and vanquish the rights of minorities. Hence, the Madisonian concept of democracy is predicated upon a constitutional guarantee of those minority rights, and this is important to bear in mind when assessing the motives and actions of China's government.

It is only natural that the oppressed resent the oppressors, and, after gaining sufficient strength, challenge those oppressors. This is even more likely when a population's ruling segment consists of a plurality instead of a majority. In such a situation, if say 40 percent of the people dominate the 60 percent who are divided among several factions (Madison's word for what would later become political parties), those dominated will gain strength only to the extent that they can band together.

This describes modern-day China, where over 90 percent of the people are Han Chinese and the minorities are truly minor, yet all of the people are ruled by a small faction of communists in Beijing.

Xinjiang, China's westernmost province, was annexed in 1949, and its Muslim Uyghur population became one of the most organized and outspoken opponents of the Chinese central government. Tibetans, whose nation was absorbed by China in 1950, make up the other major ethnic opponents. In all, there are fifty-five ethnic minority entities in China, but together they account for less than 10 percent of the population. As a result, rather than being a rallying point for other dissidents, Uyghurs and Tibetans actually tend to solidify Han Chinese nationalism, if not Han Chinese unity.

The real threat to the central government comes from Han Chinese fighting Han Chinese, which is what occurred on June 4, 1989, in Tiananmen Square and elsewhere in the nation. This is not unusual. After all, the English Civil War and the American Civil War were primarily waged by people of similar races and ancestries who separated into factions for other than ethnic reasons.

China's ruling faction, the Chinese Communist Party (CCP), and its eighty-three million members make up less than 6 percent of China's 1.4 billion people, and even they wield little power. Beina Xu and Eleanor Albert, writing for the Council on Foreign Relations, put China's hierarchy in perspective:

> The CCP convenes its National Party Congress (NPC) every five years to set major policies and choose the Central Committee, which comprises around 370 members including ministers, senior regulatory officials, provincial leaders, and military officers. The Central Committee acts as a sort of board of directors for the CCP, and its mandate is to select the Politburo, which has twenty-five members.
>
> In turn, the Politburo elects through backroom negotiations the seven-person Standing Committee, which functions as the epicenter of the CCP's power and leadership. Xi Jinping, who took over from Hu Jintao in 2012, sits atop the system as general secretary; as president and head of the military, he exerts enormous influence in setting

parameters for government policy. The premier, Li Keqiang, heads the State Council, China's equivalent of a cabinet. In Xi's transition to power, he has amassed more power than his predecessors; as the sole head of a number of important leading groups, his unilateral decision making has to some extent undermined his party's prior commitment to consensus-based rule.

This is the opposite of Madisonian democracy. He warned of the tyranny of the majority, with the tyranny of a plurality, by definition, being even more dangerous. Worse, still, is the tyranny of the minority down to the worst of all, the tyranny of one. Where does China's system fall among this pyramid of tyrannies? Somewhere in the realm of a tyrannical minority, which may fluctuate between one—the general secretary of the party—and twenty-five, the number of Politburo members. But as incomes rise and fall and freedoms come and go, the ruling minority could potentially expand to include the 370 members of the Central Committee and beyond. The question is whether a growing dispersion of power will keep up with the public's expectations.

In 1989 those expectations grew into peaceful demonstrations, and the communist leadership overreacted. Considering the absence of threats or weapons among the demonstrators, civil war fears, which were utterly implausible then, have become real today because never again will such an outpouring of dissent come unarmed to the streets of China.

China's leaders, Deng Xiaoping and Li Peng, tragically miscalculated when they issued the fatal order to disperse the student and worker demonstrators occupying Beijing's Tiananmen Square: "Use any means." That loaded phrase led to the military use of lethal force and reverberating repercussions. Hundreds, if not thousands, of demonstrators were killed. MIT professor Stephen Van Evera, noting that "the Chinese People's Liberation Army (PLA) is highly civilized," made clear that the Tiananmen Square massacre was a civilian leadership-initiated event.

The uprising came at a time of reform, following the death of Mao Zedong and the demise of his violent and reactionary Cultural Revolution. Seemingly counterintuitive or at least ironic, Tiananmen Square was, in fact, neither. Equal sparks are created whether the dreams of the hopeful outpace reality or the dreams of the hopeless replace reality.

In the immediate aftermath of Tiananmen Square, repression, censorship, leadership purges, arrests, and trials were the order of the day. Then something extraordinary transpired. Deng Xiaoping overruled hardliner Li Peng and reinstituted economic reforms, especially in the realm of private ownership and profits. This coincided with the coming turnover of Hong Kong from British to Chinese rule scheduled for 1997 under Deng's banner of "one country, two systems."

Interestingly, a non-Chinese influence was at play. According to Ezra Vogel's biography of Deng Xiaoping, the late Prime Minister Lee Kuan Yew of Singapore was the "individual outside China who had the greatest impact on Deng and on China's march to the market . . . and every Chinese leader since Deng has consulted Lee when making critical decisions." Capitalism was coming to China. Harvard professor Joseph S. Nye saw this as one part evolutionary and one part leadership self-preservation because in contrast to the days of Mao, "the legitimacy of the Chinese government depends on a high rate of economic growth."

Even the practice of religion was tolerated, and independent newspapers mushroomed. Political parties did not. The Communist Party remained the nation's party, and the people remained disenfranchised. Even so, this left the free nations of the world to hope capitalism would eventually breed democracy, and businesses, large and small, flocked to China.

So despite the initial economic setbacks following 1989, including trade sanctions imposed by several nations, the United States and Great Britain among them, China's economy began expanding at a rapid pace.

But will economic freedom lead to political freedom? Not likely, and when it does not, the ghosts of Tiananmen Square will return, and not as peaceful protesters. They tried that route and were slaughtered for their naïve idealism.

The concept of "one country, two systems" ominously masked within its quaint wording underlying and unintended meanings beyond the description of a communism-capitalism economic hybrid. It was actually describing what would become a political-economic hybrid of heavy-handed communist rule overseeing a command-control capitalist economy.

"Extend the sphere," Madison wrote, and so the Chinese leadership did, economically, not politically, creating in the process an untenable situation not unlike what the Soviet Union experienced in its own unique manner with perestroika (restructuring) and glasnost (openness) before its downfall.

Today, the central government is not cherished; it is tolerated, and that toleration has a half-life measured in prosperity. But as the Chinese economy and currency continue the slide begun in 2014–15, discontent will rise in opposite tandem. The cost of coveted foreign goods will begin to rise beyond the average worker's financial reach, while the foreign appetite for Chinese manufactured goods simultaneously hits a saturation point, causing decreasing demand to face an increasing supply of unsold goods. A ripple effect will be seen in tenantless buildings, while pollutant-spewing plants and vehicles continue to jeopardize public health with dangerous levels of blinding smog. A January 9, 2016, *New York Times* editorial declared, "Ultimately, however, China's leaders must realize that they need to modernize their policies by encouraging more private initiatives and greater competition. Their nation has changed dramatically over the last three decades, and a command-and-control approach to economic management will not produce the results of the past."

Chinese leaders' attempts to explain that lower levels of prosperity are still phenomenal compared with the situation twenty, thirty, and forty years before matters little to people who never lived through the bankrupt economies foisted upon their parents and grandparents by the false prophets of a flawed communist system in such fiascos as Mao's "Great Leap Forward" and the "Cultural Revolution," lethal experiments responsible for the deaths of millions and the impoverishment of millions more.

Today's hybrid system promoting economic prosperity without political freedom is also failing. "Under President Xi, China is rapidly retreating from rights reforms and the Party's promise to 'govern the country according to law,'" said Sophie Richardson, China director at Human

Rights Watch. "Repression of critics is the worst in a decade, and there appears to be no end in sight.

"What the Communist Party refuses to permit, however, is intellectual freedom, democratic participation, governmental transparency and a reliable rule of law, which are indispensable ingredients for a truly prosperous market economy."

This will result in a revolt of the "haves," and the "have nots" will be mobilized to suppress it in a dangerous game of Tiananmen Square Redux, albeit with a twist. In 1989 protestors rose up in support of democratic reform as an end in itself; now they will rise up in support of democratic reform to safeguard prosperity. As the economy falters, the "haves" will increasingly have less, and worse, not know how much less is in the offing.

As in 1989, troops will be brought in from the countryside to quell what authorities downplay as an urban disturbance, which a disturbed public and the world will rightly recognize for what it is: an armed revolution. Peasant soldiers, who at least have a job—though far removed from the prosperous "haves"—and military prestige, can be expected to have no compunctions about firing on the city dwellers they resent. Likewise, those educated and relatively affluent city dwellers are not going to be thwarted by semiliterate, backward farmers-turned-soldiers from the hinterlands.

The result will be an urban vortex in the middle of the Middle Kingdom, where the nation's major eastern commercial cities unhappily attract envious, hostile peasant soldiers from across the country. This will correspondingly remove them from the nation's border defenses. Long a nation devoid of allies except for North Korea, militarily, and Pakistan, scientifically and economically, China is surrounded by countries ranging from uninterested neutrals to active belligerents, all of them eyeing China's increasingly denuded borders.

In 1949, at the end of the last Chinese Civil War, the Republic of China (Nationalists) forces retreated to the island of Formosa (Taiwan), and the mainland became the People's Republic of China (Communists). Harking back to that period, and with an eye toward a Taiwan alliance and also to differentiate themselves from the communist system, the new rebels will also call themselves Nationalists.

As the fighting in the east intensifies, cross-border skirmishing will commence, starting with Kazakh probes aimed at helping their fellow Eurasian Muslims in western China's Uyghur Autonomous Region. This initially minor event will have far-reaching repercussions when the Communist Chinese Army in the region proves to be too weak to counter it.

Meanwhile, communist North Korea's large army—the Korean People's Army (KPA), never truly threatened by a South Korean or US invasion—will be free to send help to its embattled communist neighbor. The urban insurgents did not count on this, and the surprise move of more than 500,000 KPA troops into Manchuria in northeastern China will come as a shock. These forces are easily replaced on the North Korea–South Korea DMZ (demilitarized zone) with ideologically infused, but militarily inferior, reserves and paramilitary troops whose sole objective is to bluff the United States and its allies into inertness.

Depending upon the count comparisons, the KPA and its auxiliary forces constitute the fourth- or fifth-largest army in the world, an organization just brimming for a fight, but since the 1953 Korean War Armistice Agreement (a "temporary" cease-fire), its only bordering foes are the US and South Korean troops, who, like themselves, are dug in along the DMZ behind some of the most formidable defenses ever devised.

North Korea's entry into Manchuria will dramatically change the military balance, especially in the fight for Beijing. Russia could intervene but will not, at least not at this stage, in part because it is not clear which side it would choose and in part because North Korea will have preempted it in the one piece of northeast China that Russia has long coveted.

Taiwan's army has been severely pared back from the days when it fostered hopes of returning to the mainland in a bid to defeat the communists. Now, emphasis is on defense, not offense, and military spending priorities have gone to the navy and air force. Consequently, Taiwan cannot begin to offset North Korea's intervention, and the beleaguered Nationalists besieged in Beijing will have to look beyond like-named Nationalists on Taiwan for help.

The bad news gets worse. Pakistan, a staunch friend of the Communist Chinese government, will suddenly put pressure on fellow Muslim

Kazakhs to withdraw from Uyghur, a move that will immediately free up additional Chinese Communist troops to join the fight for the eastern cities. Pakistan's longtime foe, India, not facing an imminent threat from either China or Pakistan, will, like Russia, sit things out, though that second most populous country in the world and its more than two-million-man active and reserve army will continue to pose an ongoing wild-card threat.

This will leave the considerably smaller, but superbly trained Vietnam People's Army (VPA) as the Nationalists' last real hope from a contiguous nation, though such intervention would come with its own set of unique problems. First, although many Chinese insurgents might welcome the help, they fear that the Vietnamese may not depart when peace is achieved. Further, there is a great deal of Chinese-Vietnamese racial hostility that transcends politics, creating doubts and questions alike. What would Vietnam's objective be? The conquest of territory inhabited by hostile Chinese? The installation of a friendly Chinese government opposed to communism, an interesting leap of logic and optimism because communism is the only legal party in Vietnam? Further, there is obvious major concern in reverse: There is nearly a fifty-fifty risk that the Nationalist movement might collapse, and the full weight of the Chinese Communist Army would suddenly descend upon Vietnam. So, for now, Vietnam will also join those who stand and wait.

Another element is nuclear weapons. As the nation splits, its nuclear arsenal will split, with both sides in the Chinese Civil War remaining nuclear powers, though neither side is about to use them on Chinese territory, a fact that neutralizes their deterrent effect.

One bright spot for the insurgents will be Hong Kong, which easily falls to them through a local revolt at the outset of the war and thereafter generally will be ignored, an island city easily supplied and defended and the destruction of which would benefit no one.

With no other assistance appearing, North Korea's intervention is likely to swing the pendulum of war in the Communists' direction. It would take a massive movement from another direction to alter this, and it will come from a surprising source: the United States, where an unexpected public clamor in favor of the insurgents emerges. However, in keeping with America's distaste for large ground operations, the war fervor will manifest itself in air and sea operations, coalition building, and lucrative deliveries of critical arms and supplies funded through Nationalist control of the treasury and large cities, especially from financial centers Hong Kong and Shanghai, the New York and London of the East.

Coalition building after hostilities have commenced entails a set of unique problems, generally connected to and dependent upon the changing fortunes of war, military and monetary, as well as ally reliability. Potential allies are also motivated by objectives. Some might be swayed by "make-the-world-safe-for-democracy" altruistic goals, others by the traditional pursuit of gain. Bearing these divergent ends in mind, attainable objectives agreeable to and believable by every member of the alliance must be found, beginning with the most beneficial deployments of allied forces.

The Communists' two most heavily defended regions are also the most likely avenues for allied offensives: the DMZ in Korea, even though it is being manned in part by second-line troops, and the Chinese-Vietnamese border. The Communists' 2.3 million–man PLA, the world's largest army, will have lost about one quarter of its strength due to deserters going over to the Nationalists, but most of this loss will have been replaced by North Korean reinforcements, although another 500,000 to 600,000 Communist troops will remain tied down in border defenses. This will leave a combined PLA-KLA force of approximately 1.6 million soldiers facing around 800,000 Nationalists, a less professional army made up of disaffected Communist soldiers and insurgent-trained militias. Planes, tanks, artillery, and all the other systems and matériel typically found in modern armies will be split along the same percentages.

The key to a Communist victory will be speed because it will be incumbent upon them to employ their superior numbers to defeat the Nationalists before the Nationalists can draw upon the large city populations to fill their ranks. Since soldiers in a modern army must be well trained in both military and technological endeavors, the Communists will have around four to six months to prevail.

Because the Nationalist path to victory will lay in their ability to turn city dwellers into soldiers, the course for the US-led allies becomes clear. They must use sea and airlift capabilities to help hold those Nationalist-held cities by inserting allied soldiers, beginning with Shanghai, China's largest city with a population of more than twenty million people. As a coastal city, it can easily be reinforced under the protection of the US Seventh Fleet, while a massive airlift operation uses it as a base to leapfrog troops into other major cities. This plan is seemingly viable from both a manpower and matériel perspective, entailing as it does the least risk for the most gain, making it acceptable to America and its diverse collection of military partners alike, including Japan, the Philippines, South Korea, Taiwan, Australia, New Zealand, and Vietnam (the Allies).

The Taiwanese Army has fewer than 150,000 soldiers, but almost all of them could be dispatched by air to Beijing, where North Koreans are making significant headway against the surrounded Nationalists. Taiwan could do this due to reaffirmed guarantees that the US Seventh Fleet will continue to defend the island nation. However, the airlift will be an especially dangerous operation because both the PLA and KPA have mobile ground-to-air missile batteries, which US Air Force–led suppression missions are going to be strained to locate and neutralize. Realizing this, high-ranking political and military Taiwanese leaders are going to expose the airlift as a suicide mission.

The relief of Beijing will quickly be understood by all sides as the key to Nationalist victory, but finally accepting the legitimacy of the Taiwanese complaint, the US-led Allied command will be compelled to find another way to take the pressure off of the Chinese capital. They could launch a major campaign out of Shanghai, but that would entail even higher casualties than the discarded airlift approach. They could initiate an amphibious landing in North Korea and thereby force that nation to recall its army from China, but North Korea has spent more than half a century building up its coastal as well as its DMZ defenses. So no obvious or low-casualty options will seem readily available.

Then, with Allied and Nationalist forces stymied, the most unexpected of events will occur. Russian troops and tanks will pour across the border into Manchuria, not to aid their North Korean allies, not even to aid their on-again, off-again Chinese Communist friends, but to aid the Nationalists. The reasons should have been obvious. Russians realize that democratic nations pose no threat to them, but authoritarian governments such as Communist China do. Further, Russia has long opposed North Korea's advances in nuclear weaponry even while friendly relations were maintained. All this will have come into increasing focus as they watched the likelihood of a Nationalist collapse in Beijing.

Interestingly, Russia will not coordinate its invasion with the Allies, creating a quandary as to its goals and objectives. From the Allied perspective, Russian military campaigns have historically been conducted with territorial acquisitions in mind. At the end of World War II, Russia's predecessor, the Soviet Union, attacked an already defeated Japan and gobbled up land that it never relinquished. What now would be its end game? Manchuria or even Beijing? Allied overtures will be rebuffed. Could it be that the old adage "the enemy of my enemy is my friend" will be turned on its head, becoming "the enemy of my enemy is my enemy?"

In fact, the Russian campaign will concentrate on the destruction of the KPA in China, bringing immediate relief to the Nationalists holding Beijing. An utterly shocked and disillusioned North Korea will have no choice but to rush troops away from the DMZ and its coastal defenses to establish a defensive line along its Yalu River border with China. Simultaneously, Communist forces will fall back from the western edge of Beijing into defensive positions after the KPA front on the eastern side of the city collapses in the wake of Russia's onslaught. These developments will uncover the port city of Tianjin, the nearest ocean port to Beijing.

In an odd twist, the time necessary for the Allies to take advantage of the strategic voids at Tianjin and North Korea will turn on the willingness and ability of the KPA in China to hold out against the Russians. Those North Korean forces, cut off from their homeland and facing overwhelming Russian armies, could surrender, stand and fight, or retreat into the Communists' lines.

Meanwhile, in moves reminiscent of MacArthur's Inchon Landing during the Korean War, Allied forces will rapidly put together an amphibious force to land at Tianjin while South Korea, supported by US air and ground units, finally attacks the greatly weakened North Korean forces remaining along the DMZ. In this highly fluid situation, the speed and directional intent of Russian forces will prove critical.

As these new campaigns in North Korea and northeast China form, they will begin to resemble melees more than planned operations. In quick succession the Russian Army will ease off of its attacks against the KPA outside of Beijing and begin to move south toward Tianjin while also commencing river assaults across the Yalu into North Korea, in both instances coming increasingly closer to confrontations with Allied forces. Thoroughly disheartened, and despite the Russian semidisengagement, the KPA in China will continue its retreat toward Communist lines now pulling farther away from the western side of Beijing. All the while, their comrades defending along the Yalu against the Russians and on the DMZ and coastal defenses against South Korea and the Allies will begin to surrender in droves, creating a strategic void of the entire North Korean nation. Into this mix a strong Nationalist force is going to sally out of Beijing—the eastern side being nearly devoid of enemy troops—to link up with the Allied invasion at Tianjin, which will place the Nationalists and Russians on converging paths toward that port city.

Disarray in the north will create strategic opportunity in the south. At last Vietnam will launch its invasion of southern China, prompted by Allied promises of postwar economic benefits. Vietnam's objective will be to pull Chinese forces away from the Nationalist-held cities rather than to conquer territory. This will be Communist Vietnam's opportunity to rid itself of a hostile—though communist—Chinese government that had so often threatened its borders in the past.

In conjunction with these offensives, the Allies will open another front, successfully breaking out of their Shanghai defenses.

Suddenly threatened with total defeat, the Chinese Communists are going to raise the specter of nuclear war, though it is unclear what access they have to their nuclear arsenal or to the command-and-control systems and sites necessary to implement such a conflagration. Neither the concept of mutually assured destruction (MAD) nor mutually assured survival (MAS) can be assumed to be operative with all of China's major cities being in Allied, Nationalist, or Russian hands. A Communist nuclear campaign would never target them, but Vietnamese, South

Korean, Russian, Japanese, and other nations' cities would certainly offer lucrative targets—but to what end? With the Vietnamese clearly not pressing for a deep penetration of Chinese territory, and Russia's armies, having turned away from the KPA, and seemingly turning against the Nationalists and the Allies, why would Chinese Communists interfere? Faced with unclear or illogical objectives and unknowable repercussions, the Chinese Communists may not choose to play a game of high-stakes nuclear poker, but none of the belligerents can be certain of this.

Such situations call for an honest broker, and neutral India, a nuclear power, will step up to fill the role. But before it can do so, Tibet and Uyghur, sensing the dismemberment of China, will erupt in revolt. With Allied and Russian forces on collision courses north of Tianjin and south of the Yalu and Chinese Communist–controlled land shrinking by the hour, Indian diplomatic skills are sure to be tested as never before.

After sorting out the players and their objectives, capabilities, and threats, India will propose the following solutions that essentially recognize the legitimacy of territory won and held:

1. Russia pulls out of North Korea and away from Tianjin, but is allowed to keep its massive Manchurian conquest.

2. Korea is united under the flag of South Korea.

3. Tibet receives its independence.

4. The Uyghurs are allowed to break away from China and form a new nation or join the Kazakhs as their people determine in a plebiscite.

But what is to become of the Chinese Communist government? It may not control the major eastern cities, but it does control most of the countryside, and it is still sitting on that nuclear arsenal. Communist China cannot be allowed to become a trapped animal with nuclear claws.

Once again, the dynamic will be altered from an unexpected direction, a coup d'état that overthrows the Communist Chinese government, replacing it with a coterie of generals and politicians. Their outreach to Indian negotiators will include an agreement to replace the Communist Party with a form of social democrats who are given a voice in the new

Nationalist-controlled government—an apparently reasonable request, but the Nationalists will not agree, and the fighting will recommence, but without Russian, Vietnamese, Allied, or North Korean involvement.

The thoroughly disheartened and betrayed North Koreans remaining in China will be voluntarily disarmed by Russian forces and repatriated to Korea. Russia, having accepted the Indian recommendations and terms, will pull in its armies to fully consolidate its newly won Manchurian territory. The Vietnamese will return to Vietnam. The Allies will retain control of Tianjin, the critical gateway to Beijing, but otherwise return to their ships and homeland. Except for Hong Kong, which will become independent, Shanghai and the other major cities will be turned over to the Nationalists. A purely Chinese civil war will continue.

This will allay fears of nuclear war because neither side is going to use such weapons against their own countrymen. India's bifurcated truce will have achieved this. What it will not prevent is an ongoing, pointless bloody civil war. Side changing will become commonplace as some Nationalists disappointed with democratic liberalism and commotion will switch to the now moderated former Communist side, whose only other remaining assistance is coming from its old friend, Pakistan. Yet, with Tibet and Uyghur gone, the Pakistani aid can reach them only by air and then only by violating the air space of those former Chinese territories. Conversely, many troops from the former Communist side will defect to the Nationalists in part from ideology, more likely from a sense of which way war's winds are blowing.

Adding to this mix, Russia will once again change sides, primarily due to the belligerent attitude of the Nationalists over its conquest of Manchuria. Already, the Nationalists will have swallowed the loss of China's claim to the disputed islands in the South China and East China Seas, which will have been divided up among the other claimants, who took the action unilaterally without consulting peacemaker India.

Once again, Russia's reentrance into the conflict will have a positive effect, this time because it will force the Nationalists to accept the former Communists into the reconfigured nation's polity, and, of course, confirm Russia's acquisition of Manchuria.

In time the Allies will also depart from Tianjin, their occupation there resembling the days of the Boxer Rebellion, when foreign nations controlled China's port cities.

In the end China will once again claim its place as the Middle Kingdom, this time not as an isolated nation surrounded by barbarian enemies, but as a new democracy spreading the doctrines of freedom to its neighbors, a surprising turn of events for communist Vietnam. This is what newly democratic Russia was supposed to have become after the fall of the Soviet Union, but the United States and the West had in general failed to assist to the degree necessary for such a difficult transition, and Russia became more autocracy than democracy. If the Allies repeat this mistake in China, all will have been for naught. Special care must be taken to create a Madisonian democracy that constitutionally enshrines and guarantees individual and minority rights, but such a system is created in the minds of man as well as in documents and institutions. Much care must be taken as it was when Japan was guided in its post–World War II transition from authoritarianism to democracy. The optimum result will be the creation of a Chinese democracy that is in many ways superior to that form of government anywhere else because its constitution will be an improvement rather than a replica of the American Constitution. With the codification of such changes, China's economy will expand to such a degree that the nation, although reduced in size and population, becomes stronger than it was before the war, proof that a merging of democracy and free enterprise is indeed the finest form of nationhood yet devised.

World War 4: The Polar War

While we prefer to act in concert with others, we will act unilaterally if the situation demands. In the event of an attack, the U.S. military will respond by inflicting damage of such magnitude as to compel the adversary to cease hostilities or render it incapable of further aggression. War against a major adversary would require the full mobilization of all instruments of national power and, to do so, the United States sustains a full-spectrum military that includes strong Reserve and National Guard forces. They provide the force depth needed to achieve victory while simultaneously deterring other threats.

—THE UNITED STATES MILITARY'S CONTRIBUTION TO
NATIONAL SECURITY, JUNE 2015
COURTESY US DEPARTMENT OF DEFENSE
(SEE APPENDIX A FOR THE COMPLETE TRANSCRIPT)

TWO YEARS FOLLOWING THE FIRST VOYAGE OF CHRISTOPHER COLUMbus, Pope Alexander VI announced Lines of Demarcation dividing new western discoveries between Spain and Portugal. Portugal objected, and the Treaty of Tordesillas renegotiated the lines, effectively granting Spain all rights to most of the New World and Portugal rights to Africa and what would become Brazil.

Following Ferdinand Magellan's explorations, a similar agreement dividing Asia and the Pacific, the Treaty of Saragossa, was signed in 1529.

Of course, neither treaty was respected by other powers, England in particular. The economics of rich resources trumped papal edicts and Spanish-Portuguese presumptions of world hegemony.

Today, another resource rush is on, and as five hundred years ago, a treaty has been signed to allocate sovereignty. And just as before, it will be ignored. It is being ignored. And as before, conflict will ensue, first with words, which have already begun, later by other means.

The South Pole sits on land; the North Pole sits on ice, with only sea and seabed below—a seabed sitting atop riches to turn the heads of men and nations alike, although neither man nor nation owns those resources—yet. At no time in the history of the world has so much unclaimed wealth enticed so much power. In the gold rush days, they called the impact of this lure "gold fever" because it turned the rational into the irrational. And when this phenomenon is manifested in national psyches and leaders, anything is possible. War is possible because gold fever has a way of turning people into crazed prospectors and law-abiding nations into aggressive Machiavellians.

Even so, there is at least the framework of law at work, even if it is unlikely to be followed. Indeed, this framework might even engender the opposite of its intent, encouraging claims, creating spheres, and thereby providing excuses for conflict.

Because water, not land, is at issue the framework has evolved from the United Nations Convention on the Law of the Sea (UNCLOS), which became effective in 1994 and is the governing treaty—theoretically. The treaty's Preamble reads in part: "Desiring by this Convention to develop the principles embodied in resolution 2749 (XXV) of 17 December 1970 in which the General Assembly of the United Nations solemnly declared inter alia that the area of the seabed and ocean floor and the subsoil thereof, beyond the limits of national jurisdiction, as well as its resources, are the common heritage of mankind, the exploration and exploitation of which shall be carried out for the benefit of mankind as a whole, irrespective of the geographical location of States. . . ."

UNCLOS now has 162 signatory nations with only one major country not included: the United States. To date, the US Senate has not ratified the treaty due to concerns about sovereignty issues dating back to the Reagan Administration. Since then, all administrations, Democratic and Republican, have supported ratification but failed to find a sufficient number of senators to agree. In truth, it is a complex treaty which makes it all the more likely to be ignored when the stakes are high, and nowhere are the stakes higher for it than in the Arctic.

Modern technology and global warming have combined to open the inhospitable region to mining, drilling, and fishing endeavors that were previously too difficult to economically employ. So plentiful are the estimated deposits of oil, gold, and other resources that a resource rush has been spawned as the five Arctic nations (not including Iceland, Finland, and Sweden, whose claims are limited to areas far removed from the North Pole) lay overlapping claims to the region. And where unclaimed and untapped natural resources are found, the military is not far behind. All the while, the nations of the non-Arctic world seem blithely unaware of the catastrophic potential a resource rush of this magnitude could wield.

The Arctic nations—Canada, Russia, Norway, Denmark through its semiautonomous possession, Greenland (Denmark controls its military and monetary policies), and the United States—are salivating over the riches of the region, and while generally subscribing to the tenets of UNCLOS, these nations will in the end stretch the limits of self-interest. Already, Canada has laid claim to the Northwest Passage, that elusive northern water route between the Atlantic and Pacific Oceans that baffled explorers for centuries, even unto watery graves for some.

Meanwhile, on the other side of the North Pole, the Russian Bear is treading heavily, planting flags, conducting military maneuvers, and laying claims to disputed areas.

And like a lottery that increases in value, the Arctic draws more interest with each new resource discovery or estimate.

On August 4, 2007, the Russian daily *Kommersant* reported: "The world does not doubt that Russia's interest is not purely scientific. According to the U.S. Geological Survey (USGS), the Arctic Ocean's seabed contains nearly 25 percent of the world's deposits of oil and natural gas. It is also rich in diamonds, gold, platinum, tin, manganese, nickel, and lead. Besides, experts predict that the Arctic Ocean's major part will be free from ice by 2040, due to the global warming. It will make seabed mineral resources extraction significantly easier, and their transportation much cheaper."

On March 17, 2015, Duncan Depledge, writing on the news website The Conversation, placed a value on these resources: "The Russian Arctic contains significant reserves of hydrocarbons, diamonds, metals and other minerals with an estimated value of more than $22.4 trillion." There has never been anything like it.

Under UNCLOS, coastal nations have a 12-mile territorial limit and a 200-nautical-mile exclusive economic zone (EEZ). The EEZ provides nations with exclusive fishing rights as well as rights to mine and drill in the ocean seabed, but not to control air or seaborne transit in the area, except for one major exception: ice-covered areas as established in Article 234 of UNCLOS. Also, the continental shelf can extend beyond the 200-nautical-mile limit "if the geophysical configuration allows," but rights are confined strictly to the seabed.

In all this the seeds of dissension have been sown, specifically through Article 4 of UNCLOS: "Where a coastal State intends to establish, in accordance with article 76, the outer limits of its continental shelf beyond 200 nautical miles, it shall submit particulars of such limits to the [UN] Commission along with supporting scientific and technical data as soon as possible but in any case within 10 years of the entry into force of this Convention for that State." This provision allowed signatories to the treaty to extend their continental shelf limits to 350 miles if they could prove to the UN that their existing continental shelves stretched beyond the 200-nautical-mile EEZ limits.

Four of the five Arctic nations used this provision in their race to the North Pole and the immense wealth lying en route. The deadlines for each were: Norway, 2006; Russia, 2007; Canada, 2013; and Denmark, 2014. In an odd twist, the United States has prolonged its ten-year window by not ratifying the treaty. On the other hand, there may be little left to claim after the other nations' claims receive UN sanction. With so much at stake, the process has not been orderly. The claims vary as do the actions—diplomatic, political, and military—and although the United States is prevented from taking a proactive role, it is taking a

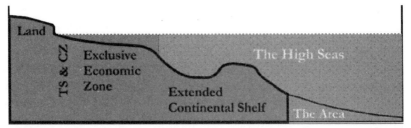

Article 76 of UNCLOS defines the conditions under which a country can determine the delimitation for an extended continental shelf beyond 200 nautical miles. The maritime zones as outlined by UNCLOS are the territorial sea (TS), the contiguous zone (CZ), the exclusive economic zone, the continental shelf, the high seas, and the "Area" (seabed outside national jurisdiction).

reactive role, and doing so against none other than Canada. While it is inconceivable that the United States and Canada could become hostile, their dispute effectively opens the door for Russian intrusions. In other words, if Canada prevails in its unilateral action to claim sovereignty over disputed territory, so might Russia.

There are no passive participants in this game of claims. Here, then, is a capsulation of those claims and actions, competing and otherwise:

CANADA

Under UNCLOS, Canada has laid claim to the Arctic resources from its northern border to the North Pole. It also has claimed total sovereignty over the Northwest Passage as a Canadian waterway within Canadian borders. Words have flown; "foreign" incursions have been made.

In 2007 Russia initiated the Arktika 2007 expedition to the North Pole and planted a flag on the seabed, which Canadian Foreign Affairs Minister Peter MacKay rejected: "This is posturing. This is the true north strong and free, and they're fooling themselves if they think dropping a flag on the ocean floor is going to change anything. There is no question over Canadian sovereignty in the Arctic. We've made that very clear. We've established—a long time ago—that these are Canadian waters and this is Canadian property. You can't go around the world these days dropping a flag somewhere. This isn't the 14th or 15th century."

Russian Minister of Foreign Affairs Sergey Lavrov responded:

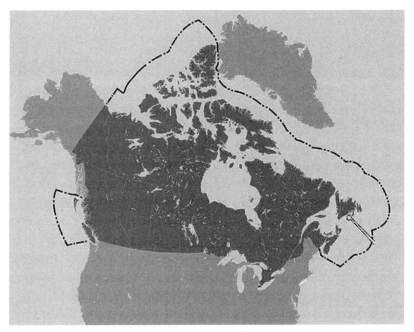

Canadian 200-nautical-mile EEZ
MAPS AND DESCRIPTIONS COURTESY OF FISHERIES AND OCEANS CANADA

I read reports of the statements made by my Canadian colleague, Peter MacKay. I know him quite well—it's very unlike him. I was sincerely astonished by "flag planting." No one engages in flag planting. When pioneers reach a point hitherto unexplored by anybody, it is customary to leave flags there. Such was the case on the Moon, by the way.

As to the legal aspect of the matter, we from the outset said that this expedition was part of the big work being carried out under the UN Convention on the Law of the Sea, within the international authority where Russia's claim to submerged ridges which we believe to be an extension of our shelf is being considered. We know that this has to be proved. The ground samples that were taken will serve the work to prepare that evidence.

Canadian Prime Minister Stephen Harper weighed in on September 25, 2007: "President Putin assured me that he meant no offence, nor had any intention to violate any international understanding or any Canadian sovereignty in any way. Needless to say, I always listen carefully when Mr. Putin speaks."

However, added to Canada's North Pole claims and disputes is Canada's claim to the Northwest Passage, which has been challenged not only by the United States, but by Japan, most European nations, and, of course, Russia. Several of these nations, including the United States, have ignored Canada's assertion of sovereignty and sent vessels into what they consider to be an international waterway.

In response, Harper raised the military ante, announcing that Canada would build "eight Arctic patrol ships, a new army training center in Resolute Bay, [and refurbish] an existing deep water port at a former mining site in Nanisivik."

Alice Zorzetto, in a case study for American University's Inventory of Conflict and Environment, reported: "This potential conflict [between the United States and Canada over the Northwest Passage] is unique in the fact that it is occurring between two nations that possess strong economic, social and political alliances relative to each other. The cultural similarities, and the fact that they are both highly developed nations encourages a diplomatic form of conflict resolution. This diplomatic resolution may not be feasible with nations that are experiencing a higher degree of economic and political instability."

KINGDOM OF DENMARK

On December 15, 2014, the BBC headline was "Denmark Challenges Russia and Canada over North Pole." Denmark's claim is based upon the Lomonosov Ridge that "splits the Arctic in two" and extends from a point north of Greenland, through the North Pole, and ends north of Russia. No area of the Arctic will prove to be more divisive than the Lomonosov Ridge.

On December 14, 2014, Denmark submitted its claim to the UN. If it is upheld, Denmark will have attained the rights to the entire length of the underwater Lomonosov Ridge, a claim that is certain to be ignored by Russia and possibly by Canada because it effectively encompasses the entire North Pole. The situation is further complicated because the claim is based upon Greenland's proximity to the ridge, but Greenland

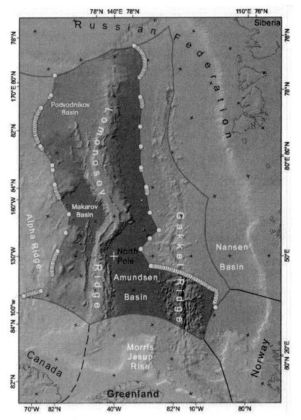

Lomonosov Ridge.
PHOTO COURTESY OF PARTIAL SUBMISSION OF THE GOVERNMENT
OF THE KINGDOM OF DENMARK TOGETHER WITH THE GOVERN-
MENT OF GREENLAND TO THE COMMISSION ON THE LIMITS OF THE
CONTINENTAL SHELF

is already autonomous and there is a substantial movement afoot for
independence. In this event, would the Dane's Arctic claim remain with
Denmark or be ceded to Greenland? If the latter, Greenland would have
no means of defending the claim unless it turned elsewhere for assistance,
and it must be noted that the United States not only maintains an air base
at Thule (now Quaanaaq), Greenland, but also attempted to purchase
the island from Denmark for $100 million in 1946. The Danes refused

then, and the local population is concerned about US weapons stationed there now. Even so, the calculus could quickly change if Greenland gains Lomonosov Ridge and is compelled to address a Russian threat.

THE RUSSIAN FEDERATION

On March 17, 2015, Duncan Depledge wrote: "Tensions have increased a notch in the Arctic with the news that the Russians have started a major military exercise in the region. Nearly 40,000 servicemen, 41 warships and 15 submarines will be taking part in drills to make them combat-ready—a major show of strength in an area that has long been an area of strategic interest to Russia."

Although Russia has come to terms with its Arctic neighbors on several issues, such as its agreement with Norway concerning Barents Sea claims, it has been unrelenting and aggressive on all major points. Chief among them is the Lomonosov Ridge all the way to the North Pole, which Russia claims is an extension of its Siberian continental shelf.

Russia submitted its claims to the UN in 2001, and that body asked for further justification. In 2007 Russia dispatched its Arktika North Pole expedition, which was simultaneously scientific, geological, exploratory, and provocative. At the time, *National Geographic* reported: "Rock samples retrieved last month from beneath the Arctic Ocean indicate that the North Pole is part of Mother Russia, the Russian government announced yesterday. The Russians contend that the Lomonosov Ridge, an undersea structure running across the Arctic Ocean beneath the pole, is a geological extension of the Russian region of Siberia."

Viktor Posyolov, of Russia's Ministry of Natural Resources, told the Telegraph Agency of the Soviet Union (TASS): "With a high degree of likelihood, Russia will be able to increase its continental shelf by 1.2 million square kilometers [460,000 square miles] with potential hydrocarbon reserves of not less than 9,000 to 10,000 billion tonnes of conventional fuel beyond the 200-mile (320 km) [322 kilometer] economic zone in the Arctic Ocean."

And Todd L. Sharp invoked a thinly veiled euphemism in *Defence Studies*: "[S]hould Russia fail to gain the Arctic resources it expects through legal and procedural means, there is so much at stake in terms of Russia's economic security, that other Arctic actors need to plan for the contingency that Russia might attempt to assert its control over Arctic resources and territory through alternate means."

KINGDOM OF NORWAY

Norway has resolved issues with Russia over Barents Sea claims, but the western Nansen Basin remains an open question and has been included in the country's UN claims. Its significance comes from the fact that it lies adjacent to the Lomonosov Ridge. And although Norway is claiming only the western portion, it lies parallel to the North Pole.

As a result, what happens to Denmark's claim for the ridge is certain to impact Norway's claim to the adjoining basin, and once again, Russia is not likely to honor either claim.

THE UNITED STATES

The United States has no direct dispute with Russia's Arctic claims, but acknowledges that such claims could significantly impact allies Canada, Denmark, and Norway. Further, if Russia's claims are approved by the UN or through bilateral negotiations (which are the only negotiations Russia has said it would accept), the United States will undoubtedly be concerned about such wealth falling into the hands of an aggressive state and such ocean territory being occupied by the Russian Navy.

At present, the primary Arctic concern for the United States is Canada, especially concerning that nation's assertion of sovereignty over the Northwest Passage.

POTENTIAL CONFLICT

Russia's initial Arctic claims have already been rejected by the UN, and Russia has announced that it will not abide by that decision, even as it prepares revised claims for submission. Meanwhile, Russia is the only nation to have sent a significant naval force into the Arctic and the only nation to have planted a flag on the seabed of the North Pole. Such aggressiveness can only evoke a response as the Arctic nations grapple with issues of sovereignty, a wealth of natural resources, strategic positioning, and the validity of UNCLOS.

The Russian nuclear icebreaker *50 Let Pobedy* and the Swedish research icebreaker *Oden* in difficult ice conditions during the LOMROG I expedition in 2007 in the Arctic Ocean north of Greenland.
MARTIN JAKOBSSON, STOCKHOLM UNIVERSITY COURTESY OF PARTIAL SUBMISSION OF THE GOVERNMENT OF THE KINGDOM OF DENMARK TOGETHER WITH THE GOVERNMENT OF GREENLAND TO THE COMMISSION ON THE LIMITS OF THE CONTINENTAL SHELF

The United States, Canada, Norway, and Denmark are NATO nations, and when their Arctic claims are validated partially or in full by the UN, the claimed areas, including seabed rights, will become part of each country's sovereign domain, if not its sovereign territory. If any of that domain is then violated by Russia or any other nation, the NATO charter will require all NATO nations to provide military assistance to the violated nation. As a result, even though the United States is the least likely nation to come into conflict with Russia over Arctic claims, it will be embroiled nonetheless if Russia threatens its allies.

WAR

Despite all the diplomacy and talk of goodwill, the rule of law, and rational behavior, the fact remains that the riches of the Arctic are drawing the Arctic nations like miners to a gold rush. Further, if the polar ice cap continues to melt as predicted due to global warming, access to those riches will increase in direct proportion to the receding ice.

Russia has already deployed a flotilla to the region, employed submarines to explore the North Pole seabed, and even planted a flag there. These provocative actions will only increase as extractions of natural resources proceed.

The competing claims over the Lomonosov Ridge are the most likely to create a flash point. Denmark claims the entire ridge, while Norway claims the adjacent Nansen Basin, and Russia claims the eastern half of the ridge, including the North Pole. Canada is also claiming rights up to and including the North Pole as well as sovereignty over the Northwest Passage. The passage will become an increasingly vital waterway as global warming progresses, and the right of passage as an international waterway will be claimed by Russia as a primary route for delivery of the seabed resources it extracts. This will be justified, in part, because the United States also refuses to recognize Canadian sovereignty over the Northwest Passage. However, the United States will very likely drop such objections as Russian belligerency heats up.

In the end, the natural resources of the region will simply be too alluring for Russia to back down. The Russian economy has been built on natural resources, especially oil and gas, and the NATO nations, not fully comprehending the extent of such dependence, will likely downplay the Russian threat until it is too late.

It will all begin when the UN rejects a substantial portion of Russia's revised claims. Russia will then attempt bilateral and regional negotiations, complete with threats, bullying, and disruptions in other world hotspots. This will fail. The price will be too high.

Greenland will join the United States either as a territory or protected region, and the United States will inherit its Lomonosov Ridge claim, placing the nation in direct confrontation with Russia. By then Russia will have commenced underwater expeditions, polar overflights, mining operations, and an ever-increasing surface fleet presence. This will be countered by like moves from the United States and its NATO allies.

Unlike the Cuban Missile Crisis in 1962, when the Soviet Union had little to gain from a confrontation over Cuba, the Arctic riches will likely overwhelm rational thought. On the other hand, the United States will assume, as in 1962 that Russia will step back. Russia, however, will be looking at a different set of historical precedents where the United States was perceived as the nation in retreat. Russian leaders will point to Ukraine, Afghanistan, and Iraq, and they will look at the United States' Pivot to Asia and its consequent efforts to contain China.

As a means of distraction, the Russian Pacific Fleet, operating out of Vladivostok and the Kamchatka Peninsula, will commence diversionary maneuvers in the disputed waters of the East China Sea, where EEZs under UNCLOS are also being contested. And, of course, there will be the usual saber-rattling in Europe.

Both sides will have miscalculated. Russia will not, and the United States cannot, back down. It will be a matter of a drive for national wealth versus the imperative of national defense: greed versus safety, two competing and conflicting motivations that will add up to a casus belli.

The spark that finally ignites the war could come over or under the North Pole, in the Northwest Passage, between fleets in the East China Sea, or even in Europe. However, because neither homeland would initially be threatened, it is conceivable that such a conflict will be waged with conventional weapons. Unlike the surrogate wars of the late twentieth and early twenty-first centuries, a new nuclear restraint could evolve in which the major powers go to war, but specifically avoid attacks of any nature against the home nations, proving once again that nuclear weapons have made the world safe for conventional warfare.

OPTIONS

Of the options available, waiting will not be one of them. Russia is the threat, and the creation of a solid front by the other four Arctic nations, all NATO allies, could begin the path toward deterrence. But first, those four nations must come to terms about their respective Arctic claims. A compromise solution for those nations would include recognition of Canada's claim of sovereignty over the Northwest Passage in exchange for relinquishing its claims over the North Pole.

The United States, having acquired Greenland, will assert its rights for the Danish claim to Lomonosov Ridge. Norway will retain its claim to the Nansen Basin.

At the completion of these negotiations, these nations, led by the United States, would present a consensus front to the UN, leaving only Russia to contest their Arctic claims. However, like Russia, these allies should not wait for a UN decision before sending scientific expeditions and military forces into their claimed regions, followed by the commencement of resource extractions.

In this manner, as in Western Europe, lines will be drawn and appropriately defended, presenting in the process an overwhelming force to potential Russian military designs, and one of the shortest wars in history will end almost before it begins.

World War 4:
The Blue Gold War to Nowhere

Youth populations are rapidly growing in Africa and the Middle East, regions that face resource shortages, struggling economies, and deep social fissures. . . .

Complexity and rapid change characterize today's strategic environment, driven by globalization, the diffusion of technology, and demographic shifts.

Globalization is impacting nearly every aspect of human activity. People, products, and information are flowing across borders at unprecedented speed and volume, acting as catalysts for economic development while also increasing societal tensions, competition for resources, and political instability.

—THE UNITED STATES MILITARY'S CONTRIBUTION TO
NATIONAL SECURITY, JUNE 2015
COURTESY US DEPARTMENT OF DEFENSE
(SEE APPENDIX A FOR THE COMPLETE TRANSCRIPT)

RIVAL IS DERIVED FROM THE LATIN WORD *RIVALIS*, WHICH MERRIAM-Webster defines as "one who uses the same stream as another" and later, with metaphorically sexual overtones, as "a man in love with the same woman as another man." *Rival* then came to describe "one of two or more trying to get what only one can have."

As the director of the Central Intelligence Agency (1997–2004), George Tenet gave a speech surprising to everyone, including this author, who was in attendance. He did not warn us about a resurgent Russia, an expansionist China, or Islamic fundamentalism. He did not paint a picture of collapsing cultures and failing political institutions, nor did he wax ominous about the prospect of a nuclear winter. No, George Tenet spoke of that mundane essential element of life—water—stating that the greatest threat to world peace eventually would be freshwater scarcity.

That was before polar ice cap melting became a topic of widespread concern and discussion and before California and other western states endured a multiyear drought of historic proportions. "Demand in our key rivers systems are outstripping supply," said Caren Trgovcich, the [California] State Water Resources Control Board's chief deputy director. Additionally, groundwater problems are multiplying there, but also in Mexico and worldwide, according to journalist Victoria Burnett: "As California guzzles groundwater and Saudi Arabia rents land [to grow alfalfa] in Arizona because its own aquifers are depleted, Chihuahua [Mexico] is a study in the costs of overusing a resource and the tensions that flare as it becomes scarce." It is a place "where links between organized crime, mining and farming are murky" and where farmers face "difficulty getting permits for wells, and soaring costs for irrigated lands."

This is an age-old problem reminiscent of micro disputes over water rights in the American West or the international macro disputes arising from the diverting of rivers. Europe, for example, is strewn with canals, while rivers such as the Rhine and Danube traverse numerous national boundaries. Aaron Schwabach of the *Berkeley Journal of International Law* addressed the problem inherent in international rivers:

> *We live in a time when demand for fresh water is rapidly surpassing available resources. Nations compete with each other for these resources under rules of international law that are often conflicting or vaguely defined. . . .*
>
> *Under the community theory, the waters of an international drainage basin would be managed as a unit, without regard to*

national territorial boundaries. . . . Because this involves a consid-erable sacrifice of sovereignty by all of the basin states, it appeals to very few, although the European Union seems to be moving in that direction with regard to the rivers which lie within its boundaries. . . .

For the most part, the United Nations has been an enthusiastic promoter of community management of freshwater resources. . . . At the same time, the United Nations approach has been to try to please all, with the inevitable result that it ends up pleasing none. . . .

The Danube is one of the world's great international rivers; few rivers in the world can match the diversity of peoples and nations within its basin. This distinguishes it from Europe's other great international river, the Rhine, which flows only within the developed West and, with the historically intermittent exception of France, only within the Germanic world. Other great rivers, such as the Amazon, the Nile, the Mekong, and the Ganges/Brahmaputra system, are much less developed; the waters of these rivers are put to different uses than the waters of the Danube. They also differ geo-graphically. The Nile, especially, crosses borders rather than forming them, and is virtually without tributaries in its lower reaches. Each international river is unique. This uniqueness renders it difficult and perhaps undesirable to create a single body of international law governing all of them. . . . .

The problem of protecting fresh water is thus fundamentally different from that of protecting other global environmental resources such as the oceans or the atmosphere, which are global rather than local in nature. General rules of customary international law are ulti-mately less satisfactory than carefully designed treaty regimes which take into account the geographical peculiarities. . . .

This does not mean that treaty regimes are always better than customary international law. In many cases, the bargaining power of the parties may be grossly unequal. The treaty regime will then reflect this inequality, rather than the most rational allocation of resources. In other cases, the treaty regime may be founded on an incorrect understanding of the extent or relative importance of resources such as subsurface water.

The unequal nature of bargainers is at the root of potential disputes, which is why an analysis of the most likely places of conflict must center first on inequality—the large-nation, small-nation alliances and the likelihood they will draw large nations into war.

Beginning with South Asia, it is of note that disputes have been ongoing between India and Bangladesh over the Ganges River, compounded because some of the river's tributaries originate in China. Bangladesh, a poor nation plagued by flooding and other natural disasters, won its independence from Pakistan with the aid of India in 1971. China and Pakistan are allies and both nations have fought wars with India. And despite its defense agreement with China, Bangladesh has become a pawn in the Sino-Indian-Pakistani differences, and control of the Ganges could play into this.

The Nile delta is entirely in Egypt, but the headwaters and subsequent route to the delta are found in a variety of countries. Egypt would certainly employ force to keep the waters flowing, which is why none of the other nations involved—all them considerably weaker—would risk manipulating the river, which is to say no rational leader would do so. This, of course, leaves room for the dangerous and erratic behavior of an irrational leader. Even in such an event, it is difficult to envision any of the great powers becoming embroiled there.

China's massive Xiaowan and Nuozhadu dams on the Mekong River have the ability to wreak havoc on its southern river-sharing neighbors, Myanmar (Burma), Thailand, Laos, Cambodia, and Vietnam. Already, when the dams open the spillways, water levels unexpectedly rise. Conversely, those levels can just as quickly drop when the spillways are closed. Either way, the economic impact is felt all the way to the South China Sea. And ever since China's 1979 border war with Vietnam and the more recent disputes over the Spratly Islands in 2016, relations between them have been chilly. The Mekong is the single most critical element in the life of Southeast Asia's nations, and to have it controlled by a hostile China creates one of the world's more ominous geopolitical confluences. However, China cannot use those waters as a weapon against Vietnam without simultaneously harming the other nations in the region, a fact that would compel a Southeast Asia alliance of necessity.

Among the other great rivers, the Amazon is too encompassed within the borders of Brazil to provide nefarious opportunities for its neighbors, and the same may be said for China's Yangtze and Yellow Rivers, America's Mississippi and Missouri Rivers, and all of Russia's great rivers. The various problems arising over European rivers have all been peacefully resolved and are likely to continue to be for the foreseeable future.

In short, when a war over freshwater comes, it will not be over river water, although the inability of rivers to supply humanity's needs will have other ramifications.

In Case Study Number 185, American University's Inventory of Conflict and Environment (ICE), Alicia Zorzetto wrote of resource depletion in 2006:

> It appears that in addition to the issue of commercial travel, other concerns regarding natural resources, abundantly scattered throughout Canada's northern territories, are related to determining the stewardship of the Northwest Passage [see Scenario 5]. Col. Leblanc, Canada's military commander in the North, is convinced, for example, that the pristine waters of the North (which make up 10 percent of the world's freshwater) will eventually become a significant international commodity worth more than oil. The fresh water is formed from Arctic halocline (slope) separating cold, low-saline water from warmer, saltier levels. Canada's northern archipelago is also believed to contain substantial oil/gas resources, and valuable mineral deposits. Thus, if [former] Prime Minister Harper is defeated in his objective to protect what he firmly believes to be Canadian territory, a massive quantity of newly accessible natural resources will be available to any nation interested in exploring the waters of Canada's arctic region.

Clearly, Canada is concerned about encroachments into what it considers its sovereign right to the "pristine waters," but the population of Canada only makes up 0.5 percent of the world's population while controlling 10 percent of the world's freshwater. By definition, Canada is bound to be a water exporter, presumably via pipelines across the Bering

Strait to Asia. Such a pipeline, however, would be subject to interruption as it crosses through Russia, China, and elsewhere.

The alternative would be to use supertankers. Saudi Arabia and the other Middle East oil exporters have extremely low extraction costs, a fact that allows them to economically utilize supertankers to span the oceans and deliver their black gold. The analogy is not precise, but the concept is close enough to apply the same economics to the transportation of water, a commodity the world may soon describe as blue gold, a low-cost commodity made expensive through transportation, distribution, protective services, administrative overhead, and profits. And if the economics do prove to be analogous, how will people afford water at a price of more than $2.00 per gallon when the average Californian in one district, for example, uses water at the rate of 220 gallons per person per day? Even if imported water could be purchased for $1.00 per gallon and usage could be reduced to 50 gallons per person per day, the average person could not afford the $1,500 per month price tag.

In reality, imported water would be supplemental, and when merged with local water and sold by local water authorities, the price for the combined blue gold might be around $500 per month. Further, only those areas devoid of abundant local water would face the higher price tag.

The days of ten-minute showers will be over; water recycling will be in; swimming pools will become private reservoirs.

The other method described in Zorzetto's case study is desalination. In a period of global warming with the consequent rising oceans encroaching upon coastal and lowland freshwater, desalination offers a solution. Israel, a nation with limited freshwater sources, is a leader in the process.

"Production capacity of all of Israel's desalination plants will soon reach 600 million cubic meters of water—nearly 70 percent of the country's domestic water consumption," noted Zafrir Rinat in *Haaretz*, a Jerusalem daily. "Although Israel experienced an unprecedented drought in 2014, there will be no need to build more major desalination plants this decade, according to a new Water Authority report."

Israel's normally limited freshwater supplies would have been sorely tested in 2014 had it not been for desalination: "Water Authority director

Alex Kushnir noted that last year saw record drought conditions. 'Various countries are dealing with a situation of extreme drought by drastic means, to the point of declaring emergencies and making sharp cuts in water supply. In contrast, due to early assessments, Israeli consumers have not been impacted at all by the lack of rainfall,' Kushnir wrote."

Yet, just as imported water is expensive, so is desalinated water, which is why it is not a water source readily available to most of the underdeveloped world.

Further, oil refineries and wells are targeted in wartime, and this also would be the fate of desalination plants. Whereas people can survive without oil, they cannot survive without water, which means a military disruption of water supplies could prove to be fatal for a nation under attack.

Clearly, pipelines, supertankers, and desalination plants all have their benefits and all have their vulnerabilities. This brings the discussion back to the Wild West scenario as played out in the modern world. Property owners who control water can make friends or enemies of their neighbors. Israel, for example, could subsidize its desalination plants and offer inexpensive water to its Arab neighbors, a peaceful gesture far less expensive than war.

Where then, in all these scenarios, will there be a cause of war? Blue gold like black gold or yellow gold will be coveted. Water wells will pop up like oil derricks, and as with them, there will be the infamous angle and horizontal drilling seeking water sources under other nations' lands.

This, then, is the not-so-pretty picture of a future thirsty world. Nations and neighbors will thirst for the freshwater of nations and neighbors. The irony is that such a coveted commodity could actually bring peace to the Middle East. Unable to defeat or coerce Israel, the surrounding nations will need to come to terms with their longtime enemy, who will have become their primary source for freshwater, and conducting cross-border raids and rocket attacks are not going to prove conducive toward that end.

However, because freshwater is a necessity, not a choice, those without it will be forced to obtain it one way or another, peaceably if they can, forcibly if they must. Not all situations will lend themselves to an Arab-Israeli solution, essentially a black gold for blue gold trade. And many of the most waterless regions are among the poorest, which will leave them little bargaining power, and they will resort to piracy.

Water tankers plying the waters between Canada and Japan will have little trouble, but once they move south through the South China Sea to China and on through the Strait of Malacca toward India, they will come into contact with an already active Asian piracy sphere. From there it will be on to the Middle East and Africa and the reconstituted and thirsty Somalian pirates infesting the coastal regions. In fact, much of the sea lane traversing the stretch from Asia to the Horn of Africa and the Red Sea is teeming with pirates. As a result, increased naval protection and patrolling will be essential, and the US Navy will have little reason to be either the only or even the dominant force involved.

Instead, the onus for naval police operations is going to fall on China and India. So, by default, both of those nations would be compelled to commence massive shipbuilding programs, which in time would allow them to match or even surpass the US naval presence in the region. Reminiscent of Germany's fatal decision to compete with British naval dominance in the years before World War I, the United States would almost accidently find itself in a naval arms race in the Pacific and Indian Oceans.

Even wealthy but tiny Singapore would get into the act, building a sizable regional fleet to protect shipping passing through the Strait of Malacca, one of the busiest sea lanes in the world. Ever the capitalist country, Singapore would begin to treat that passage as territorial water and begin charging fees for transit.

The idea will catch on, and China will do likewise in return for escorting civilian convoys through the dangerous expanses of the South China Sea. All the while, the United States will have stood aside as these other nations established naval hegemony over their contiguous waters.

Tantamount to protection money, transit fee excesses will increase suspicions that China is in league with the pirates because any vessel refusing to pay for an escort will almost be guaranteed to fall prey to pirates.

To the south, the large oil-producing, water-independent Indonesia, a Muslim nation, will confront its non-Muslim neighbor, Singapore, over those fees. Indonesia had long benefitted from the Strait of Malacca traffic, which will begin to fall off as transit fees rise. The confrontation will take the form of religious, ethnic, and economic competition culminating with Indonesia's entry into the transit fee racket.

Canada's response to all this will be unexpected. The world's foremost water-exporting nation will design and build the largest ships ever constructed: water tankers dwarfing the size of large oil tankers. With such increased capacity and its commensurate value, the ships will include armaments and a small contingent of government troops. This merging of military and civilian crews on civilian ships will be unique to the times, but not to history. The Canadian Merchant Navy was created in 1939, just prior to World War II. Earlier, the United States had enacted the Merchant Marine Act of 1936 (an expansion of the 1920 Jones Act), Chapter 27, which read in part:

> It is necessary for the national defense and development of its foreign and domestic commerce that the United States shall have a merchant marine
>
> (a) sufficient to carry its domestic water-borne commerce and a substantial portion of the water-borne export and import foreign commerce of the United States and to provide shipping service essential for maintaining the flow of such domestic and foreign waterborne commerce at all times,
>
> (b) capable of serving as a naval and military auxiliary in time of war or national emergency,
>
> (c) owned and operated under the United States flag by citizens of the United States, insofar as may be practicable,
>
> (d) composed of the best-equipped, safest, and most suitable types of vessels, constructed in the United States and manned with a trained and efficient citizen personnel, and
>
> (e) supplemented by efficient facilities for shipbuilding and ship repair. It is declared to be the policy of the United States to foster the development and encourage the maintenance of such a merchant marine.

Unlike those World War II merchantmen and their dual civilian-military roles, the new Canadian megatanker crews will include single-purpose military personnel in addition to dual-purpose civilian crewmen trained to act as onboard militias.

This militarization of Canadian mega–water tankers will inject a new element into the increasingly complex array of competing navies and their pirate antagonists off the Asian and African coasts.

Yet, just as these megaships appear, large, sophisticated pirate vessels will also pop up, almost as a confirmation of foreign government collusion. Overnight the clock will have turned back to the age of Spanish gold bullion–carrying galleons and their English privateer tormentors (government-sanctioned pirates).

The Canadians will counter the threat by running their big tankers in convoys, and when these fail to deter the pirates, regular Canadian Navy warships are going to be added to the mix. This will prove to be insufficient, and Canada will call upon its longtime ally, the United States, and its large, powerful navy to assist.

Having secretly subsidized, encouraged, and even passed on longitudes and latitudes of Canadian tankers to the pirates, China will recognize the situation is beginning to escalate out of control. Too late. The illicit trade will have significantly increased the flow of blue gold to Chinese ports, filling a demand that dare not be interrupted, and filling it through the work of Chinese privateers and their now-large semi-independent navy.

Canadian and US intelligence agencies will pinpoint the hidden coves on the Chinese coast where pirates bring their captured quarry and pump out the liquid gold. But they cannot notify the Chinese government of this; they know that government will only respond by denying the accusations while secretly warning the pirates to move their operations. Instead, Canada and the United States will have no choice but to plan and execute punitive expeditions. They will look at these in the same vein as President Woodrow Wilson viewed the dispatch of General Pershing's army into northern Mexico to punish Pancho Villa and his land-based version of privateers who had been raiding across the US border in the years before World War I. The Chinese will take a different view. To them it will be a foreign invasion comparable to the 1588 Spanish Armada campaign against England.

Once the action begins, the campaign will split the difference between the analogies. The Chinese Navy, patrolling its coastline, will provide the first line of defense for the pirates, and when the US-Canadian armada strikes, it will strike this Chinese picket line, and easily brush it aside, in part through armed action, in part through sheer intimidation. The pirate fleet, caught in a given sheltered port, will be far too weak to put up a fight, and the pirate crews will fade into the Chinese interior, leaving their vessels and captured ships as nothing more than burning hulks. After all, they know the wealthy Chinese government, their not-so-secret patron, can simply build new vessels.

The whole operation will have been an Allied gamble, and that gamble will begin to fail as Chinese land-based missiles suddenly slam into their ships. Allied missiles, planes, and drones will engage in counterbattery fire, while marines pour ashore to secure a foothold in the pirates' abandoned bases.

To the south, Singapore, Indonesia, and India, seeing where their transit fare games can lead, will quickly discontinue the practice. Besides, the flow of Canadian mega–water tankers, now threatened by Chinese missiles as well as Chinese pirates, will have come to a halt. This will have reverberating repercussions because blue gold consumers cannot survive without the continuous flow of the precious cargo. These countries, from India to the Mideast to Africa, will immediately put diplomatic pressure on China to allow the unhindered transit of the tankers. China will respond that the pressure ought to be placed on Canada and the United States, whose forces have violated Chinese sovereign territory.

With its water reserves rapidly running out, India will have no choice but to exert military pressure against China, at first with border skirmishes, and when those fail to achieve the desired result, with a full-blown invasion.

Meanwhile, the mega–water tankers will divert, bypassing the Strait of Malacca and moving south of Indonesia before proceeding on to their thirsty customers. But such a diversion will increase the time, distance, and costs of the product.

All the while, the US-Canadian joint operation will have landed forces at three Chinese pirate enclaves, and all of those forces will come under Chinese missile attacks, but not ground assaults. The Chinese government will still foster hope of a peaceful solution that satisfies the population's demand for water, the pirates' demand for profits, and its own demand for power. Further, once engaged in open conflict with India, China does not want to be involved in a two-front war. On the other hand, the United States and Canada will have little to gain by holding on to destroyed pirate villages, and their forces will depart, claiming—as Pershing did in Mexico—the punitive expedition a success. In fact, it will not have been. The pirates will return, and the pirating will recommence.

This will leave India on its own, facing the full force of the Chinese Army, a situation too enticing for Pakistan to ignore. Pakistan, long allied with China and long hostile toward India, will enter the war. The idea of running increasingly short on water and paying higher and higher prices for rerouted water while confronting both China and Pakistan on the battlefield will be unendurable for India.

India had played it coy throughout the Cold War, remaining friendly with the Soviet Union while claiming to be strategically nonaligned, which is to say, devoid of military allies. Now, in dire straits, that aloof nation will find itself alone. No other nation will see its national interests at stake in the Indian Subcontinent War, and India will be forced to rely upon its technological arsenal: nuclear weapons. This fact combined with the clamoring for water coming out of Africa and the Middle East will suddenly awaken the world to the importance of saving India.

The North African nations, especially populous Egypt and Algeria, are among the most water-deprived nations on earth, but they can get their Canadian and other Arctic water through the safe Atlantic Ocean route. Besides, they are Sunni Muslim nations, and they are not about to side with predominantly Hindu India against Sunni Muslim Pakistan. This same problem exists for the thirsty desert nations of the Middle East. And the water-deprived African nations do not have the military power to offer help against a behemoth like China.

The solution will come from a reincarnated SEATO, the Southeast Asia Treaty Organization, which disbanded in 1977. Like NATO,

SEATO was formed as a bulwark against communist expansion, but its members held too many divergent views about the threat and it lacked a joint military command. Further, Pakistan was one of its members; India was not.

The new SEATO will coalesce around a threat the whole region can perceive: Chinese expansionism. Neither religion nor political philosophy will prove to be factors. China's support of piracy and consequent disruption of the sea lanes; its island seizures in the East China and South China Seas; its previous border wars with India, Russia, and Vietnam; and its current threat to India will provide sufficient rationales for collective security. Every nation from India to Japan will have reason to fear China, and every Asian nation from India to Japan as well as Canada, the United States, New Zealand, Australia, and water-hungry South Africa—another nuclear power—will join SEATO. This eclectic combination of communist, monarchial, democratic, and autocratic nations of Buddhists, Taoists, Muslims, Hindus, Christians, Jews, Animists, Shintoists, and other religions or atheists of every race will require masterly diplomatic suasion and military coordination.

Even though this coalition of the willing could rapidly take shape, some time will still be required, and to help buy that time, the United States will introduce its airpower to the Indian Subcontinent War, while, simultaneously, the US-Canadian armada remains intact as a potential amphibious threat to China. The armada will also pose an actual threat by occupying Hong Kong, in part to distract China from its Indian operations, in part to help secure the sea lanes, in part to deprive China of an economic powerhouse, in part because its population would welcome the allies with open arms, and in part because China will not unleash its missiles against a Chinese population center as it had against the pirate-abandoned villages. With Hong Kong secure, the armada will move up and down the Chinese coast, about 200 miles out, forcing China to tie up large troop formations in defense of its long coastline.

Meanwhile, SEATO troops will be landing in India in ever greater numbers, while a second front will be opened on the China-Vietnam border, where Vietnamese, Cambodian, Laotian, Thai, and Malaysian forces will launch an offensive. With the pendulum once again swinging, this time China will be in trouble.

This will set the scene for a SEATO-favored truce, one that would cause China to lose territory, hegemony, and prestige. Most of all, it would establish a US-led SEATO in control of the Pacific Rim—those nations bordering that great ocean. All this would prove to be too much, not for China, which would have no choice, but for Russia. Already hemmed in by NATO to the west, Russia would now be equally stunted from expansion or influence in the east. And Russia cannot stand by while the Pacific Ocean is turned into an American lake.

So, much to the surprise of all belligerents, Russia will enter the conflict, becoming China's ally, an event China neither sought nor expected, and will only grudgingly accept.

The Russians will begin by providing air cover to North Korea as, at Russia's insistence, that nation finally makes good on its threats and attacks South Korea. The first stage will witness North Korea's unleashing of a massive artillery barrage on Seoul, the South Korean capital so near the DMZ. This had been in the planning for years, but fear of retaliation always sufficed to inhibit the Hermit Kingdom, once an appellation applying to all of Korea, but now just to self-isolated North Korea. With Russian support the calculus will change, although that support would so far be of a defensive nature only. Russian planes will not cross the DMZ. The primary purpose, from Russia's point of view, will be to divert the United States and its allies away from their increasingly successful campaigns against China on the Indian and Vietnamese fronts.

With Russia's entry into the war, six nuclear powers would be engaged, three on each side: Russia, China, and Pakistan against the United States, India, and South Africa. Here, then, with the conflict spreading, and nuclear war becoming an existential threat, the thirsty nations of the world—mostly in Africa—will have all but abandoned the Pacific and Indian Ocean trade routes in favor of the safe Atlantic. Those megatankers full of freshwater coming out of Canada will seek cargos for the return trips, and technology will provide the answer. Previously, it would have been unheard of for megatankers of freshwater to return with holds full of oil (although tanker trucks and ships commonly cleanse between loads of dissimilar commodities). Contamination of water on succeeding trips would negate such trade, but with new methods and chemicals to scour the holds, or through the use of water-only bladders, this trade will materialize and prove to be the most cost-efficient sea trade in history. West African, North African, and Mideast oil will fill the tankers, and the non-oil producers of the region will also increase their exports with various raw materials as well as manufactured goods to replace the Asian markets that had previously dominated this sector. The war had disrupted this trade as Asian nations committed more and more of their resources to war making. Further, the contiguous Asian lanes were no longer safe.

So, once again war will have created unexpected consequences. For centuries Africa had languished, the victim of colonization, exploitation, tribal warfare, corrupt governments, and stalled economies. Ironically, Africa's need for freshwater will be the catalyst for positive change, and most of the African nations will see their economies grow as never before, their governments becoming receptive to freedom as well as capitalism, and a rising middle class asserting increasing influence. The affluent Northern Hemisphere will be moving southward.

Meanwhile the War to Nowhere will continue unabated along the periphery of China, all sides understanding how their nuclear weapons foreclose any possibility of total victory. Already, the North Korean destruction of Seoul, the devastating equivalent of a nuclear attack without the ongoing effects of radioactive fallout, will have provided a graphic display of an unimaginable future.

The Russian gambit will have achieved a desired result in a manner soon to be undesired. The United States and its SEATO allies will divert military assets from the China fronts to Korea and launch a major counteroffensive, eliminating the North Korean Army as an effective force. Having come out of their deeply entrenched defenses along the DMZ and into the open as they pressed south without Russian air cover, the North Koreans had become easy targets. It would be 1950 repeating itself, when the North Korean Army was all but destroyed after attacking South Korea and Chinese forces replaced them in defense of the North. This time it will be the Russians.

As the allied forces begin to move north of the DMZ, the Russian Air Force, having committed to providing defensive cover for the North Korean Army, will soon see there is no army of consequence remaining to be covered. Will the Russians commit their ground forces as the Chinese did in 1950?

At this point all of the belligerents, from the Indo-China front to the Vietnam-China front to what is left of the Korean front, will mentally, if not physically, pause to reassess the situation, realizing:

1. The war began when China's support of piracy interdicted the traffic of Canadian freshwater megatankers through East Asian seas, but most of that traffic has now shifted to the Atlantic Ocean.

2. The primary beneficiary of this has been Africa, where increased trade fostered increased output of manufactured goods, which took market share away from the Asian nations.

3. China's advance against India was halted when the United States reconstituted SEATO and counterattacked.

4. Russia then entered the fray, but only halfheartedly and only to provide defensive air cover for North Korea, which, in turn, prompted North Korea to attack South Korea, flattening Seoul in the process. This action pulled allied troops away from the other fronts, bringing those drives to a halt.

5. The question this brief history poses for the future is a question of objectives: Where are the Indians, the United States, and SEATO going? What does China want? It appears that only Russia has achieved its objective by interrupting the Allied advances. However, this led to the destruction of the North Korean Army. Will Russia now defend that country with ground troops, knowing its army will come into direct contact with US forces?

6. These unclear objectives are why the pundits began calling the conflict the War to Nowhere. But casualties have been high, and the destruction of Seoul unforgivable.

7. At least the terms for peace are obvious: Russia should allow the unification of Korea to go forward under South Korean leadership. In exchange, Indian and SEATO forces should withdraw from China, while the United States withdraws from Hong Kong. But here is the sticking point: The citizens of Hong Kong want to be free from China, and the United States says that is the price China must pay for its blatant support of piracy that set the world to war in the first place.

In this way, peace could be achieved, but not harmony. After such a bloody struggle and loss of trade, the populations of India and the SEATO nations will clamor for more than the status quo ante. Political turmoil will ensue; governments will fall, and new governments will demand reparations in the form of money and land. China's leadership will also change, and the new government will disclaim responsibility for the conflict and further note that its forces had not been defeated. So the War to Nowhere will end in a Peace to Nowhere, in some degree not unlike the Treaty of Versailles that ended World War I only to lay the groundwork for World War II.

SCENARIO 7

World War 4: The Lunar War

*Of particular concern are the proliferation of ballistic missiles, pre-
cision strike technologies, unmanned systems, space and cyber capabilities, and weapons of mass destruction (WMD)—technologies
designed to counter U.S. military advantages and curtail access to the
global commons. . . .*

*Key homeland defense capabilities include resilient space-based
and terrestrial indications and warning systems; an integrated intelligence collection, analysis, and dissemination architecture; a Ground-
Based Interceptor force; a Cyber Mission Force; and, ready ground, air
and naval forces.*

—THE UNITED STATES MILITARY'S CONTRIBUTION TO
NATIONAL SECURITY, JUNE 2015
COURTESY US DEPARTMENT OF DEFENSE
(SEE APPENDIX A FOR THE COMPLETE TRANSCRIPT)

JUST AS THE SMALL ISLANDS OF THE PACIFIC WERE LOOKED UPON AS
unsinkable aircraft carriers during World War II, so the moon has come
to be viewed as a permanent low-gravity satellite.

In a 2012 Senate hearing, the Defense Intelligence Agency director,
Lt. Gen. Ronald Burgess Jr., testified: "China is beginning to develop and
test technologies to enable ballistic missile defense. The space program,
including ostensible civil projects, supports China's growing ability to
deny or degrade the space assets of potential adversaries and enhances

China's conventional military capabilities. . . . China successfully tested a direct ascent anti-satellite weapon (ASAT) missile. . . . A prerequisite for ASAT attacks, China's ability to track and identify satellites is enhanced by technologies from China's manned and lunar programs. . . . Beijing rarely acknowledges direct military applications of its space program and refers to nearly all satellite launches as scientific or civil in nature."

Anthony H. Cordesman at the Center for Strategic and International Studies wrote: "China's growing capabilities translate into military capabilities that affect all aspects of conventional and nuclear targeting, ground-air-sea operations, precision conventional strike capacities, and missile defense."

The Treaty on Principles Governing the Activities of States in the Exploration and Use of Outer Space, Including the Moon and Other Celestial Bodies—known as the Outer Space Treaty—was ratified by the US Senate on April 25, 1967, and, to date has been signed by more than one hundred countries, including all of the major powers. The US Department of State issued a narrative, explaining that "its concepts and some of its provisions were modeled on its predecessor, the Antarctic Treaty."

Like that Treaty it sought to prevent "a new form of colonial competition" and the possible damage that self-seeking exploitation might cause. . . .

The substance of the arms control provisions is in Article IV. This article restricts activities in two ways:

First, it contains an undertaking not to place in orbit around the Earth, install on the moon or any other celestial body, or otherwise station in outer space, nuclear or any other weapons of mass destruction.

Second, it limits the use of the moon and other celestial bodies exclusively to peaceful purposes and expressly prohibits their use for establishing military bases, installation, or fortifications; testing weapons of any kind; or conducting military maneuvers.

After the treaty entered into force, the United States and the Soviet Union collaborated in jointly planned and manned space enterprises.

(See Appendix C for the full treaty text.)

As described in Scenario 5, Pope Alexander VI announced the Treaty of Tordesillas, dividing interests in the New World only to witness the treaty's impotence as national self-interests took precedence. And such will be the case with the Outer Space Treaty. It is only a matter of goals and deterrents.

When one of the world's major powers decides sovereignty in space is critical for national survival, the treaty will be scrapped. This could be triggered for a variety of reasons, first among them being another nation's unacknowledged violation of the treaty.

More likely, it will happen when the world's major powers simultaneously realize the importance of space to national defense and deep-space exploration. This is where the unsinkable aircraft carrier analogy comes into play because the nation occupying the moon will control Earth-centric space.

It will begin with the establishment of permanent US, European, Russian, and Chinese moon installations, all of them manned, all of them defended with an assortment of weapons. However, the weapons and tactics will of necessity be geared to a new dimension. Whereas Earth combat—including air combat—is tied to the x-y plane defined by land, no such limitation exists in three-dimensional space. In this environment the moon is simply another satellite, albeit a large satellite, in an infinite void.

Retired Department of Energy physicist Dr. Thomas Finn said, "Low Earth orbit satellites are only 300–600 miles up and provide continuous monitoring of the Earth because of their number. Geosynchronous (fixed-position) satellites are 22,500 miles up. The moon is 240,000 miles away and covers the Earth in a lunar month. It takes a long time to deliver a weapon from the moon."

The two models—Earth and space—intersect only when control of the moon leads to military ascendency on Earth, a strategic event reached only after tactical success is attained in the limitless expanse of space. This realization will be the primary motivation for nations to abrogate the Outer Space Treaty and strive for lunar conquest.

Interestingly, when the first conflict does occur on the moon, it will not be compounded by a corresponding conflict on Earth since only lunar outposts, rather than cities, will be at risk. The United States and Europe will become allies; Russia and China will not.

Preconflict logistics will be both the key and the spark to war in space. This will begin as each nation understands the urgency of building up a lunar infrastructure, fuel and food reserves, and weaponry because once fighting commences all will turn on the ability of the belligerents to reinforce and resupply their lunar outposts. This will be critical because the buildup of reserves on the moon will provide vulnerable and inviting targets. Only the continuous flow of men and matériel can keep the outposts viable, and this will raise the fighting from the moon's surface to the vast space between the moon and Earth.

Ground-to-air and air-to-air combat on Earth consists of anti-aircraft fire, drone, plane, and missile attacks, all of which are dependent upon direct hits or, more likely, near misses that disable the targets. In space near misses would entail a much larger blast area to have any hope of being incapacitating, and this is where nuclear weapons come into the calculus. However, according to Dr. Finn, "There is no blast from a nuclear weapon in space because there is no atmosphere. The lethality comes from the electromagnetic pulse (EMP), which damages electronics. Satellites are very vulnerable. Power grids are also vulnerable to some extent. Nuclear weapons are lethal to spacecraft. Hardening spacecraft is an important component of the design. In space the nuclear explosion generates X-rays which impinge on the skin of the spacecraft (knocking out electrons) and create the EMP that damages the satellite. There was an agency dedicated to the nuclear threat, the Defense Nuclear Agency (DNA). It has evolved to become DTRA—Defense Threat Reduction Agency."

Although such weapons will continue to have a deterrent effect on Earth, space is another matter so long as any nuclear explosion in that arena is sufficiently out of Earth's orbit and there is no likelihood of radioactive debris falling to Earth. The same would apply to the lunar surface because radioactive material would make the moon's surface inhospitable to all nations.

However, nuclear attacks conducted in open space against logistical spacecraft intended for moon outposts, while increasing the odds of disabling or destroying those target craft, will not affect the nuclear peace on Earth.

All this is logical, but theory and practice rarely coincide. Once nuclear weapons are exploded in space, the genie bottled up since the US attacks on Hiroshima and Nagasaki in 1945 will have escaped. As usual with nuclear weapons, it will be assumed that no nation would directly attack another nation's homeland for fear of reprisals, resulting in a nuclear holocaust. But the threat of deviation from this self-interest will increase once the nuclear war in outer space commences. Even so, the threat will remain just that; self-destructive nuclear war will not spread to either Earth or the moon.

In this scenario China will be the first nation to begin the weaponization of its lunar outpost, quickly followed by Russia, the United States, and Europe, creating an arms race in space. When it appears that China or Russia is on the verge of gaining the upper hand through the accumulation of moon-based weapons, the United States and Europe (the Allies) will have no choice but to respond. Diplomacy will fail in a barrage of denials, and military action will follow.

The Chinese and Russians will be put on notice that the moon is to be quarantined. No further weapons will be allowed, and the Allies will commence the interdiction of moon-bound weapons from both of those countries. Unlike such blockades on land or sea, the means to halt and inspect moon-bound spacecraft will not be available. In an outer space blockade, those craft can only be attacked and destroyed.

The Chinese and Russians will do likewise to Allied spacecraft, and the war will be on, with the tacit self-interest understanding by all sides that it is being limited to space.

The Chinese will employ their wealth in an attempt to swamp the Allied rocket defenses with more spacecraft than can possibly be targeted by conventional means. This is when the Allies will switch to nuclear-tipped rockets as a means of broadening the defensive EMP cloud, which would be the space equivalent of flak in Earth-borne anti-aircraft terms. The Chinese will respond in kind. Russia will await developments.

China can circumvent the Allies' nuclear shield by routing its supply spacecraft far out in space, away from the moon, then back and around to the opposite undefended lunar dark side. This will up the economic ante because the cost for the Allies to expand their nuclear shield would be exorbitant.

This will also bring about the second stage of the war: the Allied assault against the Chinese and Russian lunar outposts with conventional forces. Having anticipated this, China will employ its nuclear weapons to engage the Allied invasion fleet, causing significant casualties.

As so often happens in war, unforeseen consequences take the conflict in unexpected directions, and a lull will suddenly come over the outer space battle zone as all sides reassess their predicaments. Time will be against the lunar outposts, however, as supply craft fail to keep up with supply needs. The rerouting of spacecraft to the lunar dark side will prove to have tripled the time to destination.

This time, diplomacy will play a role as all sides find it in their mutual interests to return to the terms of the Outer Space Treaty and demilitarize the moon—but the peace will not hold. All of the belligerents will turn the problem over to their scientists, and the outer space arms race will become the outer space science race, a race reminiscent of the World War II scientific race to build the first atomic bomb.

How this will play out cannot be known. It will be the stuff of incomprehensible futurists and could include anything from a means to neutralize nuclear weapons to building even more powerful weapons. It might include the development of spacecraft capable of catapulting through a nuclear shield or of manmade satellites surrounded by their own protective shields. Lockheed Martin's Space Fence is being built to track potentially threatening space debris, including parasite satellites capable of infecting US military satellites. Meanwhile the Pentagon is planning to create target dispersion by flooding space with large numbers of satellites. However the science race turns out, the winner of the race will be the winner of the war, and, like the Cold War, it may end through the acknowledgment of technological superiority, which is what opponents of the attacks on Hiroshima and Nagasaki had in mind when they advocated a demonstration instead of the military use of atomic power.

World War 4: The Nuclear Terrorist War

Iran also poses strategic challenges to the international community. It is pursuing nuclear and missile delivery technologies despite repeated United Nations Security Council resolutions demanding that it cease such efforts. It is a state-sponsor of terrorism that has undermined stability in many nations, including Israel, Lebanon, Iraq, Syria, and Yemen. Iran's actions have destabilized the region and brought misery to countless people while denying the Iranian people the prospect of a prosperous future.

North Korea's pursuit of nuclear weapons and ballistic missile technologies also contradicts repeated demands by the international community to cease such efforts. These capabilities directly threaten its neighbors, especially the Republic of Korea and Japan. In time, they will threaten the U.S. homeland as well. North Korea also has conducted cyber attacks, including causing major damage to a U.S. corporation.

—THE UNITED STATES MILITARY'S CONTRIBUTION TO
NATIONAL SECURITY, JUNE 2015
COURTESY US DEPARTMENT OF DEFENSE
(SEE APPENDIX A FOR THE COMPLETE TRANSCRIPT)

Admiral Giampaolo di Paola, chairman of the NATO Military Committee, said, "We live in a world where threats have no borders and borders have no threats," which begs the question: Can the United States and its NATO allies be allied with a nation's people, but not the nation? In fact, NATO has done just that in the Balkans and the Middle East, but more often the opposite has been true. Several countries come to mind: Turkey, Saudi Arabia, and Pakistan. In each of these countries and others, Americans are less popular with the populace than with the leadership, but only one of them, Pakistan, has a nuclear arsenal.

Professor Stephen Van Evera, a member of the MIT Security Studies Program, wrote, "The rogue military danger . . . is very alive in a dangerous place: Pakistan. . . . Today it [the Pakistani military] dominates public discourse and shapes politics from behind the scenes. . . . The Pakistani army has long engaged in hidden but close cooperation with al-Qaeda" and "supports the Afghan Taliban in killing U.S. troops, even while it receives U.S. foreign aid."

Pakistan is simultaneously allied with the United States and China, and a longtime foe of India and Russia. One of the country's top nuclear physicists, A. Q. Khan, provided atomic bomb technology to Libya, Iran, North Korea, and China, theoretically without government sanction, yet he is a free man in Pakistan today.

Meanwhile, Pakistan's Inter-Service Intelligence Directorate (ISI) appears to act as an almost autonomous agency, aiding US friends and foes alike, possibly supporting nuclear proliferation, possibly supporting A. Q. Khan.

On November 8, 2015, a *New York Times* editorial provided a full-throated warning of the dangers posed by Pakistan's growing nuclear arsenal:

> *With as many as 120 warheads, Pakistan could in a decade become the world's third-ranked nuclear power, behind the United States and Russia . . . and it has become even more lethal in recent years with the addition of small tactical nuclear weapons that can hit India and longer-range nuclear missiles that can reach farther. . . .*

The fact that Pakistan is also home to a slew of extremist groups, some of which are backed by a paranoid security establishment obsessed with India, only adds to the dangers it presents for South Asia and, indeed, the entire world. . . .

During the Soviet occupation of Afghanistan, ISI coordinated with the United States to supply and train the Pakistan-based Mujahideen in its cross-border insurgent war against the Russians. However, when the Soviets departed, ISI continued to support the Mujahideen Taliban off-shoot, which in turn played host to al-Qaeda training camps. Then came al-Qaeda's 9/11 terrorist attacks against the United States, soon followed by the Taliban's defeat at the hands of Afghanistan's Northern Alliance, an operation conducted with American assistance in a brief war that witnessed the United States and ISI on opposing sides.

Later, it was discovered that the most wanted man in the world, al-Qaeda leader Osama bin Laden, the man responsible for the 9/11 terrorist attacks, was living in Pakistan, ostensibly with ISI knowledge. On this assumption, the insertion of US special operations forces to eliminate him was launched without first seeking permission from Pakistan's government.

Next, a resurgent Taliban, based in Pakistan, fought Afghan, US, and allied forces, also with the apparent support of ISI.

All of this adds up to a nation within a nation: ISI within Pakistan, as *New York Times* correspondent Carlotta Gall wrote: "'The madrasas [Islamic fundamentalist schools] are a cover, a camouflage,' a Pashtun legislator from the area told me. Behind the curtain, hidden in the shadows, lurked the ISI. . . . The [Haqqania] madrasa is a notorious establishment, housing 3,000 students. . . . Ninety-five percent of the Taliban fighting in Afghanistan have passed through its classrooms, a spokesman for the madrasa proudly told me. . . . The strategy that has evolved in Pakistan has been to make a show of cooperation with the American fight against terrorism while covertly abetting and even coordinating [the] Taliban."

If ISI gains control of that nation's nuclear arsenal, the threat to India, also a nuclear power, will become significant. However, ISI's proclivity to support Islamic fundamentalists is where the real threat lies. It is this combination of ISI, Islamic terrorists, and nuclear weapons that threatens world peace in myriad ways, possibly including a nuclear attack against Israel, Russia, or even the United States, all through terrorist surrogates.

In this scenario ISI would disclaim all culpability, and the Islamic terrorists would be too dispersed to present a viable retaliatory target. Confusion will reign, accusations will move at Internet speed, and World War 4 will have begun among an intermingling of belligerents reminiscent of the Thirty Years War. In fact, this amounts to more of a theoretical threat than a reality. It would take a far more war zealous entity than ISI to execute such a strategy, and that enemy would soon emerge.

In the meantime, Iran continued to pursue the development of a nuclear arsenal, which, in turn, brought about the Joint Comprehensive Plan of Action signed by Iran, the United States, the United Kingdom, China, Russia, France, Germany, and the European Union on July 14, 2015. The signatories believe the agreement will be sufficient to forestall Iran's nuclear weaponry ambitions. Not all nations agree, and Iran's support of several terrorist organizations poses a proliferation factor.

Israeli ambassador to the United States Ron Dermer wrote, "Because states throughout our region know that the deal paves Iran's path to the bomb, a number of them will race to get nuclear weapons of their own. The most dangerous region on earth would get infinitely more dangerous. Nuclear terrorism and nuclear war would become far more likely. In fact, if someone wanted to eviscerate the global nuclear nonproliferation regime, this deal is definitely a great place to start."

As antagonistic as Sunni Muslim Pakistanis are toward Hindu-dominated India, they apparently dislike Shiite Muslims even more, and Iran is a Shiite nation. Syria and Iraq became Sunni-Shia battlegrounds with Iran supporting Syria's dictator Bashar al-Assad and Shiite militias in Iraq, both of which fought ISIS (the extremely violent Sunni Muslim offshoot of al-Qaeda known as the Islamic State of Iraq and the Levant—or ISIL or ISIS, not to be confused with Pakistan's ISI). The United States and various allies joined in the fight against ISIS but also opposed al-Assad, while generally discouraging Iranian involvement.

Meanwhile, Pakistan's ISI, whose support of Sunni extremists is well known, played a confusing role in a confusing environment. ISIS and al-Qaeda have become increasingly hostile to one another as they compete for adherents. Al-Qaeda and Afghanistan's Taliban are allies. ISI surreptitiously supported the Taliban, even as it played an occasional role in suppressing that organization as it operated from Pakistani bases. US drone attacks joined in such operations, but not in coordination with ISI. What role ISI played in Syria and Iraq, if any, is unknown.

With an array of forces opposing ISIS in Syria and Iraq, that terrorist organization, unable to hold on to its conquered territory, will be far from admitting defeat. ISIS simply chose the wrong target. Already realizing its mistake long before the tables were turned, ISIS began supplanting al-Qaeda in Afghanistan, which was conducting an ongoing insurgency against a weak government virtually devoid of allies. The Russians had fought and lost there in the 1980s, and the United States and its allies reverted from field operations to an advisory role in 2014. Now, if neither Russia nor the United States intervenes, Afghanistan will fall, not to al-Qaeda, but to ISIS, viewing its Syria and Iraq campaigns as nothing more than diversions.

With ISIS controlling a sovereign nation and covertly being supported by ISI in Pakistan, the world will have found in its midst an Islamic fundamentalist state more brutal, extremist, and dangerous than any other country since Nazi Germany was defeated in 1945. A move will be made to prevent ISIS-controlled Afghanistan from taking that nation's seat at the UN, but this will fail when too many nations, dreadful of terrorist repercussions, ignore their duty and vote their fears. Further, Pakistan, coming out of the shadows, will recognize ISIS as the legitimate rulers of Afghanistan, an option no other nation, not even North Korea, chooses.

Not content with legitimacy, ISIS will proceed to foment Sunni revolutions throughout the Muslim world while continuing its reign of terrorism in Europe in an attempt to sow fear and disunity in the West, though what is reaped may be the opposite. Pakistan will attempt to control its uncontrollable ally and surrogate only to discover ISIS influence being directed at the madrasas that heretofore had often been privately funded by Saudi adherents of Islam's ultraconservative Wahhabi sect and occasionally served as a breeding ground for al-Qaeda. With ISIS supplanting both Saudi and al-Qaeda influence in the madrasas, Pakistanis will suddenly discover that they have become the target of ISIS student-infused propaganda. This will quickly spread, inspired by the youthful Red Guard movement during China's 1966–76 Cultural Revolution.

Whereas Pakistan's ISI wielded much power, it only helped to sap the power of the government, dispersing lines of authority and leaving both ISI and the Pakistani government in a weakened and vulnerable position. Historically typical in such situations is a government's sudden collapse, and this will be the case in Pakistan. Soon, with most of the impetus for ISIS influence coming from within Pakistan's borders, another analogy will come into focus: the Nazi movement that subverted Austria and led to the 1938 Anschluss, Germany's peaceful, invited conquest of the country. Likewise, with equal speed and precision, ISIS will gain the reins of power in Pakistan, a nuclear state, and the world will shudder.

All this will occur while Russia, Iran, Iraq, and the United States and its allies are mopping up ISIS remnants in Iraq and Syria. The collapse of that ISIS "caliphate" along the Tigris and Euphrates Rivers will have been an unintended diversion that proves to be fortuitous for the organization in its worldwide designs, which will continue unabated. With success, legitimacy, and nuclear status achieved in Afghanistan and Pakistan, ISIS revolutions will erupt throughout the Sunni Muslim world.

Will ISIS-controlled Pakistan then employ nuclear weapons or use them as a terrorist threat? Previously, ISIS acted rather than threatened, relying upon zealous terror tactics to instill fear in its enemies much as Mongol hordes did in the thirteenth century. It is an instilled fear that causes armies to flee and cities to surrender. But those armies lacked a nuclear retaliatory capability. ISIS in Pakistan will resolve this problem in the same manner previously threatened by ISI in Pakistan. It will distribute nuclear weapons to remote surrogates whose dispersed forces preclude retaliation.

One positive is that there is no template for such activities. Not only must the nuclear weapon be distributed, but also the means—whether by plane, ship, truck, or rocket—of delivering it to a target must accompany the weapon. Further, both the weapon and the rocket or other means of delivery must be supported by trained personnel. In short, nuclear proliferation to far-flung terrorist cells will entail a complex logistical plan. Air and overland routes can be detected through covert means and interdicted, leaving seaborne shipments with a better chance of getting through.

So the problem is posed: With a fanatical terrorist organization in control of a nuclear nation, how is the world to respond, because respond it must. Obviously, covert actions will be attempted, but ISIS, having prepared its takeover with propaganda and indoctrination through Pakistan's madrasas, will have created a solid base of fundamentalist support. A full-blown military invasion is always on the table, but particularly fraught with risks when confronting a nuclear power. This leaves interdiction and isolation.

The United States, Russia, and India will find their interests in complete accord and commence a joint land, sea, and air blockade of Pakistan and Afghanistan, clear acts of war. ISIS-controlled Pakistan and Afghanistan will respond with attempts to secretly supply nuclear weapons to terrorist groups in Chechnya, Libya, Egypt, Yemen, and elsewhere. And since terror, regardless of its magnitude, will be the objective, ISIS will opt for the smallest nuclear devices and forego major delivery means, this being the most likely scenario to meet with success. And, indeed, it will, beginning in Chechnya because that disgruntled Russian territory of Muslim separatists will prove to be the most vulnerable, not being guarded with the US Department of Homeland Security's Human Portable Tripwire (HPT). Developed by the department's Domestic Nuclear Detection Office, the tripwire allows government personnel to "detect nuclear or radioactive material" with "small, wearable radiation detector devices that passively monitor the environment and alert the user when nuclear or other radioactive material is present. . . . The technology can also locate the source of the detected radiation and includes communication features that allow the user to easily seek additional technical assistance from experts if needed."

A handful of Chechen zealots will obtain a nuclear device from Pakistan, transport it to the nearest non-Muslim Russian town, and detonate it, destroying themselves in the process. The amount of damage will not be as important as the message: ISIS will have launched the first nuclear attack since the US attacks on Hiroshima and Nagasaki in 1945. The world will be in shock as a sense of panic grips all opponents of ISIS. Where and when will the next attack come? Calls for full nuclear retaliation against Pakistan and Afghanistan will be heard and just as quickly dismissed although only after Russia is convinced there is a more rational solution to routing out ISIS than killing millions of Pakistanis and Afghans.

However, the prestige of ISIS will have received a substantial boost from its Chechen attack, and hundreds of thousands of new recruits are going to flock to its black flag of jihad. Overnight, megalomania will drive the ISIS leaders into believing this is their moment, not just for a caliphate, but for world conquest. Then, while the world is still reeling from the nuclear shock, ISIS allies in Yemen will set off another nuclear device, this one in neighboring Saudi Arabia, not in a population center, but in the Gahwar Oil Field, by far the world's largest, intentionally creating an immediate disruption and price spike in worldwide oil markets. As in Chechnya, the HPT will not have been introduced into Yemen, where a civil war is raging.

With events spinning into an incomprehensible new reality, the United States and its partners (the Allies) will be compelled to move more rapidly than at any time in history. Fear will inflate reality. Fear will drive decisions, both military and political, unless the world's leaders can quickly devise a viable response. The unfettered free distribution of HPTs will be an important step, but it will be impossible to cover every avenue, and before the HPTs become ubiquitous, untold numbers of Pakistan's small tactical nuclear weapons will have already been placed in terrorist hands far and wide.

Years of intelligence gathering provided the United States with accurate information about Pakistan's nuclear arsenal, which is held deep in the Hindu Kush Mountains and other locations throughout the country. However, the command and control center is in the capital, Islamabad.

This then is the unprecedented situation confronting the world: A rogue zealot regime controls a nuclear nation and has already distributed tactical nuclear devices to its terrorist cells in untold regions. Meanwhile, it threatens to use large-scale nuclear weapons delivered by missiles even though this would result in retaliatory attacks—the potential scale of casualties unimaginable. Yet, a means to overthrow ISIS control of Pakistan must be found because the concept of mutually assured destruction will have no deterrent effect upon fanatics who believe jihadist martyrdom will lead to eternal life. Once understood, this will undermine the Russian option of massive retaliation.

The unimaginable and tragic reality of nuclear war is that civilians become primary targets. A corollary aspect of this is that civilian casualties will be an unavoidable consequence of countermeasures. HPTs can certainly interdict much of the ISIS distribution of tactical nuclear weapons, but for those already in terrorist hands in a variety of nations, eliminating them is going to require the use of planes, missiles, and especially drones in instantaneous attacks that are employed with pinpoint precision before the nuclear devices can be detonated. Such a plan entails striking targets wherever they are discovered as soon as they are discovered, regardless of the collateral damage inflicted on civilians in the strike zone. Special Operations forces supplied with HPTs would be inserted around the globe to detect nuclear weapons, but there will generally not be time for them to eliminate the threats before the weapons are detonated. Only immediate drone and other strikes are capable of handling such missions, which is why collateral damage in these circumstances is unavoidable.

The far more difficult problem will be the neutralization of ISIS-controlled Pakistan's primary nuclear arsenal. An outright invasion would likely end in a nuclear conflagration. India, in particular, will balk at such an idea because, as Pakistan's archenemy, its cities would be primary targets. Likewise, China, Pakistan's longtime ally, has also been its technology-exchanging nuclear ally, but its leadership is rational and can be expected to avoid a nuclear confrontation unless its own existence is placed in question. In short, the two largest nations in the world, India and China, will not participate in any nuclear confrontation with Pakistan. This will ensure China's safety, but not India's because the fear will be that once a nuclear war begins, Pakistan will automatically attack its longtime foe.

With the peripheral war gaining success against Pakistan's distributed tactical nuclear devices, the United States, NATO, Russia, and other allies will focus on the primary objective of neutralizing Pakistan's large-scale nuclear arsenal. Because an invasion will be off the table, a complex campaign will be devised. Technology will be used to disable Pakistan's electricity grid and computer communications while armed satellites are positioned to destroy launched missiles.

In contrast to the peripheral campaign, Special Operations forces will be utilized because Pakistan will not detonate nuclear devices in its own territory. They will be employed in conjunction with a plane-and drone-imposed no-fly zone over both Pakistan and Afghanistan, and they will be backed up with conventional forces.

Russia will largely be excluded from these plans because it cannot be relied upon for the timing and secrecy so essential to success.

The campaign will be executed in several parts. First will be the positioning of satellites, planes, and drones, the disabling of Pakistan's electric grid and computer communications, and the insertion of Special Operations forces against known nuclear sites. This will prompt ISIS to launch nuclear-armed missiles from sites not previously discovered by United States and Allied intelligence sources, sites that will immediately be attacked from the air and by special operations forces.

Pakistan will respond with regular army units, counterattacking the special ops units in the process of destroying nuclear sites. The reality will be that many of the special ops units are likely to sustain high casualties and even face the risk of annihilation unless the troops can be extricated, avoid capture through evasion, or be reinforced by substantial conventional forces. One advantage will be the sheer number of separate Special Op incursions, so many that it will confuse and diffuse the Pakistani response.

At this point the US Fifth Fleet, an element of US Central Command based in Bahrain on the Persian Gulf, will launch an amphibious invasion on Pakistan's Arabian Sea coast and quickly take Karachi with the assistance of some defecting Pakistani Army formations that were filled with conscripts opposed to ISIS. The Allied army and Pakistani defectors will then proceed up the Indus River toward Islamabad.

With Pakistan's nuclear capability apparently neutralized, a new geopolitical dynamic will take hold. Islamabad is only a short distance from the Indian border, and the Indian Army will suddenly join the fray, launching an offensive toward the Pakistani capital. Likewise, the Russian Army will invade Afghanistan, believing that the United States would be pleased to allow Russia's control of that difficult country, unlike the attitude that prevailed when communist Russia invaded in 1979. Then, US-supplied Islamic Mujahideen based in Pakistan forced Russia out. This time, Russia could assume no such US-supplied opposition would materialize, and the US-led attack against ISIS in Pakistan simply opened an opportunity not to be missed.

The question mark will be China, Pakistan's longtime ally. Further, China and India have had an antagonistic relationship, and China is not likely to look kindly on Russian expansionism. As a result, a large Chinese Army will have remained poised on the China-Afghan border ever since ISIS took control of Afghanistan and Pakistan.

Without warning or coordination, that Chinese Army will cross the Afghan border and proceed down the southern slope of the Hindu Kush Mountains toward Kabul and cross through the Khyber Pass into Pakistan, heading for nearby Islamabad. By following that route, the Chinese Army will beat the Russians to Kabul and confront the Indians, who are driving on Islamabad from Kashmir to the east, and the US-led Allies, who are approaching from far south down the Indus River. Further, the only army in their path will be the ISIS-led Pakistanis, who look upon the Chinese as allies. The result will be that China's incursions into Afghanistan and Pakistan will be accomplished without firing a shot. No one will know their purpose or allegiance.

This is the opposite of the ISIS/Pakistani view of Russians, Americans, and Indians, all of whom they will confront and oppose, possibly believing that China, as their friend and ally, will assist in such opposition.

In fact, all entities will literally and figuratively be advancing their own agendas, agendas that will include at least one common thread: the dismantling of ISIS-controlled nuclear weapons.

Russia, as is often the case, will prove to be the most enigmatic as it sends an army across the Caspian Sea, through a friendly "Stan" to

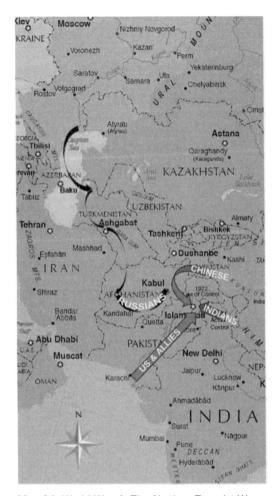

Map 14: World War 4: The Nuclear Terrorist War
© NATIONSONLINE.ORG/ONEWORLD/ASIA_MAP.HTM, WITH
MILITARY OPERATIONS BY DOUGLAS COHN

Afghanistan. Kazakhstan, Uzbekistan, Kyrgyzstan, and Turkmenistan of
the former USSR are Muslim countries. Turkmenistan's population is
not to be confused with the Turkmen, a different ethnic group found in
Syria, Iraq, and Iran. A Russian bombing campaign against Syrian Turkmen has been carried out in support of Syrian dictator Bashar al-Assad,
whom the Turkmen oppose. Turkmenistan has maintained close ties with

Russia, and it is through that nation and its rail lines that the Russian Army will quickly reach western Afghanistan, but why? When the Stans were part of the Russian Empire and later the Soviet Union, Russia's desire to conquer Afghanistan on its way to obtaining a warm-water port was undisguised. But with the dissolution of the USSR, a buffer of Muslim Stan states appeared to make such a goal all the more unrealistic and unattainable. But apparently Moscow's historical view remains. In the 1980s the Soviets failed in their attempt to hold on to Afghanistan because the United States armed the Mujahideen opposition and Pakistan provided them a safe haven. Now, with the United States, China, and India all opposing ISIS control of Afghanistan, there would be no outside help or sanctuaries, and this fact could only arouse Russia's latent interest in the region despite the existence of Stan buffer states. As implausible as this would appear to the outside world, it would be in keeping with Russia's age-old strategic goals.

India, the most obvious belligerent, has had a long-standing dispute with Pakistan, not only over borders and the Kashmir region, but also over the British-imposed partition that separated the two countries after World War II. Pakistan and India have fought wars, but their respective acquisition of nuclear technology and arsenals has had a dampening effect on their conventional military operations. This is why India would make a move against Islamabad only once it was certain that Pakistan's nuclear retaliatory ability was eliminated.

Likewise, the US and Allied invasion of southern Pakistan could be undertaken only after Pakistan's nuclear ability is neutralized. But the operation would be predictable. It must come up the Indus River, and it must secure Karachi to do it. These facts would allow the Pakistani Army to be prepared. Theoretically, India would assist the Allies, but, in fact, such assistance would interfere with Indian plans for its longtime foe. So India will demur, and the Allies would not be allowed to use Indian ports for bases of operations. This will create a long supply line across open seas, a fact that could only hamper Allied operations.

Phase 1 of the war will have been the neutralization of Pakistan's nuclear arsenal. Phase 2 will witness the introduction of Chinese, Russia, Indian, and US/Allied conventional forces. Phase 3, as often happens in war, will entail surprises and unintended consequences. ISIS will concentrate its forces in Pakistan, and this will open the door to Russian and Chinese forces overrunning Afghanistan. China will easily occupy Kabul, and Russia will occupy Kandahar and all of western Afghanistan. ISIS will welcome the Chinese Army into Islamabad as a counterweight to the Indian invasion from Kashmir, and this will free up the ISIS/Pakistani Army to concentrate against the Allies driving up the Indus River from Karachi. Karachi itself will have easily fallen to the Allies with the help of anti-ISIS local insurgents.

India will not want to become embroiled in a war with China, and it will stop and consolidate its position after occupying Pakistani-held Kashmir. As a result, the only significant fighting will be between ISIS and the Allies in the Indus Valley.

At this point, military reality will dictate events. The apparently ungovernable nation of Afghanistan with its history of warlords, jihadists, and heroin exports will now become a problem divided between China and Russia, both of which have reputations as brutal occupiers, a fact not unwelcome to the United States and its allies. Less agreeable will be China's occupation of Islamabad, but as a fait accompli, nothing could be done about it. And neither will India be pleased with this, but it can take great consolation in its acquisition of Kashmir—provided China, with whom it has several border disputes, does not contest it.

The great deterrent hanging over all these operations is the fact that China, Russia, India, and the United States are all nuclear powers, which will provide each of them with an incentive to avoid direct confrontation. Besides, China, Russia, and India will have each gained substantial territory on the cheap. Only the United States and its allies will have engaged in significant military actions, and only they will have the least to gain. After all, what possible benefit could accrue to the Allies by occupying Karachi and southwestern Pakistan?

Once ISIS is defeated, southwestern Pakistan would be too small and too weak to remain as a country sufficiently viable to stop Russian or Chinese designs on a warm-water outlet. Even neighboring India and Iran would be tempted to take a bite out of the territory.

India, a Hindu-majority nation with a sizable Muslim minority, might offer the solution. The United States could turn Karachi and southwestern Pakistan into a large city-state along the lines of Singapore and place it under Indian control, backed by a major US naval base there. China and Russia will object, but just as they control parts of Afghanistan and Pakistan, so they would have to accept the military reality of US, Allied, Indian control of Karachi and its surrounding regions.

ISIS will be the loser in all this, and it will have lost the moment it put its faith in China. When ISIS gave up Kabul and Islamabad to the Chinese, believing them to be allies, they were actually surrendering to an enemy without a fight, a fact the Chinese will quickly make apparent as they join with Russia, India, and the United States and its allies to extinguish that terrorist organization.

Of note will be the fact that the nuclear threat will have acted as a magnet, bringing together all of the nuclear powers in a common purpose for the benefit of mankind.

World War 4: The Commerce, Currency, and Cyber War

The presence of U.S. military forces in key locations around the world underpins the security of our allies and partners, provides stability to enhance economic growth and regional integration, and positions the Joint Force to execute emergency actions in response to a crisis....

In concert with all elements of national power and international partnerships, these efforts aim to disrupt VEO [violent extremist organizations] planning and operations, degrade support structures, remove leadership, interdict finances ...

—THE UNITED STATES MILITARY'S CONTRIBUTION TO
NATIONAL SECURITY, JUNE 2015
COURTESY US DEPARTMENT OF DEFENSE
(SEE APPENDIX A FOR THE COMPLETE TRANSCRIPT)

WITH THE WORLD'S ECONOMIES BECOMING MORE INTERDEPENDENT than ever before, protectionist trade policies have become more provocative than ever before. And a critical element of protectionism—albeit a positive one—is a country's protection of its currency. When currency trading turns into currency manipulation, nations must protect their money as they would protect their sovereignty. Conversely, a nation that manipulates its own currency to make its exports more competitive is simply engaging in negative protectionism.

Napoleon once said an army marches on its stomach, but today, an army marches on its currency. In the modern military world, numbers matter—not the number of soldiers, but the number of dollars, rubles, renminbi, pounds, and euros, because modern science, weaponry, and transportation define strength, and these things are attained through strong currencies, or, in the absence of strong currencies, strong foreign reserves.

China is a case in point. By keeping the renminbi artificially low, the Chinese kept their exports cheap and flowing, which, in turn, brought in huge amounts of foreign currency, especially US dollars. This trend changed after 2008, but began again in 2015. Here is how it works: a US company buys $10 million of Chinese goods, and those dollars are exchanged for renminbi by the Chinese company, leaving the Chinese bank or central bank with those dollars, which are then held as foreign reserves. This is compounded when the Chinese Central Bank uses both dollars and renminbi to help finance US debt through the purchase of US Treasury bills, debt instruments that are exchanged like a global currency. The impact of this is offset by historically low US interest rates.

Economists generally agree that the gold standard created currency devaluation, and even though China is the world's largest gold producer, it cannot possibly produce enough to keep up with its population and economic growth. This is precisely why China might just revert to the gold standard as a means of keeping its currency undervalued, which, in turn, would theoretically keep its exports competitive and thriving.

That nation's undervalued renminbi has been an on-again-off-again point of contention for its trading partners, especially the United States. But reverting to the gold standard would relieve China from accusations of unfair currency manipulation because it would no longer be in the hands of the central government. Of course, no other countries would be fooled, but neither would they have a viable objection, given that almost every nation has its own gold bug advocates, although there are no longer any nations still on the gold standard.

In 2014 Conservative Member of Parliament Kwasi Kwarteng wrote from London:

China's nearly $4 trillion in reserves—accumulated through its mercantilist trade policies—give it plenty of ammunition to claim leadership in the creation of a new monetary order. . . . For the past 25 years they have pursued a policy of aggressive export growth to drive their economy. China successively devalued its currency, from 1.50 renminbi to the dollar in 1980, to 8.72 in 1994. (Today the renminbi trades at 6.20 to the dollar, which the United States still considers artificially low.)

Could China someday peg its currency to gold, as Britain did in 1821? China has the reserves to do this. . . .

Of course, Britain's earlier adoption of the gold standard, in 1821, worsened a sharp deflationary period, during which, according to one calculation, consumer prices fell nearly 50 percent, between 1818 and 1822.

Having expanded its manufacturing base and captured international markets, China may well find a world hooked on its products.

What countries could do is denude themselves of gold bullion by using it to pay for Chinese products or to redeem their own currencies that had been tendered as payment. But this could backfire. By allowing China to corner the gold market, the expectation would be that the price of gold in renminbi would initially increase, allowing the Chinese Central Bank to maintain its renminbi/gold ratio by increasing the money supply. However, when the demand for renminbi caused by population and economic growth soon reverses this process, as it began to do in 2015, the renminbi will once again fall and exports will continue to grow.

Using rough rounded numbers, say in 2016 gold traded at $1,300 or ¥217 per ounce. (Because the symbol for the Chinese renminbi and Japanese yen are the same, the renminbi is often written CN¥.) This calculation is based upon ¥6 to the dollar. But if China increases its money supply by 25 percent while its gold reserves remain static, the price of gold in dollars will be unchanged, but in Chinese currency it would be ¥289 per ounce, causing the exchange rate to be ¥4.50 to the dollar. This can become quite confusing, because, in fact, the price of gold is not static; it fluctuates in world markets according to supply and demand. Even so, by adhering to the gold standard, China would be free to peg its currency to a fixed price of the metal, just as the United States did for so many years when it pegged the dollar to gold at $35 per ounce. Adherence to such a standard and such arbitrary pegging is successful only if the country's trading partners accept the valuation.

This brings the discussion back to the original debate. China's trading partners know the renminbi is already artificially priced because the Chinese government has not allowed it to float except in a low, narrow range most of the time. Theoretically, all that changed on November 30, 2015, when the International Monetary Fund (IMF) announced that the Chinese renminbi would join the dollar, pound, euro, and yen as a currency with special drawing rights. Christine Lagarde, the managing director of the IMF, said it is a "recognition of the progress that the Chinese authorities have made in the past years in reforming China's monetary and financial systems."

However, according to Keith Bradsher of the *New York Times*,

China was forced to give up some of its tight control over the currency, which could inject fresh volatility into the economy. . . .

China still maintains a heavy hand over the country's financial system. The country also falls short in legal protections, with the Communist Party continuing to play a strong role in deciding court cases. . . .

As the renminbi becomes more deeply woven into the global economy, it undermines the ability of the West to impose financial sanctions. . . . China remains a close business and financial partner of [rogue regimes such as] Sudan and North Korea, even inviting the president of Sudan to a recent military parade in Beijing. . . .

Most important, China began changing the way it sets the value of the renminbi each morning, allowing market forces to play a bigger role. To do so, it abruptly devalued the currency.

The IMF may have taken a too optimistic view, and by switching to the gold standard, China may prove that all else is nothing more than a charade as it continues to manipulate and justify an unrealistically low exchange rate to keep its exports unfairly competitive. In short, a China gold standard would be a propaganda tool rather than a legitimate monetary tool, a thin veil concealing only as much as other nations are willing to allow or that their gullible populations are willing to believe.

Of course, other nations could also adopt the gold standard, but history has proven the self-defeating nature of this choice and the likelihood it would lead to devaluation, tight money, and depression. In any event, those countries would be unable to match China's low-priced exports, and those exports are what keep China solvent.

China's systematic currency manipulation may have driven its commerce, but other factors are also at play, including product quality, tariffs, economic treaties, raw materials, transportation, and timeliness.

The Trans-Pacific Partnership (TPP) trade agreement was finalized on October 5, 2015 (signatory nations were then provided two years to ratify it), between the United States and eleven other Pacific Rim nations: Singapore, Brunei, New Zealand, Chile, Australia, Peru, Vietnam, Malaysia, Mexico, Canada, and Japan. Additionally, South Korea, Taiwan, the Philippines, Colombia, Thailand, Laos, Indonesia, Cambodia, Bangladesh, and India have expressed interest in the agreement. Noticeably missing is China, which was a clear signal of the agreement's intent to be a counterweight to that nation and what are regarded as its unfair currency and trade practices—an interesting game considering the fact that China is such a large trading partner for all of the signatories. In fact, the TPP is an economic leg of the Pivot to Asia strategy the United States and its allies are pursuing to address Chinese designs on the region.

While that strategy entails the repositioning of military assets in conjunction with base and port agreements being negotiated with a diverse group of Pacific Rim nations, the economic aspects could prove to be either the more important deterrent or the impetus for an unexpected Chinese military response reminiscent of the Japanese reaction in 1941 to US embargoes on oil and scrap metal—embargoes that were instituted to thwart Japanese aggression in China and Southeast Asia, but provoked the attack on Pearl Harbor, Southeast Asia, the Philippines, and various Pacific islands instead.

In the midst of all this, China has been engaging in cyber-espionage against both military and commercial targets. The fact that the Chinese have been successful at tapping into and stealing industrial and military secrets also implies their ability to disrupt those entities.

According to the *MIT Technology Review,*

> *On a wall facing dozens of cubicles at the FBI office in Pittsburgh, five guys from Shanghai stare from "Wanted" posters. Wang Dong, Sun Kailiang, Wen Xinyu, Huang Zhenyu, and Gu Chunhui are, according to a federal indictment unsealed in 2014, agents of China's People's Liberation Army Unit 61398, who hacked into networks at American companies—U.S. Steel, Alcoa, Allegheny Technologies (ATI), Westinghouse—plus the biggest industrial labor union in North America, United Steelworkers, and the U.S. subsidiary of SolarWorld, a German solar-panel maker. Over several years, prosecutors say, the agents stole thousands of e-mails about business strategy, documents about unfair-trade cases some of the U.S. companies had filed against China, and even piping designs for nuclear power plants—all allegedly to benefit Chinese companies.*
>
> *It is the first case the United States has brought against the perpetrators of alleged state-sponsored cyber-espionage, and it has revealed computer-security holes that companies rarely acknowledge in public. Although the attackers apparently routed their activities through innocent people's computers and made other efforts to mask themselves, prosecutors traced the intrusions to a 12-story building in Shanghai and outed individual intelligence agents. There is little chance that arrests will be made, since the United States has no extradition agreements with China, but the U.S. government apparently hopes that naming actual agents—and demonstrating that tracing attacks is possible—will embarrass China and put other nations on notice, inhibiting future economic espionage.*

Most nations, including the United States, undoubtedly engage in varying degrees of cyber-espionage, probably against friends and foes alike. However, the publicizing of such activities and indictments of government-connected individuals is unusual, and it may be surmised this was done in China's case due either to the egregiousness of the acts or the criticality of the scope and sensitivity of the material involved. Even so, such revelations can result in unforeseen consequences. Reciprocal revelations would carry the least impact. Overt responses against cyber-sensitive assets such as satellites or military communications would ratchet up the likelihood of some form of conflict. But worst of all would be confirmation that a nation's defenses had been compromised.

Taken together, interrupting or stunting commerce, undermining another nation's currency, and compromising its cybersecurity could—and in all likelihood, would—lead to war because no country could stand idle while its economy and security were shredded. For these reasons, acknowledgment of such breaches would be tantamount to a declaration of war. All will turn on the magnitude of the breaches and the readiness of a target nation to confront them.

Yet, while the world focuses on the obvious—Russian and Chinese targeting of US commerce, currency, and cybersecurity—sparks will ignite elsewhere. This will happen due to US technological experts' ability to thwart the cyber-threats, US monetary strength, US aggressiveness to counter currency threats, and US economic dominance backed by military policing of sea lanes to maintain the United States' position as the world's economic powerhouse.

Surprisingly, war will erupt as a result of collateral damage to Asia's Pacific Rim nations. Led by Japan, the other nations in the region, Vietnam, Thailand, Malaysia, the Philippines, Singapore, South Korea, Taiwan, and Indonesia, will be forced to respond to Chinese and Russian economic and cyber-threats against the United States. It will be their currencies, which are closely tied to the dollar; their commerce, which is reliant upon trade with both China and the United States; and their cybersystems, which were primarily developed in the United States, that will feel the greatest shocks from blows intended for the United States. The impact of these shocks will also soon be felt in Australia, New Zealand, India, and beyond.

These will be the unintended consequences of the Chinese and Russian economic and cyber-assaults against the United States.

Post–World War II Japanese pacifism prevailed under the protection of the US nuclear umbrella and Seventh Fleet, but those military bulwarks will prove to be inadequate in the face of economic and cyber onslaughts. Japan and the other Pacific Rim nations will know that the United States is not going to launch a nuclear war over such issues. They will also know that their own countermeasures will take time to develop and employ, and time will prove to be the enemy. All nations understand that long-term strategies are irrelevant when faced with short-term disasters.

Initially, Japan will attempt to convince the United States and its other allies to impose embargoes against Chinese and Russian products, but the economic repercussions, especially in America, where prices will skyrocket, will be too great to bear.

Having for many years anticipated the need to rearm, the Japanese Navy and Air Force will prove to be technologically superior to the Chinese Navy and Air Force even though the number of vessels will be fewer. And recognizing China as the primary threat, Japan will simply ignore Russia. On the other hand, Japanese ground forces, although highly trained and armed, cannot come close to matching the size of China's massive army.

The Japanese strategy will be to unilaterally strike a relatively isolated Chinese economic target, one it could then defend with its limited means. If successful, other Pacific Rim nations are likely to join Japan.

Hong Kong, an island city with continued strong cultural and financial links to the West dating from its long history as a one-time member of the British Empire, will be the Japanese target. Long a major center of Asian commerce, Hong Kong became a critical element contributing to China's economic success after Britain ceded control in 1997 following the expiration of its ninety-nine-year lease. Only New York and London are equivalent world financial capitals.

For the Japanese attack and occupation to be successful, it would have to be conducted without warning and in such a surgical operation with internal Hong Kong assistance as to be presented as an irrevocable fact along the lines of Russia's occupation of Ukraine's Crimea in 2015.

But to reach there, the Japanese fleet must fight its way past the Chinese East and South Seas Fleets, and this will require an extreme effort. Neither country's navy has seen significant action since the Chinese briefly engaged the Vietnamese in 1988. The ships of both fleets are mostly manned with sailors who have never been under fire led by leaders who have never experienced anything more than theoretical combat. The larger and equally untried Chinese Navy, while appearing to be the product of decades of development, has actually only been modernized since the nation's economy began to flourish after capitalism was embraced in the 1990s, which a thriving Hong Kong had facilitated.

The Japanese Navy is even newer, the country having been virtually demilitarized since the end of World War II. On the other hand, Japan has a long naval tradition, and that combined with latent naval knowledge allowed the country to rapidly build up its fleets to modern standards. Even so, numbers alone will put the Japanese at a disadvantage unless esprit de corps drawn on a revered naval history can make the difference.

To signal its naval resurgence, the Japanese fleet will ominously raise the Z flag as it goes into action against the Chinese covering fleet defending Hong Kong in what its leaders hope will culminate in an epic battle reminiscent of the 1905 victory at Tsushima when Russia's Second Pacific Squadron was destroyed at the hands of Japan's Admiral Togo Heihachiro. It was he who first raised the famous flag to signal, "The fate of our empire depends upon this fight. Every man is expected to act with his utmost efforts."

The Japanese had developed their navy along British lines, and Captain (later Admiral) William Pakenham (whose grandfather's sister was the Duke of Wellington's wife, and whose brother was killed leading the British Army against Gen. Andrew Jackson at the 1815 Battle of New Orleans) was an observer and trusted advisor aboard Togo's flagship, *Mikasa*, which may have influenced the Japanese admiral to emulate British Admiral Horatio Nelson's signal flags raised at the Battle of Trafalgar precisely one hundred years earlier: "England expects every man to do his duty."

However, the United States only remembers that the Japanese also hoisted the Z flag in 1941 when launching the surprise attack on Pearl

Harbor. So, its employment at Hong Kong could conceivably alienate Japan's indispensable ally, but it will be a risk worth taking, the symbol carrying so much history and meaning that it could increase the Japanese morale and resulting combat effectiveness at a critical time. And so it will. The Chinese fleet will be crushed.

Unlike events following the Russian occupation of Crimea, China will aggressively react. With the US umbrella firmly in place, nuclear war will be off the table as will a Chinese invasion of Japan due to the presence of the US Seventh Fleet and the buildup of the Japanese Navy, not to mention its near-annihilation of the Chinese fleet at the just-concluded Battle of Hong Kong. A counterattack to retake that all-important city will be considered, but a Hong Kong turned to rubble will be of little benefit. However, with Chinese prestige greatly damaged and such an important financial metropolis lost, China will be compelled to make a move somewhere.

The answer will be to emulate the Japanese strategy and seek a soft target, and that target need not be on Japanese soil. Japan, an island nation, is heavily dependent on foreign trade—the primary reason it was forced to act against China in the first place—and an action against one or more of its major trading partners would likely cause the Japanese abandonment of Hong Kong. But if the gambit fails, it will succeed only in expanding the war. The soft target of choice will be weakly defended, prosperous Singapore.

China will demand and receive the right of transit for its army through Thailand, Burma (Myanmar), and Malaysia to enable it to quickly drive on Singapore in a move eerily reminiscent of the Japanese offensive against the same target in 1942. This attack will be aided by an amphibious operation undertaken by a Chinese task force based in the Spratly Islands, those same South China Sea islands that had been partially occupied in 2012–15 despite objections from the United States as well as all the nations laying claim to some of them, including Brunei, Vietnam, Taiwan, Malaysia, and the Philippines. Ignoring those claimants, China had built air bases and ports on several of the islands.

With the US Seventh Fleet and the Japanese fleet focused on Hong Kong, the Singapore soft target is especially soft from the Strait

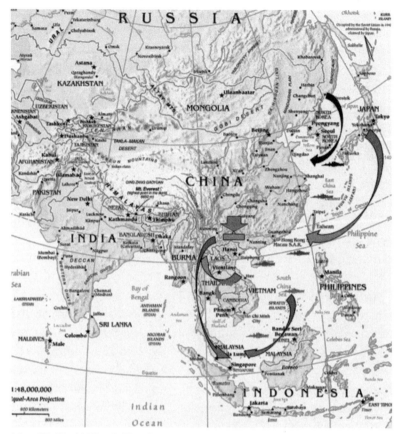

Map 15: World War 4: The Commerce, Currency, and Cyber War
COURTESY OF UNIVERSITY OF TEXAS LIBRARIES, WITH MILITARY OPERATIONS BY DOUGLAS COHN

of Malacca sea approach, making it vulnerable to a naval offensive, and it accordingly will fall to China's combined land, sea, and air campaign.

In short order, the Japanese and Chinese operations will begin to emulate a chess match in which both sides lose their queens, Hong Kong and Singapore. And as in a chess match, such losses are offsetting, not fatal. The war will continue.

Shanghai would be an obvious next target for Japan, so obvious that China will sufficiently beef up its defenses to deter any such action.

Instead, Japan will revert to causal remedies such as attacking the renminbi, and Hong Kong will be the key. As a major financial center, Hong Kong acts as the hub for billions of renminbi transactions, and Japan will halt those, replacing them not with Japanese yen, but with US dollars. The result will be a flood of renminbi hitting the market as people exit the currency in favor of dollars, yen, and euros. This would appear to be self-defeating because it causes the renminbi's value to drop and the corresponding price of Chinese exports to become even more competitive, one of the underlying causes of the war. However, the Chinese will have understood there was a point of diminishing returns because trade is two-way, and the Japanese action will cause import prices to soar. So China will counter the Japanese move by selling gold, specifically by exchanging the metal for renminbi, the clear signal being China's intent to go off the gold standard.

Worldwide, these currency tactics will be highly disruptive with the renminbi crashing, Chinese exports soaring, and Chinese imports falling before the situation suddenly reverses as gold floods the market, renminbi are redeemed, and import and export prices reverse from high-low to low-high. The nation to unexpectedly be hard-hit by all of this will be Russia, the world's third-largest gold producer behind China and Australia, and China's tenth-largest trading partner. Of more significance is the reverse fact that China is Russia's second-largest trading partner.

Russia and its oil- and gas-heavy economy have long been susceptible to resource and monetary fluctuations, and the Sino-Japanese War can only exacerbate this situation. The conundrum will come when Russia feels forced to choose a side. The Russo-Japanese history is one of belligerence, especially following the humiliating Russian defeat in the 1904–05 Russo-Japanese War—which came on the heels of Japan's victory in the 1894–95 Sino-Japanese War—and Russia's retribution, when it declared war against a defeated Japan at the end of World War II. In a brief vulture-like campaign aimed at taking advantage of Japan's prostrate position, Russia occupied the Japanese half of Sakhalin Island, which Japan had annexed in 1905. But, in modern times, Russia has also engaged in border conflicts with China.

The Russian dilemma will not easily be solved. Russia cannot stand by while its economy is wrecked. Neither can it resolve the problem through misdirected military action. A certain maturity became attached to modern Russia that had been missing from some of the tsarist regimes. In post–World War II times, Russian foreign policy generally was motivated by attainable objectives—the Cuban Missile Crisis being a glaring exception. So, when Russia took the Crimea from Ukraine, it calculated its opponent, not being a NATO country and virtually devoid of allies, to be too weak to intercede. Likewise, as Russia's leaders eye the Asian situation, they must come to the conclusion that China is the problem, even if this entails an alliance with Japan.

Ever the guileful nation, Russia will offer its services to China to counter the potential threat the US Seventh Fleet and Japanese fleet pose to Shanghai. China, being more than ready to gain an ally and in need of additional sea power, can only too readily accept. After all, the Russians and Chinese have held joint naval exercises each year since 2012, with the 2014 exercise being based in the Usun naval base in Shanghai. And so a Russian fleet will move to Shanghai, and to keep up the facade, the Russian government will not advise the United States or Japan of its true intent. So complete will this duplicitous move be that both the United States and Japan are going to warn Russia to stay away. This will have no effect other than to reinforce Russian credibility with China, because the Russians know that neither the United States nor Japan is going to take any overt action to stop the move.

Shanghai is the world's busiest container port (Singapore was first until 2010), which was accomplished through the construction of the Yangshan deepwater port connected to Shanghai by the 20.2-mile long Donghai Bridge, the world's longest ocean bridge.

Panoramic view of deepwater port of Yangshan
© 2010 CREATIVE COMMONS ATTRIBUTION-SHARE ALIKE 3.0, BY PERMISSION OF BIGG(G)ER

Control of Yangshan and the surrounding waters of Hangzhou Bay means control of Shanghai and bottles up China's East Sea Fleet at Ningbo. The Russian fleet will arrange to establish its headquarters at Yangshan, followed by the landing of increasing numbers of Russian sailors and soldiers, ostensibly to provide security. This, in turn, will lead to a variety of Russian requests and demands, including export fees to help defray the cost of the very naval "assistance" that is actually occupying the harbor, the lifeblood of the city.

The United States and Japan will become increasingly aware of Russia's objective, as will China. In response, Chinese submarines will sortie out from the Usun naval base and torpedo one of the patrolling Russian ships, blaming the attack on Japan. The ploy will fail, Russian technology confirming the truth.

Russian forces are inadequate to defeat the PLA (China's People's Liberation Army) in Shanghai, but with the main Chinese fleets defending other Chinese ports while shadowing Japanese fleets at Hong Kong and the Spratly Islands, their naval forces remaining in port or at anchor at the Usun naval base will be vulnerable. Even so, the Russian fleet will

Donghai Bridge
© 2007 PUBLIC DOMAIN BY W:USER:ZHANG 2008

have no need to engage Chinese vessels, the Russian objective having been achieved simply by blockading Yangshan and bringing Shanghai export traffic to a halt.

By this point very little fighting will have taken place, with Hong Kong easily falling to the Japanese, Singapore likewise falling to the Chinese, and the Chinese and Russians at Shanghai reaching a standoff. The war began over economic considerations, and, accordingly, the military objectives were economic objectives. And so successful will all sides be in securing those economic objectives that the world economy will be thrown into chaos. The dollar and euro will increase as the renminbi and yen fall while the ruble holds steady.

The downward pressure on the dollar and euro emanating from the absence of cheap Chinese imports will be offset by transitioning trade to other Pacific Rim, South Asian, and South American nations. Further, the United States and Europe will benefit, as neutral nations often do in wartime, by selling arms and foodstuffs to the belligerents.

At this point China will face a critical decision. Should it widen the war or sue for peace? Suing for peace will entail acceptance of a diminished role in the world, economically and militarily. Widening the war will be fraught with risks. How and where and against whom would it widen? If it fails, its government could collapse and its territory could be partitioned. Survival being the first rule of both political and military strategy, there will be considerable domestic pressure placed on the Chinese government to negotiate. On the other hand, there are always hardliners, and they often carry the day with autocratic governments. China will continue.

Unable to confront the Japanese, Russian, and US fleets while simultaneously protecting its conquest of Singapore, China will deem naval action out of the question. So, stymied in the Pacific, China will turn landward, striking the resource-rich lands of Southeast Asia. Having already compromised the territorial integrity of Thailand, Burma, and Malaysia in its drive to Singapore, China will expand that theater by invading its traditional enemy, Vietnam, and, if successful, press on to take Cambodia and Laos, while consolidating its position in Thailand, Burma, and Malaysia.

This is where the plan will stall. Vietnam has fought China before, and if not always with complete success, at least with the ability to forestall disaster. Knowing this, China is going to mass overwhelming forces on the China-Vietnam border, and this cannot be accomplished in secrecy, creating an invitation for a preemptive strike.

Vietnam will accommodate, not moving north against the main Chinese Army, but west into Thailand to cut the Chinese supply line with Singapore in an operation requiring few Vietnamese troops because (a) China, with few troops in that area of operations, is not going to be expecting it, and (b) the Thai Army, not having been fully neutralized by the Chinese, can join the campaign. This would appear to disrupt China's strategy, but its attack against Vietnam will proceed as scheduled, leaving its occupying corps in Singapore and its naval covering force temporarily to their own devices.

China's air superiority will prove decisive unless it can be countered, prompting Vietnam to call on the United States, Japan, Russia, and even nonbelligerents such as the Philippines to assist in bolstering its air forces, but they will demur. The United States has not yet engaged China militarily and is going to see no benefit in aiding Vietnam, its one-time foe. Japan, focused on its own defenses and its newly acquired Hong Kong territory, will be unable to assist. Russia, like the United States, also has not actually commenced a shooting war with China and is going to make clear it has done its part by bottling up Shanghai. In fact, all of these nations will be keeping their options open, content to stand aside and await the outcome of events in the Sino-Vietnamese Campaign. It is not going to be a long wait as the Chinese Air Force dominates the battlefield, clearing the skies of Vietnamese planes and wreaking havoc on their infantry and armored formations.

It will not be a rout. The Vietnamese only give ground grudgingly, but with mounting casualties approaching the critical point, only the United States will have ability to reverse the situation, and yet it will not move. Preferring, instead, to be the arbiter of peace and the postwar friend to all, the United States will step into the fray as the peacemaker, convincing China to temporarily suspend its campaign against Vietnam by implying

America's willingness to come to Vietnam's aid and by convincing the Chinese that a true opportunity for an honorable peace actually exists.

Hong Kong is sure to be the sticking point, Japan having no incentive to give it up, and the Hong Kongers overwhelmingly desiring independence, but preferring democratic Japan to Communist China. Of course, the Russian blockade of Shanghai must be lifted, but that was always a given. Likewise there was never any doubt that China would be compelled to relinquish Singapore.

The impasse will be solved by settling the issue of disputed islands in the East China Sea and South China Sea. Chinese sovereignty will be recognized over those islands where China has already established a presence, such as on the Spratly and Paracel Islands, while Japan, South Korea, Taiwan, Vietnam, and the Philippines will confirm their claims to other islands in those seas. No longer can China be allowed to turn those seas into Chinese lakes, but neither can China be excluded from exploiting resources in its areas of control. None of the countries gaining rights to the islands is going to be entitled to the normal Law of the Seas territorial rights, in that all nations will be allowed free transit in both seas. However, any nation legally occupying one of the islands will be allowed to retain fishing and resource rights within the internationally recognized limits.

Implementation of the peace terms could be expected to entail complications, yet Russia's withdrawal from Shanghai and China's withdrawal from Singapore will be carried out with meticulous adherence to the terms as all sides are anxious to win the peace through edges gained and concessions granted in the resumption of lucrative trade relations. Hong Kong will become an autonomous protectorate of Japan and a reliable democracy, and it will enjoy the same city-state status that has been so beneficial to Singapore.

The economic factors originally driving the war will be resolved when China reverses course and goes off the gold standard, allowing the renminbi to float, and vows to end its cyber and industrial espionage, even agreeing to oversight from the World Court in The Hague.

It will be a complex ending to a complex war.

PART III
HISTORICAL PERSPECTIVE

The Atomic Bomb—
Weapon of War, Deterrent of War,
or Limiter of War*

THE SENSITIVE AND CONTROVERSIAL NATURE OF FOUR FATEFUL DAYS IN
August 1945 has long fanned misconceptions and myths, foremost
among them the debate over projected casualties to be suffered by US
forces engaged in the invasion of Japan's home islands. In fact, the figures,
ranging from 40,000 to one million, influenced military planners' decisions as to invasion sites, but not the decision to use atomic bombs since
the Joint Chiefs of Staff, created in 1942, was clearly prepared to advise
the use of any means available to lessen casualties whether estimates were
on the low or high side.

The Manhattan Project, initiated in 1942, culminated with the successful test of the first atomic explosion on July 16, 1945, code-named
Trinity. The results were reported to President Harry S. Truman, then
in Potsdam, Germany, meeting with British Prime Minister Winston
Churchill (who would be replaced by Clement Attlee on July 26) and
Soviet Premier Joseph Stalin, whose forces were in the process of turning
Eastern Europe into Soviet satellite states ruled by unelected communists in violation of the February 1945 Yalta Agreement. An element of
that agreement was the Soviet promise to declare war on Japan within
three months following the defeat of Germany. It was a promise that
would be inexorably linked to the Potsdam Declaration by the United

---

* Including passages from the author's book *The President's First Year*

States, the United Kingdom, and Nationalist (anti-communist) China demanding Japan's unconditional surrender.

Stalin took the full three months between Germany's May 8 surrender and August 9, 1945, before launching his attack against Japanese forces in Manchuria. In part this was due to the time necessary to reposition armies from Europe to the Far East, but more likely because Stalin believed the USSR had borne the brunt of the campaign against Germany, while the United States, Britain, and France came late to garner a share in victory's spoils. In light of that assumption, he intended to turn the tables and gather up Japanese-held territory after Japan was already on its last legs. In fact, Japan had been sending peace feelers to the West through then-neutral Soviets. Stalin never passed these on to President Truman, but US code breakers did.

It was, therefore, a matter of coincidence that the atomic bombs were ready for use at approximately the same time Stalin was prepared to declare war on Japan. This would lead to the ongoing debate about whether the Soviet attack or America's atomic bombs brought about the Japanese surrender.

As these events rushed toward the war's denouement, Truman, thrust into office and driven by a thousand predecessor decisions, was faced with one of the most critical dilemmas in human history: Should the United States use the most destructive weapon ever devised to save American lives? Certainly. To deter Soviet expansion? Probably. But against what targets? The momentum of momentous events had condensed time, clarified options, and obscured morality. Andrew J. Rotter wrote in *Hiroshima: The World's Bomb*, "A kind of bureaucratic momentum impelled the bomb forward. . . . It would have taken a president far more confident, far less in awe of his office and his predecessor, to reflect on the matter of whether the atomic bomb should be used. . . . [because] ethical erosion had long collapsed the once-narrow ledge that had prevented men from plunging into the abyss of heinous conduct during war."

Following Potsdam, nuclear advice descended upon the president from those few people who had both the security clearance and a need to know the secret, which, prior to President Roosevelt's death on April

12, 1945, had not included then–Vice President Truman. Chief among those tasked with providing nuclear advice were the members of the all-important Interim Committee: Secretary of War Henry L. Stimson; chairman, former Senator and future Secretary of State James F. Byrnes; Under Secretary of the Navy Ralph A. Bard (the only dissenter); Assistant Secretary of State William L. Clayton; Director of the Office of Scientific Research and Development and president of the Carnegie Institution Vannevar Bush; Chief of the Office of Field Service in the Office of Scientific Research and Development and president of the Massachusetts Institute of Technology Karl T. Compton; Chairman of the National Defense Research Committee and president of Harvard University James B. Conant; and New York Life Insurance Company President George L. Harrison.

The committee, obviously underestimating the potential magnitude of nuclear destruction, recommended "that the Secretary of War should be advised that, while recognizing that the final selection of the target was essentially a military decision, the present view of the Committee was that the bomb should be used against Japan as soon as possible; that it be used on a war plant surrounded by workers' homes; and that it be used without prior warning."

This view was supported by a faction of scientists from the Manhattan Project led by project head Dr. J. Robert Oppenheimer (boldface added):

> *Recommendations on the Immediate Use of Nuclear Weapons, by the Scientific Panel of the Interim Committee on Nuclear Power, June 16, 1945.*
>
> *The opinions of our scientific colleagues on the initial use of these weapons are not unanimous: they range from the proposal of a purely technical demonstration to that of the military application best designed to induce surrender. Those who advocate a purely technical demonstration would wish to outlaw the use of atomic weapons, and have feared that if we use the weapons now our position in future negotiations will be prejudiced. Others emphasize the opportunity of*

*saving American lives by immediate military use, and believe that such use will improve the international prospects, in that they are more concerned with the prevention of war than with the elimination of this specific weapon. We find ourselves closer to these latter views; **we can propose no technical demonstration likely to bring an end to the war; we see no acceptable alternative to direct military use.***

This left in doubt whether military or civilian targets were intended, the confusion coming from the fact that the destruction of cities in both Germany and Japan by conventional bombing had by then been legitimized as militarily appropriate.

In contrast, Dr. Leo Szilard, who, with Albert Einstein, had originally proposed the Manhattan Project to FDR, wrote along with fifty-eight other scientists (boldface added):

A Petition to the President of the United States

Discoveries of which the people of the United States are not aware may affect the welfare of this nation in the near future. The liberation of atomic power which has been achieved places atomic bombs in the hands of the Army. It places in your hands, as Commander-in-Chief, the fateful decision whether or not to sanction the use of such bombs in the present phase of the war against Japan.

*We, the undersigned scientists, have been working in the field of atomic power for a number of years. **Until recently we have had to reckon with the possibility that the United States might be attacked by atomic bombs during this war and that her only defense might lie in a counterattack by the same means. Today with this danger averted we feel impelled to say what follows:***

The war has to be brought speedily to a successful conclusion and the destruction of Japanese cities by means of atomic bombs may very well be an effective method of warfare. We feel, however, that such an attack on Japan could not be justified in the present circumstances. We believe that the United States ought not to resort to the use of atomic bombs in the present phase of the war, at least not unless the terms which will be imposed upon Japan after the war are publicly announced and subsequently Japan is given an opportunity to surrender.

If such public announcement gave assurance to the Japanese that they could look forward to a life devoted to peaceful pursuits in their homeland and if Japan still refused to surrender, our nation would then be faced with a situation which might require a re-examination of her position with respect to the use of atomic bombs in the war.

Atomic bombs are primarily a means for the ruthless annihilation of cities. Once they were introduced as an instrument of war it would be difficult to resist for long the temptation of putting them to such use.

The last few years show a marked tendency toward increasing ruthlessness. At present our Air Forces, striking at the Japanese cities, are using the same methods of warfare which were condemned by American public opinion only a few years ago when applied by the Germans to the cities of England. *Our use of atomic bombs in this war would carry the world a long way further on this path of ruthlessness.*

Atomic power will provide the nations with new means of destruction. The atomic bombs at our disposal represent only the first step in this direction and there is almost no limit to the destructive power which will become available in the course of this development. ***Thus a nation which sets the precedent of using these newly liberated forces of nature for purposes of destruction may have to bear the responsibility of opening the door to an era of devastation on an unimaginable scale.***

In view of the foregoing, we, the undersigned, respectfully petition that you exercise your power as Commander-in-Chief to rule that the United States shall not, in the present phase of the war, resort to the use of atomic bombs.

This dissent was supported by America's top uniformed officers, including the commanders of the war's primary theaters of operations, Generals Eisenhower and MacArthur and Admiral Nimitz.

• Adm. William D. Leahy

Leahy, the highest-ranking officer, serving as what would later be called chairman of the Joint Chiefs of Staff, later wrote:

Once it had been tested, President Truman faced the decision as to whether to use it. He did not like the idea, but he was persuaded that it would shorten the war against Japan and save American lives. It is my opinion that the use of this barbarous weapon at Hiroshima and Nagasaki was of no material assistance in our war against Japan. The Japanese were already defeated and ready to surrender because of the effective sea blockade and the successful bombing with conventional weapons. . . . My own feeling was that in being the first to use it, we had adopted an ethical standard common to the barbarians of the Dark Ages. I was not taught to make wars in that fashion, and wars cannot be won by destroying women and children.

• Gen. George Marshall, Army chief of staff

According to a national security memorandum, Marshall "said he thought these weapons might first be used against straight military objectives such as a large naval installation and then if no complete result was derived from the effect of that, he thought we ought to designate a number of large manufacturing areas from which the people would be warned to leave—telling the Japanese that we intended to destroy such centers."

• Adm. Ernest J. King, commander in chief of the US Fleet and chief of Naval Operations

King stated that the naval blockade and prior bombing of Japan, in March of 1945, had rendered the Japanese helpless and that the use of the atomic bomb was both unnecessary and immoral.

• Gen. Dwight D. Eisenhower, commander of the European Theater of Operations (ETO)

Eisenhower later wrote:

SECRET ~ *File with S1*

MEMORANDUM OF CONVERSATION WITH GENERAL MARSHALL
May 29, 1945 - 11:45 a.m.

Present: Secretary of War
          General Marshall
          Mr. McCloy

C/S has noted and has no further suggestions. —

Subject: Objectives toward Japan and methods of concluding war with
          minimum casualties.

The Secretary of War referred to the earlier meeting with the
Acting Secretary of State and Mr. Forrestal on the matter of the President's speech and the reference to Japan. He felt the decision to
postpone action now was a sound one. This only postponed consideration
of the matter for a time, however, for we should have to consider it
again preparatory to the employment of S-1. The Secretary referred to
the burning of Tokyo and the possible ways and means of employing the
larger bombs. The Secretary referred to the letter from Dr. Bush and
Dr. Conant on the matter of disclosing the nature of the process to
other nations as well as to Dr. Bush's memorandum on the same general
subject. General Marshall took their letters and stated he would read
them and give his views on their recommendations as soon as possible.

General Marshall said he thought these weapons might first
be used against straight military objectives such as a large naval installation and then if no complete result was derived from the effect
of that, he thought we ought to designate a number of large manufacturing
areas from which the people would be warned to leave - telling the
Japanese that we intended to destroy such centers. There would be no
individual designations so that the Japs would not know exactly where
we were to hit - a number should be named and the hit should follow

DECLASSIFIED
E.O. 11652, Sec. 3(E) and 5(D) or (E)
OSD letter, May 3, 1972
By ___ FN ___ NARS Date ___

SECRET
DOD Dir. 5200.9, Sept. 27, 1958
NWD by ___ date ___

SECRET

shortly after. Every effort should be made to keep our record of
warning clear. We must offset by such warning methods the opprobrium
which might follow from an ill considered employment of such force.

The General then spoke of his stimulation of the new
weapons and operations people to the development of new weapons and
tactics to cope with the care and last ditch defense tactics of the
suicidal Japanese. He sought to avoid the attrition we were now
suffering from such fanatical but hopeless defense methods - it requires new tactics. He also spoke of gas and the possibility of using
it in a limited degree, say on the outlying islands where operations
were now going on or were about to take place. He spoke of the type
of gas that might be employed. It did not need to be our newest and
most potent - just drench them and sicken them so that the fight would
be taken out of them - saturate an area, possibly with mustard, and
just stand off. He said he had asked the operations people to find
out what we could do quickly - where the dumps were and how much time
and effort would be required to bring the gas to bear. There would
be the matter of public opinion which we had to consider, but that was
something which might also be dealt with. The character of the weapon
was no less humane than phosporous and flame throwers and need not be
used against dense populations or civilians - merely against these last
pockets of resistance which had to be wiped out but had no other military
significance.

The General stated that he was having these studies made and
in due course would have some recommendations to make.

SECRET

- 3 -

The Secretary stated that he was meeting with scientists
and industrialists this week on S-1 and that he would talk with the
Chief of Staff again after these meetings and the General repeated
that he would shortly give the Secretary his views on the suggestions contained in the letter above referred to.

J. J. McC.

In [July] 1945 . . . Secretary of War Stimson, visiting my headquarters in Germany, informed me that our government was preparing to drop an atomic bomb on Japan. I was one of those who felt that there were a number of cogent reasons to question the wisdom of such an act. . . .

During his recitation of the relevant facts, I had been conscious of a feeling of depression and so I voiced to him my grave misgivings, first on the basis of my belief that Japan was already defeated and that dropping the bomb was completely unnecessary, and secondly because I thought that our country should avoid shocking world opinion by the use of a weapon whose employment was, I thought, no longer mandatory as a measure to save American lives. It was my belief that Japan was, at that very moment, seeking some way to surrender with a minimum loss of "face." The Secretary was deeply perturbed by my attitude.

Eisenhower later said: "It wasn't necessary to hit them with that awful thing . . . to use the atomic bomb, to kill and terrorize civilians, without even attempting [negotiations], was a double crime."

• Gen. Douglas MacArthur, commander of the Southwest Pacific Area (COMSOWESPAC)

Norman Cousins wrote: "When I asked General MacArthur about the decision to drop the bomb, I was surprised to learn he had not even been consulted [although he was informed of the bomb the day before it was dropped on Hiroshima]. What, I asked, would his advice have been? He replied that he saw no military justification for the dropping of the bomb. The war might have ended weeks earlier, he said, if the United States had agreed, as it later did anyway, to the retention of the institution of the emperor."

This was confirmed by William Manchester: "MacArthur was appalled. He knew that the Japanese would never renounce their emperor, and that without him an orderly transition to peace would be impossible anyhow, because his people would never submit to Allied occupation unless he ordered it. Ironically, when the surrender did come, it was conditional, and the condition was a continuation of the imperial reign."

- Adm. Chester W. Nimitz, commander of the Pacific Ocean (CINCPOA) and the subordinate Central Pacific Area (COMCENPAC)

On October 5, 1945, Admiral Nimitz said, "The Japanese had, in fact, already sued for peace before the atomic age was announced to the world with the destruction of Hiroshima and before the Russian entry into the war."

- Gen. Curtis LeMay, commander of the XXI Bomber Command

The architect of the area bombing that killed hundreds of thousands of Japanese civilians, including the fire-bombing of Tokyo that claimed the highest toll of the war in a two-day raid (100,000 mostly civilian deaths), said: "We felt that our incendiary bombings had been so successful that Japan would collapse before we invaded. We went ahead and dropped the bombs because President Truman told me to do it. He told me in a personal letter."

- Adm. William F. Halsey, commander of the US Third Fleet

On September 9, 1945, the acclaimed US Navy commander said, "The first atomic bomb was an unnecessary experiment. . . . It was a mistake to ever drop it."

- US Bombing Survey, Paul Nitze, vice chairman

"Based on a detailed investigation of all the facts, and supported by the testimony of the surviving Japanese leaders involved, it is the Survey's opinion that certainly prior to 31 December 1945, and in all probability prior to 1 November 1945, Japan would have surrendered even if the atomic bombs had not been dropped, even if Russia had not entered the war, and even if no invasion had been planned or contemplated."

In 1998 the CIA's Center for the Study of Intelligence published *The Final Months of the War with Japan*, a monograph by former CIA Deputy Director for Intelligence Douglas J. MacEachin. He weighed the arguments and offered a cogent analysis, which is reprinted with permission:

The Argument for Staying the Course

He [Gen. Douglas MacArthur] favored going ahead with the Kyushu invasion [of southern Japan] as planned.

When told that alternatives to Kyushu would be the main issue at a coming JCS [Joint Chiefs of Staff] meeting, [Army Chief of Staff Gen. George C.] Marshall sent a personal cable to MacArthur soliciting his views. Marshall emphasized the large Japanese land and air buildup on Kyushu that had been reported in intelligence, noting that, if the Japanese were in fact deployed in such numbers there, US landing forces risked heavy losses in their amphibious attacks. Pointing out that the buildup on Kyushu had been carried out at the expense of reductions in other locations, Marshall queried MacArthur about "possible alternative objectives" at less defended sites, pointing to the three that the Joint War Plans Committee's 4 August memo had characterized as "under intensive study here."

MacArthur's response was dismissive of the reported buildup:

- *He said he did "not, repeat not, credit the heavy strengths reported to you in southern Kyushu."*

- *He reiterated that airstrikes would cut off Japanese reinforcement, despite reports from his own intelligence staff—and from the Joint Intelligence Committee in Washington—that so far this had demonstrably not occurred.*

- *He rejected the alternatives suggested by Marshall as either not feasible without air bases closer to the homeland (in the case of the Tokyo Plain) or requiring substantial delay for preparations (in the Northern Honshu case).*

MacArthur argued that "there should not, repeat not, be the slightest thought of changing the OLYMPIC [invasion of Japan] operation. Its fundamental purpose is to obtain air bases under cover of which we can deploy forces to the northward into the industrial heart of Japan. The plan is sound and will succeed." He concluded: *"Throughout the Southwest Pacific Area campaigns, as we have neared an operation, intelligence has invariably pointed to greatly increased enemy forces. Without exception, this buildup has been found to be erroneous."*

It is worth noting that MacArthur did not argue that the buildup—if true—should not be viewed as threatening the success of OLYMPIC. Instead he tried to impeach the accuracy of the reporting. This tactic could be interpreted as an indication that he recognized that if SIGINT [signals intelligence] reflecting the buildup was accurate—or if it was accepted as accurate by Washington—it would indeed have significant implications for the invasion plan.

MacArthur's practice was to not allow intelligence to interfere with his aims, and his history of complaints about Willoughby's reports resulted mainly from their contradiction of his own estimates and preferred courses of action. His denigration of the reported buildup on Kyushu directly contradicted the performance record of his G-2 under Willoughby. In those instances during MacArthur's Pacific campaign when the ULTRA-derived [code-breaking intelligence garnered from encrypted German messages; such intelligence from Japanese messages was code-named MAGIC] assessments were not entirely accurate, the errors tended to be on the low side.

In this instance, postwar information would show that there had in fact been 14 Japanese combat divisions on Kyushu—and that intercepted communications had identified all of them. The exact locations of a few of the newest arrivals had not been determined at the time of the war's end, but it is quite likely that, once their existence on Kyushu had been confirmed, finding their locations would have been accomplished within a few weeks at most. Japanese documents obtained after the war showed that at the time the US Military Intelligence Service was estimating 600,000 troops on Kyushu, there were 900,000 soldiers assigned to its defense.

Looking for a Middle-Ground Strategy

A middle ground between an invasion of Kyushu and a blockade-and-bomb strategy would have been the approach proposed by the War Plans Committee, apparently with some support from Marshall. The Committee continued to insist on an invasion of the Japanese homeland but sought a target less well defended than Kyushu.

The views of General Marshall and most of the Joint War Plans Committee on the obstacles to achieving unconditional surrender would have made it difficult for them to abandon their advocacy of an invasion of the Japanese homeland. The unconditional surrender objective was about much more than the status of the Emperor. Indeed, the latter issue was the easiest to resolve. While some Allied governments, especially the Australians and Chinese, remained opposed to retention of the Emperor, many key UK and US officials—including some members of the JCS—were not only willing to allow the Emperor to remain, but actually favored doing so in the belief that this would facilitate the administration of Japan by a postwar occupation force.

The more important Allied objectives of unconditional surrender were the unrestricted occupation of Japanese territory, total authority in the governing of Japan, dismantlement of Japan's military and military-industrial complex ("demobilization"), a restructuring of Japanese society ("demilitarization"), and Allied-run war crimes trials—in effect doing to Japan what was being done to Germany. Abandoning these goals would mean Japan would not suffer the same consequences as Germany. Truman's consciousness of the political side to this issue was indicated in his meeting with his military advisers on 18 June, in which he said that he was deliberately leaving the door open to a modification of the surrender terms but that the initiative would have to come from Congress.

Achieving the surrender and unrestricted occupation of the entire national territory of an opponent steeped in a warrior tradition and a history as a great power, without having captured any portion of that territory [a fact negated by the probability of a Soviet occupa-

tion], posed an extraordinary challenge. It had not been achieved in Germany without invasion:

- *The historical record shows that after the bomb was dropped, the Japanese civilian leadership was willing to settle for only one concession by Japan's conquerors—the Emperor's continuity.*

- *The Japanese military, however, held out on the very issues that defined the Allies' unconditional position, insisting that there be no security occupation of Japan; that disarmament and demobilization be left in Japanese hands; and that war criminals be tried by Japanese tribunals.*

- *Inasmuch as none of these concessions had been granted to Germany, Allied leaders doubtless would have had great difficulty in gaining political support at home for granting any of them to Japan.*

Whether the Allies' demands could be achieved without capturing any part of the Japanese homeland was really what the debate between invasion and bomb-and-blockade was all about. By early August the casualty costs of an invasion would have added credibility to the case for bomb-and-blockade. That strategy's downside was time: how much destruction had to be imposed, and for how long, and how many more thousands of Japanese had to be killed by bombing or starvation to achieve unconditional surrender?

Implications of Soviet Entry into the Pacific War

By this time (early August), the prospect of Soviet entry into the war against Japan would have provided arguments to both sides. For those favoring a bomb-and-blockade approach or even just a postponement of any invasion, Soviet entry could have been cited as an additional reason why surrender could be obtained without invading the main Japanese islands.

On the other hand, if Japan's surrender did not take place until after the Soviets had been in the Pacific war for some length of time, and if there were no US forces on Japanese territory (because no US invasion had occurred), how could the United States and its Allies acquire the control over occupation that they were seeking? Unless the mere entry by the USSR somehow caused an immediate surrender on the unconditional terms being demanded by Washington, the Potsdam experience was likely to reinforce the tendency among at least some US officials to see any gain resulting from Soviet entry as also carrying a serious potential cost—the possible emergence of a Far Eastern version of the Soviet hegemony that was beginning to be imposed on Eastern Europe.

Weighing Alternatives

These considerations supported the idea of searching for an alternative that still involved capturing some Japanese homeland territory. The appreciation that Marshall and many members of the Joint War Plans Committee would have had for the casualty implications of the Japanese buildup probably would have led them—MacArthur's views notwithstanding—to look for alternative invasion sites.

In addition to the choices suggested in Marshall's cable to MacArthur and in the Joint War Plans Committee paper of 4 August, there was the option of keeping Kyushu as the target but postponing the ground invasion so as to allow the increased air power from bases being set up on Okinawa to administer an extended pounding. Such an intensified air bombardment campaign had been slated to begin in mid-September; the Army Air Forces at MacArthur's request had already accelerated this timetable by 30 days because of Willoughby's recommendation based on the buildup that had been observed.

Timing and weather posed potential problems for the option of choosing an alternative invasion site. Such a major change in plans at this time presumably would have forced a delay in launching the invasion. As noted earlier, the date for invading Kyushu had already been moved up from 1 December to 1 November in response to concerns expressed by MacArthur and [Adm. Chester W.] Nimitz, among others, over the greater chance of adverse weather during an invasion that did not begin until December and the possibility that such conditions could set the invasion back to spring 1946.

From this perspective, there was little difference between seeking new invasion alternatives and opting for a bomb-and-blockade strategy. Each involved putting the invasion on hold and engaging in an intensified air and sea attack; if that did not produce a surrender within the next six months, the invasion issue might or might not be back on the planning board. The military alternative to this course of action was to go ahead with the invasion and risk the high casualties. The political alternative was to relax the terms for surrender.

Japanese Perspectives

This was exactly the dilemma that Japanese military leaders had sought to force the United States and its Allies to face. They wanted to buy time in the hope that war-weariness in the Allied countries, in combination with concerns about high casualties, would produce a softening of the unconditional surrender demands. Even for the Japanese, the issue was not whether they would be forced to surrender, but rather on what terms. The best leverage for Japan's leadership was to raise the cost perceptions—both military and political—for Allied decision makers.

The downside for the Japanese from Allied decisions dragging out the war would not only have been the devastation and loss of life that would have resulted from bombing and sea strangulation. The longer the war lasted, the longer and deeper Soviet participation would become. And attaining a satisfactory postwar settlement once the inevitable surrender did take place would probably have been more problematic.

Any attempt to conclude how the debate among US leaders over invading Japan would have come out if the atomic bomb had not been available to end the Pacific war abruptly would be a matter of guesses and probably preferences. The planned JCS meeting that was

> *to examine alternatives to an invasion of Kyushu did not take place because the atomic bomb was dropped at the very time the meeting was being scheduled.*
>
> *This potentially historic meeting had been proposed in direct response to the picture of an accelerating Japanese buildup portrayed by signals intelligence. Had the bomb not been ready when it was, and had the meeting gone ahead, history may well have judged this critical re-examination of strategic choices as one of the most pivotal contributions of SIGINT to the outcome of the Pacific war.*

Clearly, the belligerents, including the Japanese, understood Japan was defeated before atomic bombs were dropped and before the Soviet Union declared war. As a result, in the absence of the bomb and the Soviets, it would have been difficult to do other than proceed with the conventional bomb-and-blockade strategy to end the war. The only motivation to do otherwise (invade) was the Soviet entrance into the conflict and the likelihood of a Soviet occupation of Japan. Only this scenario could have motivated generals such as MacArthur to insist upon a costly US-led invasion of the Japanese home islands.

Further, Eisenhower and others acknowledged that Japanese overtures were being attempted. As would soon be proven, it was also clear that an understanding of Japanese culture anchored by retention of the emperor, in contravention to the unconditional surrender terms, offered the most likely path to Japanese submission, but that was a political consideration as was dropping the bomb, according to General Marshall. Though there did appear to be some comprehension of the emperor's engrained status; why else was the Imperial Palace spared in the bombing raids? All turned on time.

It was August, and options began to peel away. Japan was finished; expansionist Soviet Russia was emerging to pose a new and dangerous threat. And almost no one who knew about the atomic bomb was even considering a US invasion of Japan. The Soviets were about to attack, and Operation Olympic—the US invasion of the southern Japanese island of

Kyushu—could not be launched until November 1, 1945, far too late to deter the Russians. These facts narrowed and clarified options: enhance the bomb-and-blockade strategy with the introduction of nuclear war or negotiate a Japanese surrender by softening the unconditional Potsdam Ultimatum clause concerning the emperor. Australia and New Zealand opposed softening, and there was no way of knowing if it could actually end the conflict in any event. Further, negotiations take time, and time was vanishing because events were suddenly accelerating. Successful on July 16, Trinity was announced on July 21, the Potsdam Declaration came on July 26, and the Soviet declaration of war against Japan was scheduled for any time before August 9. It was simply too late for the United States to convince its allies, let alone the Japanese, that retention of the emperor was a possibility. The time for that had passed before Potsdam began. This left the bomb-and-blockade strategy as the only remaining option offering hope of ending the war before Russian armies overran large pieces of Japan and its conquered territories, and the atomic bomb made that viable—unless, of course, the initiation of the Soviet campaign itself were to compel Japan's surrender.

The only questions were where and when to use it. The imminent Soviet attack answered the when question. It must be soon, and it came eleven days after the Potsdam Declaration. Only the where question remained.

Into this mix crept the demon of bigotry. Japanese fear and hatred of Americans led to fanatical behavior, including brutal treatment of prisoners and the mass suicide of civilians who jumped to their deaths from Saipan's cliffs in 1944. So Japanese racial epithets were common in a way never employed against the Germans, and this led to a deeply ingrained hatred that relegated morality to a secondary consideration. Whatever the motivation or reason, Truman accepted the views of the Interim Committee and its Scientific Panel and authorized the use of atomic bombs against civilian centers as proposed by the Target Committee:

"Hiroshima is the largest untouched target not on the 21st Bomber Command priority list. Consideration should be given to this city. . . .

"It should be remembered that in our selection of any target, the 20th Air Force is operating primarily to lay waste all the remaining Japanese cities. . . . The 20th Air Force is systematically bombing out the following cities with the prime purpose in mind of not leaving one stone lying on another: Tokyo, Yokohama, Nagoya, Kyoto, Kobe, Yawata & Nagasaki."

It was the culmination of General Douhet's "total war" and "strategic bombing" concepts, rooted as they were, not within the context of the modern rules of war, but in the terror campaigns of Genghis Khan.

The bombs were dropped on August 6 and 9, 1945, to utterly devastating effect. In an instant at least 80,000 people were killed in Hiroshima and 40,000 in Nagasaki, with more dying later from the effects of wounds and radiation. Clearly, this same slaughter would never have been inflicted by ground force personnel, most of whom would have refused to carry out an unlawful order calling for the wholesale killing of noncombatant men, women, children, and babies.

But with the deed done, the most revealing communication came from Truman himself:

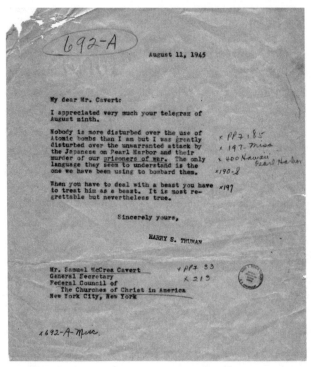

COURTESY HARRY S. TRUMAN LIBRARY AND MUSEUM

Truman was prone to hyperbole, and it is difficult to comprehend a description of old men, women, children, and babies as "beasts." Of course, he was referring to Japanese soldiers and politicians, but soldier deaths were greatly exceeded by civilian deaths at Hiroshima and almost nonexistent at Nagasaki, a city nearly devoid of a military presence. The bombing was nothing less than the wholesale slaughter of civilians. Indeed, Secretary of Commerce (and former vice president) Henry Wallace recorded in his diary the following from the cabinet meeting held the day before the Cavert telegram was sent: "Truman said he had given orders to stop atomic bombing. He said the thought of wiping out another 100,000 people was too horrible. He didn't like the idea of killing, as he said, 'all those kids.'"

This juxtaposition of the president publicly justifying the nuclear slaughter of Japanese "beasts" while acknowledging his horror of it in the confines of a cabinet meeting was revealing. His cancellation of the nuclear attack scheduled for August 17 indicated his actual position. Apparently, his bigotry was a public act in keeping with war propaganda rather than an actual belief. In the end his concern for "all those kids" became paramount and signaled an end to the Douhet-inspired theories of total war that had been taken to their logical and horrible nuclear conclusion with the strategic bombing of Hiroshima and Nagasaki.

Truman wrote another letter on August 18, this time to Joseph Stalin, categorically turning down the Soviet dictator's plan to invade Hokkaido, Japan's second-largest island, in a campaign that had originally been supported by the United States when Operation Olympic was still scheduled. Hiroshima and Nagasaki changed all that. A stunned Stalin called off the invasion on August 22, two days before it was to kick off. Truman assumed the bomb had cowed the extraordinarily cruel and aggressive dictator, but, according to Sergey Radchenko, "Seventy years on, evidence suggests that even if Truman did intend to intimidate Stalin, he was unsuccessful. Stalin's retreat at Hokkaido was a major concession made in spite of Hiroshima—a late effort by the Soviet dictator to patch up the rapidly unraveling relationship with the United States."

The use of atomic bombs surfaced again and was rejected again five years later when Chinese Communist forces were overrunning US-led

UN troops in Korea and General MacArthur pleaded for nuclear intervention. Truman refused, perhaps because the Soviet Union, China's ally, then had the bomb; more likely because he was haunted by the ghosts of "all those kids" from August 6 and 9, 1945.

There would be other instances of nonnuclear strategic bombing in the future, but the only significant such campaign was waged against North Vietnam during the Vietnam War. And, once again, Douhet was proven wrong. Just as the German bombing of British cities and the Allied bombing of German and Japanese cities had only steeled the people's resolve and resentment, so North Vietnamese civilians responded to the bombing they endured. Those populations under the yoke of fascist or communist dictators were simply instilled with a greater sense of nationalism, one that transcended politics.

And so, following their shocking use on Hiroshima and Nagasaki, the most terrifying weapons ever devised did not become the feared weapons of future wars, but deterrents of wars that could threaten the existence of a nuclear-armed belligerent. Ironically, nuclear weapons have made the world safe for limited wars—large or small.

PART IV

CONCLUSION

World War 4

HUMAN FOLLY IS THE GREAT IMPONDERABLE. YET, DOES FOLLY UPSET the calm or is the storm the natural state in the sea of humanity? Either way, folly or nature ensures a future filled with conflict.

During the Cold War when the possibility of superpower nuclear war fluctuated between the probable and the improbable, rationality prevailed. On the other end of the scale is zealotry, especially inherently irrational religious zealotry, and the world has shuddered since the dawn of the nuclear age that zealots might one day gain access to nuclear weaponry.

Yet, between these extremes lies inexplicable irrationality. It was witnessed during the 1962 Cuban Missile Crisis when Cuban dictator Fidel Castro urged his Soviet allies to launch a nuclear attack against the United States from their arsenals on his island. Whereas Soviet Premier Nikita Khrushchev was using nuclear missiles as leverage, Castro fanatically advocated their employment even though it would have meant nuclear war and the almost certain destruction of his nation. This was not religious zealotry or even Marxist fanaticism. It was geopolitical insanity—irrationality on an Armageddon scale.

At the January 1992 Havana conference, former Secretary of Defense Robert McNamara asked Castro:

1. *Were you aware the nuclear war-heads were in Cuba?*
2. *If so, would you have recommended their use?*
3. *If the nuclear weapons had been used, what would have been the outcome for Cuba?*
    President Castro's answer sent a chill down my spine. He replied:

"Now, we started from the assumption that if there was an invasion of Cuba, nuclear war would erupt. We were certain of that . . . we would be forced to pay the price, that we would disappear. . . . Would I have been ready to use nuclear weapons? Yes, I would have agreed to the use of nuclear weapons."

The subset of such thinking is miscalculation. It is the overplayed hand, the called bluff, the erroneous assumption. An example was Khrushchev's decision to place nuclear missiles in Cuba in the first place.

In the end, human folly offers many roads to war, and deterrence is only one preventive measure, a measure only applicable against a rational foe. The opposite extreme is accelerated preemptive military action. However, the real world, made up as it is of billions of individual human minds, driven by billions of human emotions and psychologies, rarely offers such clear distinctions. Aggressors often exceed their abilities when faced with compliant foes or defenders who often overestimate their enemies' abilities.

For these reasons a nation must prepare for the whole gamut of possibilities and be prepared to employ them even in the face of domestic dissent because providing for public safety is the primary purpose of government. In the United States the 1973 War Powers Resolution (in actuality an act, not a resolution) provides both presidential leeway and follow-up congressional oversight, all as a means of providing latitude of action while dampening the public passions of the moment. It was originally passed over President Richard Nixon's veto and has been both adhered to and contested by subsequent presidents, with the courts generally coming down on the executive branch, although the issue is occasionally tested as it was when a US Army captain sued the president in May 2016 over the conflict with ISIS. Even so, the resolution does help fill the gap between the constitutional power of Congress to declare war and the president's constitutional mandate to conduct foreign policy. As such, President George H. W. Bush denied the resolution's applicability to launch Desert Storm in 1991, but, on the other hand, requested and received congressional "support" for the action in the form of Public Law 102-1. President Bill Clinton reported to Congress but otherwise sidestepped the resolution in the 1993–99 operations in Bosnia and Kosovo, while George W. Bush fully complied with it following the events of 9/11. What the resolution did accomplish was to temporarily untether the president while instilling the need for executive-branch communication with Congress when military action is necessary.

World War II was America's great altruistic war, albeit a war of conquest for the Soviet Union. Initially fought as a defensive war against the fascist aggression of Germany, Italy, and Japan, it ended with the creation of the Soviet Empire, the dissolution of the British Empire, and the establishment of Pax Americana, a peace founded on the American rehabilitation and rebuilding of its enemies and the renunciation of conquest. So effective was that rehabilitation that an individual lacking an education in history might conclude that Germany and Japan were the victors. It was a scenario repeated or attempted throughout the Cold War and beyond in places such as Korea, Vietnam, the former Yugoslavia, Afghanistan, and Iraq, and while some of these conflicts were mishandled or misdirected, none of them was waged for conquest.

How much will altruism play in future conflicts? It may be enunciated at the outset of hostilities or it may creep in at the end, when the spoils of war are refused. The various scenarios described in this book are based upon history and rational self-interest as well as the human capacity for irrational behavior, which seemingly includes altruism. In truth, altruism, even if intended as a selfless act, often benefits victor and vanquished alike through future trade and alliances.

At opposite poles, the book contrasts the rational and desperate need for natural resources in the Blue Gold War with the irrational Nuclear Terrorist War, which above all the other forms of human conflict completely encompasses the reality of irrational warfare. Because the instigators are zealots, the threat of force is useless, and the use of force must be complete. In between these poles are the nuanced conflicts.

The book highlights the distinctions between xenophobia (the Great China War) and conflict resulting from a desire for land and power (the Great Russian War). It contrasts the conflicting drives of man, the age-old human flaw of greed (the Polar War and the Commerce, Currency, and Cyber War) with the eternal quest for freedom (the Chinese Civil

War). But most of all, man seeks security, which often imposes on governments the necessity for extreme self-defense measures (the Lunar War) as occurred during World War II. Yet, nothing so combines the rational with the irrational—that category falling fully in between the opposing poles—than the ongoing reality that "things fall apart" when human wants and needs are unmet by human-created boundaries, organizations, and laws (the Post-NATO War).

These World War 4 wars run the gamut and debunk the idea that national defense can be predicated upon easily defined threats. Even rational threats must first be identified and categorized to be thwarted. As often as not, such threats are nothing more than bluffs or the pushing of envelopes, and discerning the differences between those and provocative challenges requires astute analyses and rational responses.

In this respect, the irrational threats and the countermeasures to fight them are the most easily identifiable. Here the solutions tend to be found in strength and decisiveness. The technological, covert, and overt strength, especially for the United States, is generally going to be sufficient. Convincing a reticent public to act decisively can be another matter. Yet, the absence of such action will allow the ranks, infiltrations, and weapons of irrational zealots to grow because time is the enemy of the rational and ally of the irrational.

The nuanced threats falling between the fully rational and the incomprehensible irrational must be addressed with interlocking tiers of defenses. Diplomacy, technology, politics, espionage, subversion, aggressive reconnaissance, complex alliances, diverse force structures, integrated and unified commands, secure lines of supply, economic stability, secure communications, an informed and educated public, and expertise in history, geography, and ethnicity are a few of the elements critical for success. These lead to the term "flexible response," which is so key when modulating the approach to and conduct of nuanced wars.

Part V

Appendices

Appendix A

The United States Military's Contribution to National Security, June 2015

Chairman's Foreword
[Chairman of the Joint Chiefs of Staff Gen. Martin E. Dempsey]

TODAY'S GLOBAL SECURITY ENVIRONMENT IS THE MOST UNPREDICTABLE I have seen in 40 years of service. Since the last National Military Strategy was published in 2011, global disorder has significantly increased while some of our comparative military advantage has begun to erode. We now face multiple, simultaneous security challenges from traditional state actors and transregional networks of sub-state groups—all taking advantage of rapid technological change. Future conflicts will come more rapidly, last longer, and take place on a much more technically challenging battlefield. They will have increasing implications to the U.S. homeland.

This National Military Strategy [NMS] describes how we will employ our military forces to protect and advance our national interests. We must be able to rapidly adapt to new threats while maintaining comparative advantage over traditional ones. Success will increasingly depend on how well our military instrument can support the other instruments of power and enable our network of allies and partners.

The 2015 NMS continues the call for greater agility, innovation, and integration. It reinforces the need for the U.S. military to remain globally engaged to shape the security environment and to preserve our network of alliances. It echoes previous documents in noting the imperative within our profession to develop leaders of competence, character, and consequence.

But it also asserts that the application of the military instrument of power against state threats is very different than the application of military power against non-state threats. We are more likely to face prolonged campaigns than conflicts that are resolved quickly . . . that control of escalation is becoming more difficult and more important . . . and that as a hedge against unpredictability with reduced resources, we may have to adjust our global posture.

Despite what is likely to be a difficult future, we are blessed to be able to count on the young Americans who choose to serve, to live an uncommon life, and to defend their fellow citizens. Our focus must remain that they are the best-led and best-equipped force in the world. The 2015 National Military Strategy of the United States offers a blueprint towards that end.

This 2015 National Military Strategy addresses the need to counter revisionist states that are challenging international norms as well as violent extremist organizations (VEOs) that are undermining transregional security. We are working with allies and partners to deter, deny, and—when necessary—defeat potential state adversaries. Concurrently, we are leading multiple coalition efforts to disrupt, degrade, and defeat VEOs. Central to these efforts is strengthening our global network of allies and partners. This integrated strategy requires us to conduct synchronized operations around the globe, implement institutional reforms at home, and sustain the capabilities, capacity, and readiness required to prevail in conflicts that may differ significantly in scope, scale, and duration.

I. The Strategic Environment

Complexity and rapid change characterize today's strategic environment, driven by globalization, the diffusion of technology, and demographic shifts.

Globalization is impacting nearly every aspect of human activity. People, products, and information are flowing across borders at unprecedented speed and volume, acting as catalysts for economic development while also increasing societal tensions, competition for resources, and political instability.

Central to globalization is the spread of new technologies that enable a global information environment and empower people to see more, share more, create more, and organize faster than ever before. Individuals and groups today have access to more information than entire governments once possessed. They can swiftly organize and act on what they learn, sometimes leading to violent change. States, meanwhile, are using information sharing to develop advanced capabilities of their own. When applied to military systems, this diffusion of technology is challenging competitive advantages long held by the United States such as early warning and precision strike.

These changes are amplified by shifting demographics. Youth populations are rapidly growing in Africa and the Middle East, regions that face resource shortages, struggling economies, and deep social fissures. Meanwhile, populations in Europe and across northern Asia are set to decline and get older. Around the world, millions of people are flowing from the countryside into cities in search of work where they are exposed to cultural differences, alienation, and disease. They also are moving across borders and seas in growing numbers, accepting great risk and placing strain on nations that receive them.

KEY FACTORS

- Globalization
- Diffusion of technology
- Demographic shifts

Despite these changes, states remain the international system's dominant actors. They are preeminent in their capability to harness power, focus human endeavors, and provide security. Most states today—led by the United States, its allies, and partners—support the established institutions and processes dedicated to preventing conflict, respecting sovereignty, and furthering human rights. Some states, however, are attempting to revise key aspects of the international order and are acting in a manner that threatens our national security interests.

While Russia has contributed in select security areas, such as counternarcotics and counterterrorism, it also has repeatedly demonstrated that it does not respect the sovereignty of its neighbors and it is willing to use force to achieve its goals. Russia's military actions are undermining regional security directly and through proxy forces. These actions violate numerous agreements that Russia has signed in which it committed to act in accordance with international norms, including the UN Charter, Helsinki Accords, Russia-NATO Founding Act, Budapest Memorandum, and the Intermediate-Range Nuclear Forces Treaty.

Iran also poses strategic challenges to the international community. It is pursuing nuclear and missile delivery technologies despite repeated United Nations Security Council resolutions demanding that it cease such efforts. It is a state-sponsor of terrorism that has undermined stability in many nations, including Israel, Lebanon, Iraq, Syria, and Yemen. Iran's actions have destabilized the region and brought misery to countless people while denying the Iranian people the prospect of a prosperous future.

North Korea's pursuit of nuclear weapons and ballistic missile technologies also contradicts repeated demands by the international community to cease such efforts. These capabilities directly threaten its neighbors, especially the Republic of Korea and Japan. In time, they will threaten the U.S. homeland as well. North Korea also has conducted cyber-attacks, including causing major damage to a U.S. corporation.

We support China's rise and encourage it to become a partner for greater international security. However, China's actions are adding tension to the Asia-Pacific region. For example, its claims to nearly the entire South China Sea are inconsistent with international law. The international community continues to call on China to settle such issues cooperatively and without coercion. China has responded with aggressive land reclamation efforts that will allow it to position military forces astride vital international sea lanes.

None of these nations are believed to be seeking direct military conflict with the United States or our allies. Nonetheless, they each pose serious security concerns which the international community is working to collectively address by way of common policies, shared messages, and coordinated action.

As part of that effort, we remain committed to engagement with all nations to communicate our values, promote transparency, and reduce the potential for miscalculation. Accordingly, we continue to invest in a substantial military-to-military relationship with China and we remain ready to engage Russia in areas of common interest, while urging both nations to settle their disputes peacefully and in accordance with international law.

Concurrent with state challenges, violent extremist organizations (VEOs)—led by al Qaida and the self-proclaimed Islamic State of Iraq and the Levant (ISIL)—are working to undermine transregional security, especially in the Middle East and North Africa. Such groups are dedicated to radicalizing populations, spreading violence, and leveraging terror to impose their visions of societal organization. They are strongest where governments are weakest, exploiting people trapped in fragile or failed states. In many locations, VEOs coexist with transnational criminal organizations, where they conduct illicit trade and spread corruption, further undermining security and stability.

In this complex strategic security environment, the U.S. military does not have the luxury of focusing on one challenge to the exclusion of others. It must provide a full range of military options for addressing both revisionist states and VEOs. Failure to do so will result in greater risk to our country and the international order.

II. The Military Environment

The United States is the world's strongest nation, enjoying unique advantages in technology, energy, alliances and partnerships, and demographics. However, these advantages are being challenged.

For the past decade, our military campaigns primarily have consisted of operations against violent extremist networks. But today, and into the foreseeable future, we must pay greater attention to challenges posed by state actors. They increasingly have the capability to contest regional freedom of movement and threaten our homeland. Of particular concern are the proliferation of ballistic missiles, precision strike technologies, unmanned systems, space and cyber capabilities, and weapons of mass destruction (WMD)—technologies designed to counter U.S. military advantages and curtail access to the global commons.

Emerging technologies are impacting the calculus of deterrence and conflict management by increasing uncertainty and compressing decision space. For example, attacks on our communications and sensing systems could occur with little to no warning, impacting our ability to assess, coordinate, communicate, and respond. As a result, future conflicts between states may prove to be unpredictable, costly, and difficult to control.

VEOs are taking advantage of emergent technologies as well, using information tools to propagate destructive ideologies, recruit and incite violence, and amplify the perceived power of their movements. They advertise their actions to strike fear in opponents and generate support for their causes. They use improvised explosive devices (IED), suicide vests, and tailored cyber tools to spread terror while seeking ever more sophisticated capabilities, including WMD.

Today, the probability of U.S. involvement in interstate war with a major power is assessed to be low but growing. Should one occur, however, the consequences would be immense. VEOs, in contrast, pose an immediate threat to transregional security by coupling readily available technologies with extremist ideologies. Overlapping state and non-state violence, there exists an area of conflict where actors blend techniques, capabilities, and resources to achieve their objectives. Such "hybrid" conflicts may consist of military forces assuming a non-state identity, as Russia did in the Crimea, or involve a VEO fielding rudimentary combined arms capabilities, as ISIL has demonstrated in Iraq and Syria. Hybrid conflicts also may be comprised of state and non-state actors working together toward shared objectives, employing a wide range of weapons such as we have witnessed in eastern Ukraine. Hybrid conflicts serve to increase ambiguity, complicate decision-making, and slow the coordination of effective responses. Due to these advantages to the aggressor, it is likely that this form of conflict will persist well into the future.

III. An Integrated Military Environment

The U.S. military's purpose is to protect our nation and win our wars. We do this through military operations to defend the homeland, build security globally, and project power and win decisively. Our military supports diplomatic, informational, and economic activities that promote

---

U.S. ENDURING NATIONAL INTERESTS

- The security of the United States, its citizens, and U.S. allies and partners.
- A strong, innovative, and growing U.S. economy in an open international economic system that promotes opportunity and prosperity.
- Respect for universal values at home and around the world.
- A rules-based international order advanced by U.S. leadership that promotes peace, security, and opportunity through stronger cooperation to meet global challenges.

NATIONAL SECURITY INTERESTS

- The survival of the Nation.
- The prevention of catastrophic attack against U.S. territory.
- The security of the global economic system.
- The security, confidence, and reliability of our allies.
- The protection of American citizens abroad.
- The preservation and extension of universal values.

NATIONAL MILITARY OBJECTIVES

- Deter, deny, and defeat state adversaries.
- Disrupt, degrade, and defeat violent extremist organizations.
- Strengthen our global network of allies and partners.

---

our enduring national interests. As detailed in the 2015 National Security Strategy, our enduring national interests are: the security of the United States, its citizens, and U.S. allies and partners; a strong, innovative, and growing U.S. economy in an open international economic system that promotes opportunity and prosperity; respect for universal values at home and around the world; and a rules-based international order advanced by U.S. leadership that promotes peace, security, and opportunity through stronger cooperation to meet global challenges.

From the enduring national interests, the U.S. military has derived National Security Interests (NSIs) to prioritize its missions. The NSIs are: the survival of the Nation; the prevention of catastrophic attack against U.S. territory; the security of the global economic system; the security, confidence, and reliability of our allies; the protection of American citizens abroad; and the preservation and extension of universal values. NSIs guide military leaders in providing recommendations on when and where our nation should use military force, the type and degree of force to employ, and at what cost.

To secure these interests, this National Military Strategy provides an integrated approach composed of three National Military Objectives: to deter, deny, and defeat state adversaries; to disrupt, degrade, and defeat VEOs; and to strengthen our global network of allies and partners. The U.S. military pursues these objectives by conducting globally integrated operations, implementing institutional reforms at home, and sustaining the capabilities, capacity, and readiness required to prevail in conflicts that may differ significantly in scope, scale, and duration.

These NMOs support the force planning guidance prescribed in the 2014 Quadrennial Defense Review. It states that our nation requires a U.S. military with the capacity, capability, and readiness to simultaneously defend the homeland; conduct sustained, distributed counterterrorist operations; and, in multiple regions, deter aggression and assure allies through forward presence and engagement. If deterrence fails, at any given time, our military will be capable of defeating a regional adversary in a large-scale, multi-phased campaign while denying the objectives of—or imposing unacceptable costs on—another aggressor in a different region.

A. Deter, Deny, and Defeat State Adversaries

The U.S. military is the world's preeminent Joint Force. It supports the nation by providing a full range of options to protect the homeland and our interests while assuring the security of our allies. The U.S. military deters aggression by maintaining a credible nuclear capability that is safe, secure, and effective; conducting forward engagement and operations; and maintaining Active, National Guard, and Reserve forces prepared to deploy and conduct operations of sufficient scale and duration to accomplish their missions. Forward deployed, rotational, and globally responsive forces regularly demonstrate the capability and will to act. Should deterrence fail to prevent aggression, the U.S. military stands ready to project power to deny an adversary's objectives and decisively defeat any actor that threatens the U.S. homeland, our national interests, or our allies and partners.

Deterring a direct attack on the United States and our allies is a priority mission, requiring homeland and regional defenses tied to secure conventional and nuclear strike capabilities. Thus U.S. strategic forces remain always ready. U.S. military defenses are enhanced by our North American Aerospace Defense Command Agreement with Canada and close cooperation with the U.S. Department of Homeland Security. These homeland defense partnerships are complemented by growing investments in the cyber realm designed to protect vital networks and infrastructure.

In case of aggression, denying adversaries their goals will be an immediate objective. This places special emphasis on maintaining highly-ready forces forward, as well as well trained and equipped surge forces at home, resilient logistics and transportation infrastructures, networked intelligence, strong communications links, and interoperability with allies and partners. Timely interagency planning and coordination also will be leveraged to develop holistic options that serve to integrate all elements of national power.

Should any actor directly attack the United States or our interests, the U.S. military will take action to defend our nation. We are prepared to project power across all domains to stop aggression and win our nation's wars by decisively defeating adversaries. While we prefer to act in concert with others, we will act unilaterally if the situation demands. In the event of an attack, the U.S. military will respond by inflicting damage of such magnitude as to compel the adversary to cease hostilities or render it incapable of further aggression. War against a major adversary would require the full mobilization of all instruments of national power and, to do so, the United States sustains a full-spectrum military that includes strong Reserve and National Guard forces. They provide the force depth needed to achieve victory while simultaneously deterring other threats.

B. Disrupt, Degrade, and Defeat VEOs

Today, the United States is leading a broad coalition of nations to defeat VEOs in multiple regions by applying pressure across the full extent of their networks.

In concert with all elements of national power and international partnerships, these efforts aim to disrupt VEO planning and operations, degrade support structures, remove leadership, interdict finances, impede the flow of foreign fighters, counter malign influences, liberate captured territory, and ultimately defeat them. In support of these efforts, we are widely distributing U.S. military forces and leveraging globally integrated command and control processes to enable transregional operations.

Credible regional partners are vital to sustaining counter-VEO campaigns. The U.S. military contributes select combat forces, enabling technologies, and training in support of local partners that provide the majority of forces necessary to restore and secure their homelands. Timelines for these campaigns generally are long. Therefore, they must be conducted in a politically, financially, and militarily sustainable manner that optimizes the power of coalitions, as we are demonstrating in Afghanistan and Iraq.

In Afghanistan, the United States and our NATO partners are teaming with the National Unity Government to provide security by way of the Resolute Support mission, working toward establishing a long-term counterterrorism partnership. Similarly, in Iraq a broad coalition of over 60 nations is providing security assistance, training, airlift, and strike support in its struggle against ISIL.

Defeating VEOs also requires an appreciation of the nexus between such groups and transnational criminal organizations. A fuller understanding of that relationship will allow us to disrupt illicit funds, weapons, and fighters that are flowing into conflict-ridden regions. Such knowledge also will allow us to work with law enforcement officials to more effectively protect our homeland from terrorists.

Defeating VEOs ultimately requires providing security and economic opportunities to at-risk populations. Thus counter-VEO campaigns demand that our military, in close coordination with other U.S. agencies and international organizations, assist local governments in addressing the root causes of conflict. As part of that effort, the U.S. military regularly contributes to humanitarian assistance and disaster relief endeavors aimed at alleviating suffering and restoring hope.

C. Strengthen Our Global Network of Allies and Partners

America's global network of allies and partners is a unique strength that provides the foundation for international security and stability. These partnerships also facilitate the growth of prosperity around the world, from which all nations benefit.

As we look to the future, the U.S. military and its allies and partners will continue to protect and promote shared interests. We will preserve our alliances, expand partnerships, maintain a global stabilizing presence, and conduct training, exercises, security cooperation activities, and military-to-military engagement. Such activities increase the capabilities and capacity of partners, thereby enhancing our collective ability to deter aggression and defeat extremists.

The presence of U.S. military forces in key locations around the world underpins the international order and provides opportunities to engage with other countries while positioning forces to respond to crises. Therefore we will press forward with the rebalance to the Asia Pacific region, placing our most advanced capabilities and greater capacity in that vital theater. We will strengthen our alliances with Australia, Japan, the Republic of Korea, the Philippines, and Thailand. We also will deepen our security relationship with India and build upon our partnerships with New Zealand, Singapore, Indonesia, Malaysia, Vietnam, and Bangladesh.

Such efforts are essential to maintaining regional peace and building capabilities to provide for missile defense, cyber security, maritime security, and disaster relief.

In Europe, we remain steadfast in our commitment to our NATO allies. NATO provides vital collective security guarantees and is strategically important for deterring conflict, particularly in light of recent Russian aggression on its periphery. U.S. Operation ATLANTIC RESOLVE, our European Reassurance Initiative, NATO's Readiness Action Plan, and the many activities, exercises, and investments contained in them serve to underline our dedication to alliance solidarity, unity, and security. We also will continue to support our NATO partners to increase their interoperability with U.S. forces and to provide for their own defense.

In the Middle East, we remain fully committed to Israel's security and Qualitative Military Edge. We also are helping other vital partners in that region increase their defenses, including Jordan, Saudi Arabia, Kuwait, Qatar, Bahrain, UAE, Egypt, and Pakistan. Additionally, we are working to strengthen institutions across Africa, aimed at fostering stability, building peacekeeping capacity, and countering transregional extremism. And the U.S. military is supporting interagency efforts with Latin American and Caribbean states to promote regional stability and counter transnational criminal organizations.

Combined training and exercises increase the readiness of our allies and partners while enhancing the interoperability and responsiveness of U.S. forces. With advanced partners like NATO, Australia, Japan, and Korea, our exercises emphasize sophisticated capabilities such as assuring access to contested environments and deterring and responding to hybrid conflicts. With other partners, training often focuses on improving skills in counterterrorism, peacekeeping, disaster relief, support to law enforcement, and search and rescue.

Security cooperation activities are at the heart of our efforts to provide a stabilizing presence in forward theaters. These build relationships that serve mutual security interests. They also develop partner military capabilities for self-defense and support to multinational operations. Through such activities, we coordinate with other U.S. agencies and mission partners to build cultural awareness and affirm relationships that increase regional stability.

D. Advance Globally Integrated Operations

The execution of integrated operations requires a Joint Force capable of swift and decisive force projection around the world. As detailed in the "Capstone Concept for Joint Operations: Joint Force 2020," globally integrated operations emphasize eight key components: employing mission command; seizing, retaining, and exploiting the initiative; leveraging global agility; partnering; demonstrating flexibility in establishing joint forces; improving cross-domain synergy; using flexible, low-signature capabilities; and being increasingly discriminate to minimize unintended consequences. Such operations rely upon a global logistics and transportation network, secure communications, and integrated joint and partner intelligence, surveillance, and reconnaissance (ISR) capabilities.

In executing globally integrated operations, U.S. military forces work closely with international and interagency partners to generate strategic options for our nation. In doing so, military commanders use the following prioritization of military missions to advise our national leaders:

Maintain a Secure and Effective Nuclear Deterrent. U.S. strategic forces are kept at the highest state of readiness, always prepared to respond to threats to the homeland and our vital interests. Accordingly, we are investing to sustain and modernize our nuclear enterprise. We continue to implement the 2010 Nuclear Posture Review and 2011 New START Treaty while ensuring our national defense needs are met. Concurrently, we are enhancing our command and control capabilities for strategic and regional nuclear forces.

Provide for Military Defense of the Homeland. Emerging state and non-state capabilities pose varied and direct threats to our homeland. Thus we are striving to interdict attack preparations abroad, defend against limited ballistic missile attacks, and protect cyber systems and physical infrastructure. Key homeland defense capabilities include resilient space-based and terrestrial indications and warning systems; an integrated intelligence collection, analysis, and dissemination architecture; a Ground-Based Interceptor force; a Cyber Mission Force; and, ready ground, air and naval forces. We also are leveraging domestic and regional partnerships to improve information sharing and unity of effort. These capabilities will better defend us against both high technology threats and terrorist dangers.

Defeat an Adversary. In the event of an attack against the United States or one of its allies, the U.S. military along with allies and partners will project power across multiple domains to decisively defeat the adversary by compelling it to cease hostilities or render its military incapable of further aggression.

Provide a Global, Stabilizing Presence. The presence of U.S. military forces in key locations around the world underpins the security of our allies and partners, provides stability to enhance economic growth and regional integration, and positions the Joint Force to execute emergency actions in response to a crisis.

Combat Terrorism. Terrorism is a tactic VEOs use to advance their interests. The best way to counter VEOs is by way of sustained pressure

---

JOINT FORCE PRIORITIZED MISSIONS

- Maintain a secure and effective nuclear deterrent
- Provide for military defense of the homeland
- Defeat an adversary
- Provide a global, stabilizing presence
- Combat terrorism
- Counter weapons of mass destruction
- Deny an adversary's objectives
- Respond to crisis and conduct limited contingency operations
- Conduct military engagement and security cooperation
- Conduct stability and counterinsurgency operations
- Provide support to civil authorities
- Conduct humanitarian assistance and disaster response

---

using local forces augmented by specialized U.S. and coalition military strengths such as ISR, precision strike, training, and logistical support. Counterterrorism operations also involve coordinated efforts with other U.S. agencies, working together to interdict and disrupt threats targeting the U.S. homeland.

Counter Weapons of Mass Destruction. Nuclear, chemical, and biological agents pose uniquely destructive threats. They can empower a small group of actors with terrible destructive potential. Thus combatting WMD as far from our homeland as possible is a key mission for the U.S. military. Toward that end, we team with multinational and U.S. interagency partners to locate, track, interdict, and secure or destroy WMD, its components, and the means and facilities needed to make it, wherever possible.

Deny an Adversary's Objectives. Denying an adversary's goals or imposing unacceptable costs is central to achieving our objectives. This puts emphasis on maintaining highly-ready, forward-deployed forces, well trained and equipped surge forces at home, robust transportation infrastructure and assets, and reliable and resilient communications links with allies and partners. These capabilities provide the means to curtail crises before they can escalate.

Respond to Crisis and Conduct Limited Contingency Operations. Another form of power projection is teaming with partners to conduct limited contingency operations. Such operations may involve flowing additional U.S. forces and capabilities to a given region to strengthen deterrence, prevent escalation, and reassure allies. Additionally, the U.S. military sustains ready forces around the world to defend our citizens and protect diplomatic facilities.

Conduct Military Engagement and Security Cooperation. The U.S. military strengthens regional stability by conducting security cooperation activities with foreign defense establishments. Such activities support mutual security interests, develop partner capabilities for self-defense, and prepare for multinational operations. Strengthening partners is fundamental to our security, building strategic depth for our national defense.

Conduct Stability and Counterinsurgency Operations. The U.S. military also remains ready to conduct limited stability operations when required, working with interagency, coalition, and host-nation forces. Such efforts emphasize unique elements of our forces: civil military affairs teams, building partner capacity, information support teams, and cultural outreach programs.

Provide Support to Civil Authorities. When man-made or natural disasters impact the United States, our military community offers support to civil authorities in concert with other U.S. agencies. As part of that effort, we integrate military and civil capabilities through FEMA's National Planning System and National Exercise Program. During domestic events, U.S. military forces—including National Guard and Reserve units—provide trained personnel, communications capabilities, lift, and logistical and planning support. They work alongside civilian first-responders to mitigate the impact of such incidents and keep our citizens safe.

Conduct Humanitarian Assistance and Disaster Response. Over the years, U.S. Soldiers, Sailors, Airmen, Marines, and Coast Guardsmen have quickly and effectively delivered life-sustaining aid to desperate people all around the world. Such efforts sometimes last only a few weeks. At other times, they last much longer. In all cases, taking action to relieve suffering reflects our professional ethos and the values in which we believe.

E. Resourcing the Strategy

We will not realize the goals of this 2015 National Military Strategy without sufficient resources. Like those that came before it, this strategy assumes a commitment to projecting global influence, supporting allies and partners, and maintaining the All-Volunteer Force. To execute this strategy, the U.S. military requires a sufficient level of investment in capacity, capabilities, and readiness so that when our nation calls, our military remains ready to deliver success.

IV. Joint Force Initiatives

The U.S. Joint Force combines people, processes, and programs to execute globally integrated operations and achieve our National Military Objectives. This requires innovative leaders, optimized decision-making, and advanced military capabilities.

A. People and the Profession of Arms:
Improving Upon Our Greatest Advantage

Our military and civilian professionals are our decisive advantage. They are the foundation of our operational excellence and our ability to successfully innovate. Therefore, we are dedicated to building creative, adaptive professionals skilled at leading organizational change while operating in complexity. To accomplish this, we are evolving our organizational culture and strengthening our leadership.

FOSTERING INNOVATION

- Producing creative, adaptive leaders
- Adopting efficient, dynamic processes
- Developing flexible, interoperable capabilities

As we look to future challenges, the U.S. military will remain ready to meet unanticipated demands. We must prepare our Service members to fight under conditions of complexity and persistent danger, conditions that demand courage, toughness, adaptability, and endurance as well as an abiding commitment to our nation's values and professional military ethic.

We are prioritizing leader development. To retain our warfighting edge, we are stressing innovative leader development across the All-Volunteer Force—officer, enlisted, and civilian—through a combination of training, education, broad experience, and opportunity. These elements build the expertise that is the wellspring of innovation. Toward that end, our training increasingly blends physical and virtual experiences to simulate contested environments and operations in denied or degraded conditions. Our military education system also is updating how it selects and incentivizes faculty, rewards critical thought, and promotes our most innovative minds. Continuous, demanding education inspires new ideas and identifies better ways to accomplish our missions.

In developing the Joint leaders of tomorrow, we emphasize six attributes. Our leaders will:

- Strive to understand the environment in which they operate and the effect of applying all instruments of national power
- Anticipate and adapt to surprise, uncertainty, and chaos
- Work to recognize change and lead transitions
- Operate on intent through trust, empowerment, and understanding
- Make ethical decisions based on the shared values of the Profession of Arms
- Think critically and strategically in applying joint warfighting principles and concepts to joint operations

We are adapting our organizational culture. To enhance our warfighting capability, we must attract, develop, and retain the right people at every echelon. Central to this effort is understanding how society is changing. Today's youth grow up in a thoroughly connected environment. They are comfortable using technology and interactive social structures to solve problems. These young men and women are tomorrow's leaders and we need their service. Therefore, the U.S. military must be willing to embrace social and cultural change to better identify, cultivate, and reward such talent.

To do so, we are exploring how our personnel policies and promotion practices must evolve to leverage 21st century skills. We are seeking new ways to attract people with valuable civilian sector experience. We also are experimenting with giving military personnel greater access to civilian innovation practices through flexible career options. In this effort, the Reserve Components provide a critical bridge to the civilian population, infusing the Joint Force with unique skills and diverse perspectives. Also critical to building the best military possible are our efforts to further integrate women across the force by providing them greater opportunities for service.

We are promoting ethical leadership. Ethical leadership is central to protecting and strengthening our military family. This requires cultivating a professional climate that reinforces our respect for core values, promotes accountability, and appreciates the contributions of every member of our professional community. To help us meet these goals, we are moving forward with a campaign of trust that stresses mutual respect and emphasizes the importance of a positive culture enhanced by quality programs for sexual assault prevention and response, suicide prevention, and high-risk behavior avoidance.

B. Processes: Capturing Innovation and Efficiencies

Agile, efficient, and focused processes are means to accomplish our strategic objectives. Such processes include promoting greater interoperability with joint, interagency, and international partners while encouraging action through decentralized execution.

We are conducting resource-informed planning. For nearly a generation, we have consumed readiness as quickly as we have generated it. As a result, our long-term readiness has declined. Therefore, we are taking action to better balance achieving our operational goals with sustaining ready surge forces at home. We are revising operational plans to be more flexible, creative, and integrated across Combatant Commands. We also are providing the Services with time to reset, modernize, and replace vital equipment. Our goal is to strengthen deterrence while ensuring the long-term viability of our full-spectrum power projection capacity. Additionally, we are more fully coordinating requirements, plans, and operational execution at home and abroad to maximize collective capabilities against common concerns. And we are using tailored forces that deploy for limited timeframes to execute specific missions, recognizing that "campaign persistence" is necessary against determined adversaries.

We are improving our global agility. The ability to quickly aggregate and disaggregate forces anywhere in the world is the essence of global agility. We are striving to increase our agility by improving campaign planning, sustaining a resilient global posture, and implementing dynamic force management processes that adjust presence in anticipation of events, to better seize opportunities, deter adversaries, and assure allies and partners. We also are more fully sharing forces among Combatant Commands to address transregional threats. We are positioning forces where they are most needed, exemplified by our rebalance to the Asia-Pacific region as well as our evolving presence in Europe, the Middle East, Latin America, and Africa. We also are updating international agreements to assure access and provide legal protection for our people. Such agreements allow us to strengthen the relationships that are the foundation of trust.

We are demanding greater effectiveness and efficiencies. In a resource-constrained environment, we are striving to be careful stewards of our resources. Programmatic discipline by the Services has never been more important, as it is vital to generating economic efficiencies. We are working to sustain our industrial base while seeking savings through the Department of Defense's Better Buying Power 3.0 initiative. We are selectively using contractor support when it best serves the mission. We also are reducing staffs, streamlining functions, eliminating redundancies, and producing more integrated and effective organizations.

C. Programs: Sustaining Our Quality Edge

Effective programs enable our Soldiers, Sailors, Airmen, Marines, and Coast Guardsmen to fight and win. Delivering next-generation programs on schedule and within cost is vital, as our current systems increasingly are being challenged by adversary capabilities. To win against the diverse range of state and non-state threats confronting us, we must think innovatively, challenge assumptions, and embrace change.

We are improving joint interoperability. We are in the process of defining the next set of interoperability standards for future capabilities. In view of the anti-access/area denial (A2/AD) challenges we increasingly face, our future force will have to operate in contested environments. Key to assuring such access will be deploying secure, interoperable systems between Services, allies, interagency, and commercial partners. Priority efforts in that regard are establishing a Joint Information Environment (JIE), advancing globally integrated logistics, and building an integrated Joint ISR Enterprise. The results of these initiatives—particularly the enhanced connectivity and cybersecurity provided by the JIE—will provide the foundation for future interoperability.

We are investing to enhance decisive advantages. Future capabilities must sustain our ability to defend the homeland and project military power globally. Important investments to counter A2/AD, space, cyber, and hybrid threats include: space and terrestrial-based indications and warning systems, integrated and resilient ISR platforms, strategic lift, long-range precision strike weapons, missile defense technologies, undersea systems, remotely operated vehicles and technologies, special operations forces, and the Cyber Mission Force, among others. We also are improving our global sustainment capabilities and upgrading our command and control infrastructure to better support widely dispersed operations. We are modernizing our nuclear enterprise and working to protect our nation against asymmetric threats.

To improve institutional agility, we are expanding relations with American businesses, including many of the most innovative companies in the world, to learn their best practices. Further, we are aligning our programmatic efforts to take advantage of insights gleaned from the Defense Innovation Initiative, which is aimed at identifying potential strategic and operational advantages through war gaming, concept development, and a wide array of technology investments.

As we develop new capabilities to counter threats along the continuum of conflict, we also must procure sufficient capacity and readiness to sustain our global responsibilities. This may include evolving traditional platforms. Or it may require developing entirely new systems that are affordable and flexible. In all cases, our programs must allow us to quickly adapt, to counter adversaries employing unexpected techniques or weapons.

V. Conclusion

This 2015 National Military Strategy provides an overview of our strategic challenges and details how we will employ the Joint Force to keep our nation, allies, and partners safe.

It is a strategy that recognizes the increasing complexity of the global environment, driven by rapid and profound change. It also acknowledges our significant advantages, our commitment to international norms, the importance of our allies and partners, and the powerful allure of freedom and human dignity.

When placed in balance against the challenges before us, these strengths will serve us well and help us achieve a more secure future.

Appendix B

U.S. European Command
Operation Atlantic Resolve, March 2015*

OPERATION ATLANTIC RESOLVE IS A DEMONSTRATION OF OUR CONTIN-ued commitment to the collective security of NATO and dedication to the enduring peace and stability in the region, in light of the Russian intervention in Ukraine.

Land

• **3rd Infantry Division:** (Mar. 15-Jun. 15) Approximately 200 Soldiers from 3ID's 1st Brigade will assume responsibility from the 2nd Cavalry Regiment for the U.S. Army's OAR land forces training mission in Poland, Estonia, Latvia and Lithuania. On March 9, 110 vehicles were offloaded in Riga, Latvia, to be shipped to the Baltic States with the remaining equipment awaiting offload in Bremerhaven, Germany. Approximately 120 pieces of equipment will be left behind after 3ID rotates and be relocated to Germany to support the planned expansion of U.S. Army Europe's "European Activity Set" from a heavy battalion to a heavy brigade-sized equipment set.

• **4th Infantry Division Headquarters:** (Feb.-Dec. 2015) Approximately 100 Soldiers from the 4ID Mission Command Element deployed to Germany to serve as the division-level headquarters for United States Army, Europe under the Army's Regionally Aligned Forces.

• **Exercise Allied Spirit I:** (Hohenfels, Germany, Jan. 13-31) More than 1,600 participants from Canada, Hungary, Netherlands, United

---

* Courtesy Department of Defense. Reproduced without emendation.

Kingdom and the U.S. participated in Exercise Allied Spirit I, which enhanced NATO interoperability at brigade and battalion levels and tested secure communications amongst Alliance members. The exercise, which took place at the Joint Multinational Readiness Center, showcased the world class facility and highlighted its capabilities, allowing allies and partners to connect—personally, professionally and tactically—to create stronger, more capable forces.

• **2nd Cavalry Regiment** (Jan. 14-Mar. 31)—Approximately 550 Soldiers and 75 Stryker vehicles from the 2nd Cavalry Regiment are training with our allies in Poland, Estonia, Latvia and Lithuania in support of OAR. 2CR will conduct a variety of training events alongside Soldiers from NATO and partner nations. Many of these training events will focus on individual and team tasks that will culminate in joint platoon level-events, such as live fires. This is the first Stryker unit to deploy to the Baltic nations and Poland in support of OAR and it is the second brigade-sized element from U.S. Army Europe to support the mission. The 2 CR training rotation will continue through the end of March.

• **Exercise Platinum Lion 15:** (Jan. 12-Jan. 26) Exercise Platinum Lion allowed the Black Sea Rotational Force to join together with partner and allied forces in the region to build partner nation capacity, enhance interoperability and increase the overall effectiveness between them. Platinum Lion 15 included U.S. Marines and Sailors as well as Soldiers from Bulgaria, Serbia, and Romania. At more than 300 participants, Platinum Lion 15 is the largest exercise to take place in Novo Selo Training Area.

• **U.S. Marines/Moldovan Armed Forces Joint Anti-Armor Workshop:** (Balti, Moldova, Dec. 8-12) Approximately 20 U.S. Marines from the Black Sea Rotational Force based in Mihail Kogalniceanu, Romania, and members of the Moldovan Armed Forces participated in a joint anti-armor workshop in Balti designed to increase the understanding of each country's capabilities and reinforce the strong bond between our military forces. Focus was upon defensive procedures, weapons familiarization, tactics of employment, and practical application scenarios culminating with a live-fire range.

• **12th Combat Aviation Brigade Emergency Deployment Training:** (Clay Kaserne, Germany, Dec. 8) U.S. Army Europe and NATO aviators took part in an emergency deployment readiness exercise in Wiesbaden, Germany. The exercise, led by USAREUR's 12th Combat Aviation Brigade included pilots from allied and partner nations, including Sweden, Romania, Hungary and the Netherlands. The exercise emphasized the 12th CAB's ability to deploy within hours upon notification in response to crises or contingencies.

Special Operations Forces (SOF)
• **Medical Assistance Team:** (Western Ukraine, Nov.-Dec. 14) A medical team from Special Operations Command Europe deployed from Stuttgart, Germany, to Western Ukraine in order to coach and mentor Ukrainian Ministry of Defense personnel on basic battlefield medical procedures in order to enhance point of injury care. Initially the mission will focus on coaching and mentoring more than 300 Ukrainian Ministry of Defense personnel (military) to develop a pool of individuals who are capable of conducting basic battlefield medical care.

Air
• **Theater Security Package Deployment to Spangdahlem Air Base:** (Feb. 10, 2015) Twelve A-10 aircraft, 300 Airmen and support equipment from the 354th Fighter Squadron, 355th Fighter Wing from Davis-Monthan Air Force Base, Arizona, are conducting a six month deployment in support of Operation Atlantic Resolve and the new Theater Security Package mission. The term Theater Security Package, or TSP, refers to the routine deployment of additional fighter squadrons, support personnel and equipment to bolster U.S. forces in Europe on a rotating basis, conducting flying training deployments and off-station training with our NATO allies to further enhance interoperability.
• **Flying Training Deployment with Poland and Aviation Detachment (AVDET) Rotation:** (Łask Air Base, Poland, 1-26 Dec.) Two C-130 aircraft and approximately 50 personnel from the 123rd Airlift Wing, Kentucky Air National Guard, participated in an off-station train-

ing event aimed at maintaining readiness and reassuring NATO allies and regional partners.

• Ämari F-16 Exercise: (Ämari, Estonia, Nov. 13-14) Two F-16s from the 555th Fighter Squadron from Aviano Air Base, Italy, participated in bilateral training with the Estonian Air Force including range training with Estonian Joint Terminal Attack Controllers focusing on maintaining joint readiness while building interoperability capabilities.

• **USAF Aviation Detachment (AVDET) Rotation:** (Powidz Air Base, Poland, Oct. 15-31) Two C-130J aircraft and accompanying Airmen from the 182nd Airlift Wing, Illinois Air National Guard, Peoria, Illinois, conducted bilateral off-station training at this forward operating location. The Airmen are training to increase interoperability and readiness with their Polish counterparts.

Sea

• **USS Cole (DDG 67):** (Black Sea, Feb. 2015) The Arleigh Burke-class guided-missile destroyer conducted a NATO Underway Engagement with the Romanian navy ship ROS Marasesti (F 111), Feb. 12. The engagements are a series of at-sea scenarios designed to enhance maritime capabilities among participating nations and typically include tactical maneuvering exercises, passenger transfers, bridge-to-bridge communication drills, and simulated threat defenses with aircraft. Cole arrived in Constanta, Romania, Feb. 9, for a port visit and departed Feb. 13. Cole's visit to Romania provided Sailors with the opportunity to engage with their Romanian counterparts on both a professional and personal level along with reaffirming to NATO allies that the U.S. Navy shares a commitment to strengthening ties while working toward mutual goals of promoting peace and stability in the Black Sea region.

• **USS Donald Cook (DDG 75):** (Jan. 11) Conducted underway passing exercise with UKRS Hetman Sahaidachny (U130) and continued Black Sea operations through mid-January.

• **USS Ross (DDG 71):** (Black Sea, Nov. 4-13) The Arleigh Burke-class guided-missile destroyer USS Ross (DDG 71) conducted a bilateral engagement in the Black Sea with the Romanian navy. The bilateral engagement was aimed at improving maritime readiness and capability, and reaffirmed the United States' commitment to promote peace and stability with our allies and partners in the Black Sea region.

• **USS Cole (DDG 67):** (Black Sea, Oct. 16) The Arleigh Burke-class guided-missile destroyer conducted a NATO Underway Engagement with the Turkish navy Barbaros-class frigate TCG Salihreis (F 246), Oct. 16. The engagements are a series of at-sea scenarios designed to enhance maritime capabilities among participating nations and typically include fleet maneuvers, daylight landing qualifications, division tactics and communication exercises, such as a publication exercise. Cole arrived in Constanta, Romania, Oct. 21 for a port visit and departed Oct. 23. Cole's visit to Romania provided Sailors with the opportunity to engage with their Romanian counterparts on both a professional and personal level along with reaffirming to NATO allies that the U.S. Navy shares a commitment to strengthening ties while working toward mutual goals of promoting peace and stability in the Black Sea region.

• **USS Mount Whitney (LCC 20):** (Black Sea, Oct. 11) The U.S. 6th Fleet command and control ship entered the Black Sea Oct.11, to promote peace and stability in the region. The flagship's presence in the region serves to reaffirm the United States' dedication and commitment towards strengthening the partnerships and joint operational capabilities amongst U.S., NATO and regional Black Sea partners. Mount Whitney arrived in Constanta, Romania, for a scheduled port visit and participated in sporting events at the Constantin Bratescu School as part of a community relations project, Oct. 20. Mount Whitney Sailors installed new soccer nets for the school and played soccer and basketball games with the children. Mount Whitney departed Romania Oct. 23.

Support to Ukraine

• **Train and Equip Ukraine's National Guard:** U.S. Army Europe soldiers will provide training to Ukrainian National Guard security forces this year as part of a U.S. State Department initiative in order to assist Ukraine in strengthening its law enforcement capabilities, conduct internal defense, and maintaining rule of law. The training, scheduled to begin in spring, comes at the request of the Ukrainian government as they work to reform their police forces and establish their newly formed National Guard.

- Funding for the training has been authorized by Congress and is provided by the Global Security Contingency Fund (GSCF), a U.S. government mechanism enacted in the past few years to provide security sector assistance for partner countries so they can address emergent challenges and opportunities important to U.S. national security.

- This training mission meets U.S. and partner national interests by demonstrating U.S. commitment to security in the Black Sea region, and demonstrating the value of forward stationed forces accustomed to training with partner nations.

- We're still in the planning stages of determining which units will provide training and how many personnel will be required to train four maneuver companies and one tactical level headquarters unit of Ukraine National Guard forces to standard.

• **Additional $46 million in Security Assistance:** As part of the Sept. 18 White House announcement, an additional $25 million has been allocated to the Ukrainian Armed Forces through the Presidential Drawdown authority; and an additional $21 million will support to the State Border Guard through Cooperative Threat Reduction (CTR) funds. This will include military equipment and supplies such as counter-mortar radars, body armor, helmets, vehicles, night and thermal vision devices, heavy engineering equipment, advanced radios, patrol boats, rations, tents, uniforms and other items.

• **Assistance & Advisory teams:** U.S. European Command and DoD civilian and military experts have initiated a process to work with Ukraine to improve its capacity to provide for its own defense and set the stage for longer-term defense cooperation. Specifically, EUCOM deployed medical & security assistance advisory teams to Kyiv to help improve Ukraine's combat medical care and identify areas for additional security assistance.

• **Foreign Military Financing:** In addition to the 300,000 MREs delivered in March, the U.S. has also provided Foreign Military Financing to support Ukraine's armed forces with medical supplies, Explosive Ordnance Disposal equipment and various items of individual military equipment.

• **Reforming Defense Institutions:** Defense Department experts in strategy and policy continue to meet with Ukrainian defense officials in Kyiv, to assess specific defense institution building activities/programs we may want to pursue. The objective is to shape and establish an enduring program for future U.S. efforts to support the Ukrainian military, through subject matter expert teams and long-term advisors.

Appendix C

Treaty on Principles Governing the Activities of States in the Exploration and Use of Outer Space, Including the Moon and Other Celestial Bodies

Signed at Washington, London, Moscow January 27, 1967
Ratification advised by US Senate April 25, 1967
Ratified by US President May 24, 1967
US ratification deposited at Washington, London, and Moscow October 10, 1967
Proclaimed by US President October 10, 1967
Entered into force October 10, 1967

The States Parties to this Treaty,

Inspired by the great prospects opening up before mankind as a result of man's entry into outer space,

Recognizing the common interest of all mankind in the progress of the exploration and use of outer space for peaceful purposes,

Believing that the exploration and use of outer space should be carried on for the benefit of all peoples irrespective of the degree of their economic or scientific development,

Desiring to contribute to broad international co-operation in the scientific as well as the legal aspects of the exploration and use of outer space for peaceful purposes,

Believing that such co-operation will contribute to the development of mutual understanding and to the strengthening of friendly relations between States and peoples,

Recalling resolution 1962 (XVIII), entitled "Declaration of Legal Principles Governing the Activities of States in the Exploration and Use of Outer Space," which was adopted unanimously by the United Nations General Assembly on 13 December 1963,

Recalling resolution 1884 (XVIII), calling upon States to refrain from placing in orbit around the Earth any objects carrying nuclear weapons or any other kinds of weapons of mass destruction or from installing such weapons on celestial bodies, which was adopted unanimously by the United Nations General Assembly on 17 October 1963,

Taking account of United Nations General Assembly resolution 110 (II) of 3 November 1947, which condemned propaganda designed or likely to provoke or encourage any threat to the peace, breach of the peace or act of aggression, and considering that the aforementioned resolution is applicable to outer space,

Convinced that a Treaty on Principles Governing the Activities of States in the Exploration and Use of Outer Space, including the Moon and Other Celestial Bodies, will further the Purposes and Principles of the Charter of the United Nations,

Have agreed on the following:

Article I

The exploration and use of outer space, including the moon and other celestial bodies, shall be carried out for the benefit and in the interests of all countries, irrespective of their degree of economic or scientific development, and shall be the province of all mankind.

Outer space, including the moon and other celestial bodies, shall be free for exploration and use by all States without discrimination of any kind, on a basis of equality and in accordance with international law, and there shall be free access to all areas of celestial bodies.

There shall be freedom of scientific investigation in outer space, including the moon and other celestial bodies, and States shall facilitate and encourage international co-operation in such investigation.

Article II

Outer space, including the moon and other celestial bodies, is not subject to national appropriation by claim of sovereignty, by means of use or occupation, or by any other means.

Article III

States Parties to the Treaty shall carry on activities in the exploration and use of outer space, including the moon and other celestial bodies, in accordance with international law, including the Charter of the United Nations, in the interest of maintaining international peace and security and promoting international co-operation and understanding.

Article IV

States Parties to the Treaty undertake not to place in orbit around the Earth any objects carrying nuclear weapons or any other kinds of weapons of mass destruction, install such weapons on celestial bodies, or station such weapons in outer space in any other manner.

The Moon and other celestial bodies shall be used by all States Parties to the Treaty exclusively for peaceful purposes. The establishment of military bases, installations and fortifications, the testing of any type of weapons and the conduct of military maneuvers on celestial bodies shall be forbidden. The use of military personnel for scientific research or for any other peaceful purposes shall not be prohibited. The use of any equipment or facility necessary for peaceful exploration of the Moon and other celestial bodies shall also not be prohibited.

Article V

States Parties to the Treaty shall regard astronauts as envoys of mankind in outer space and shall render to them all possible assistance in the event of accident, distress, or emergency landing on the territory of another State Party or on the high seas. When astronauts make such a landing, they shall be safely and promptly returned to the State of registry of their space vehicle.

In carrying on activities in outer space and on celestial bodies, the astronauts of one State Party shall render all possible assistance to the astronauts of other States Parties.

States Parties to the Treaty shall immediately inform the other States Parties to the Treaty or the Secretary-General of the United Nations of any phenomena they discover in outer space, including the Moon and other celestial bodies, which could constitute a danger to the life or health of astronauts.

Article VI

States Parties to the Treaty shall bear international responsibility for national activities in outer space, including the Moon and other celestial bodies, whether such activities are carried on by governmental agencies or by non-governmental entities, and for assuring that national activities are carried out in conformity with the provisions set forth in the present Treaty. The activities of non-governmental entities in outer space, including the Moon and other celestial bodies, shall require authorization and continuing supervision by the appropriate State Party to the Treaty. When activities are carried on in outer space, including the Moon and other celestial bodies, by an international organization, responsibility for compliance with this Treaty shall be borne both by the international organization and by the States Parties to the Treaty participating in such organization.

Article VII

Each State Party to the Treaty that launches or procures the launching of an object into outer space, including the Moon and other celestial bodies, and each State Party from whose territory or facility an object is launched, is internationally liable for damage to another State Party to the Treaty or to its natural or juridical persons by such object or its component parts on the Earth, in air space or in outer space, including the Moon and other celestial bodies.

Article VIII

A State Party to the Treaty on whose registry an object launched into outer space is carried shall retain jurisdiction and control over such object, and over any personnel thereof, while in outer space or on a celestial body. Ownership of objects launched into outer space, including objects landed or constructed on a celestial body, and of their component parts, is not affected by their presence in outer space or on a celestial body or by their return to the Earth. Such objects or component parts found beyond the limits of the State Party to the Treaty on whose registry they are carried shall be returned to that State Party, which shall, upon request, furnish identifying data prior to their return.

Article IX

In the exploration and use of outer space, including the Moon and other celestial bodies, States Parties to the Treaty shall be guided by the principle of co-operation and mutual assistance and shall conduct all their activities in outer space, including the Moon and other celestial bodies, with due regard to the corresponding interests of all other States Parties to the Treaty. States Parties to the Treaty shall pursue studies of outer space, including the Moon and other celestial bodies, and conduct exploration of them so as to avoid their harmful contamination and also adverse changes in the environment of the Earth resulting from the introduction of extraterrestrial matter and, where necessary, shall adopt appropriate measures for this purpose. If a State Party to the Treaty has reason to believe that an activity or experiment planned by it or its nationals in outer space, including the Moon and other celestial bodies, would cause potentially harmful interference with activities of other States Parties in the peaceful exploration and use of outer space, including the Moon and other celestial bodies, it shall undertake appropriate international consultations before proceeding with any such activity or experiment. A State Party to the Treaty which has reason to believe that an activity or experiment planned by another State Party in outer space, including the Moon and other celestial bodies, would cause potentially harmful interference with activities in the peaceful exploration and use of outer space, including the Moon and other celestial bodies, may request consultation concerning the activity or experiment.

Article X

In order to promote international co-operation in the exploration and use of outer space, including the Moon and other celestial bodies, in conformity with the purposes of this Treaty, the States Parties to the Treaty shall consider on a basis of equality any requests by other States Parties to the Treaty to be afforded an opportunity to observe the flight of space objects launched by those States.

The nature of such an opportunity for observation and the conditions under which it could be afforded shall be determined by agreement between the States concerned.

Article XI

In order to promote international co-operation in the peaceful exploration and use of outer space, States Parties to the Treaty conducting activities in outer space, including the Moon and other celestial bodies, agree to inform the Secretary-General of the United Nations as well as the public and the international scientific community, to the greatest extent feasible and practicable, of the nature, conduct, locations and results of such activities. On receiving the said information, the Secretary-General of the United Nations should be prepared to disseminate it immediately and effectively.

Article XII

All stations, installations, equipment and space vehicles on the Moon and other celestial bodies shall be open to representatives of other States Parties to the Treaty on a basis of reciprocity. Such representatives shall give reasonable advance notice of a projected visit, in order that appropriate consultations may be held and that maximum precautions may be taken to assure safety and to avoid interference with normal operations in the facility to be visited.

Article XIII

The provisions of this Treaty shall apply to the activities of States Parties to the Treaty in the exploration and use of outer space, including the Moon and other celestial bodies, whether such activities are carried on by a single State Party to the Treaty or jointly with other States, including cases where they are carried on within the framework of international intergovernmental organizations.

Any practical questions arising in connection with activities carried on by international inter-governmental organizations in the exploration and use of outer space, including the Moon and other celestial bodies, shall be resolved by the States Parties to the Treaty either with the appropriate international organization or with one or more States members of that international organization, which are Parties to this Treaty.

Article XIV

1. This Treaty shall be open to all States for signature. Any State which does not sign this Treaty before its entry into force in accordance with paragraph 3 of this article may accede to it at any time.

2. This Treaty shall be subject to ratification by signatory States. Instruments of ratification and instruments of accession shall be deposited with the Governments of the United States of America, the United Kingdom of Great Britain and Northern Ireland and the Union of Soviet Socialist Republics, which are hereby designated the Depositary Governments.

3. This Treaty shall enter into force upon the deposit of instruments of ratification by five Governments including the Governments designated as Depositary Governments under this Treaty.

4. For States whose instruments of ratification or accession are deposited subsequent to the entry into force of this Treaty, it shall enter into force on the date of the deposit of their instruments of ratification or accession.

5. The Depositary Governments shall promptly inform all signatory and acceding States of the date of each signature, the date of deposit of each instrument of ratification of and accession to this Treaty, the date of its entry into force and other notices.

6. This Treaty shall be registered by the Depositary Governments pursuant to Article 102 of the Charter of the United Nations.

Article XV

Any State Party to the Treaty may propose amendments to this Treaty. Amendments shall enter into force for each State Party to the Treaty accepting the amendments upon their acceptance by a majority of the States Parties to the Treaty and thereafter for each remaining State Party to the Treaty on the date of acceptance by it.

Article XVI

Any State Party to the Treaty may give notice of its withdrawal from the Treaty one year after its entry into force by written notification to the Depositary Governments. Such withdrawal shall take effect one year from the date of receipt of this notification.

Article XVII

This Treaty, of which the English, Russian, French, Spanish and Chinese texts are equally authentic, shall be deposited in the archives of the Depositary Governments. Duly certified copies of this Treaty shall be transmitted by the Depositary Governments to the Governments of the signatory and acceding States.

Acknowledgments

I AM INDEBTED AND GRATEFUL TO THOSE INDIVIDUALS WHO DIRECTLY contributed to this project as well as to those who indirectly contributed throughout years of interaction, most of the latter not realizing the extent or impact of their influence. Life is made of memories, and the images of people fondly remembered are of those who created them.

Senior Editor: Eugene Brissie
Literary Agent: Douglas Grad
Research Assistant: Kathryn Cohn
Foreword: Lt. Gen. Harry E. Soyster, USA (Ret.)
Endorsers: Brig. Gen. Clarke Brintnall, USA (Ret.); Rear Adm. (U) J. Cameron Fraser, USN (Ret.); Lt. Gen. Henry J. Hatch, USA (Ret.); Maj. Gen. James A. Madora, USA (Ret.); Maj. Gen. Alan Salisbury, USA (Ret.); Brig. Gen. Donald P. Whalen, USA (Ret.)
Editing: Meredith Dias, Phyllis Giasson, Rachael Klein
Art & Promotion: Carol Anderson, Brian Cohn, and Colleen Elkins
Science Advisor: Dr. Thomas Finn
Insights and Facilitation: Col. J. Brian Copley, USA (Ret.); Critical Issues Roundtable; Garret Elkins; Alda Finn; Elaine Gallagher; Thomas Gallagher; Col. Charles Giasson, USA (Ret.); Craig and Suzanne Jacobsen; Dave Klein; Jay and Maureen Oliverio; Jill Schwartzman
Indirect Contributors:
Cheryl Baker; Michael Black; Beverly Bornstein; Lt. Col. Stott Carleton, USA (Ret.); Eleanor Clift; USA (Ret.); Jan Copley; Henry, Carter, H. J., and Kelly Cohn; Scott, Linda, Connor, and Carson Cohn; Marina and Cooper Cohn; Becky Christen; Col. Jonathan Dodson, USA (Ret.); Kathleen Duval; Linda Easthope; Serena, Graham, and John Elkins;

James and Ryan Gallagher; Dr. Anthony Garvey; David Gerard; Michael Hageman; Thomas and Sandy Hageman; Barbara Hanan; Dennis Holeman; John Horan; Dennis Howell; Lt. Gen. Larry Jordan, USA (Ret.); Barney and Karen Keep; Dr. Stephen Kelly; Michael and Susan Kennard; Sydney and Kenzie Klein; Dr. Thomas Laipply; James R. Locher III; Lt. Col. William and Patty Marriott III; James, Julie and Scott McKean; Mike Merrick; Fred Mihm; Lt. Gen. David Ohle, USA (Ret.); Col. LeRoy Outlaw, USA (Ret.); John and Barbara Pattillo; Gen. William R. Richardson, USA (Ret.); Lt. Col. Gordon Sayre, USA (Ret.); Col. Ann Shaklee, USAF (Ret.); John Slonaker; Linda Smull; Mike Spiegel; Stan Stanton; Camille Taylor-Sullivan; Evan Thomas; Judy Thompson; Col. Ralph Tildon, USA (Ret.); Col. Ralph Tuccillo, USA (Ret.); Janet Vehring; Elsa Verbyla; Brig. Gen. John Walsh, USA (Ret.); Laurie Washburn

Brothers-in-Arms:

2nd Platoon B Co. and Recon Platoon E Co., 5th Bn., 7th Regiment, 1st Cavalry Division, Vietnam 1969–70:

Sylvester Amey, Al Bruns, James Clark, Dan Dilts, Robert Dodge, Larry Eaton (Lucky), Eldon Erlenbach, Leo Fiegel, Ricardo Garza, Tony Gutierrez, Marcus Henson, Boyd Hines, David Larson, John (Doug) McInnes, Jim Mitchell, Mike Price, Bill Rowley, Rick Sonnenberg, William Starkey, Jack Thomas, Frank Thurston, Steve Tresemer, as well as those we unfortunately only remember as Arney, Butch, Doc, Hunley, Johnson, and Zeke, and those we remember **In Memoriam:** Captain Barry Mullineaux (company commander), Pvt. Charles Boxler, SP4 Richard Brueck, Sgt. Darrel Burns, Jim Carrel, Rick Colbert (Shorty), Leroy Conners (Pumpkin), SFC Joseph Sanchez, and James Sizemore

In Memoriam:

Annabel Ashley, Jane Cohn, Meyer and Clara Cohn, Millard and Henrietta Cohn, Brig. Gen. John Eisenhower, 1st Lt. William Ericson II, William and Elizabeth (Buzz) Headlee, Ole Johnson, Donald and Marilyn Kauffman, John and Mary Kennard, 1st Lt. Peter Lantz, Warren Rogers, Gen. H. Norman Schwarzkopf Jr., G. L. and Louise Shaw, Col. Harry Summers Jr.

ENDNOTES

I. INTRODUCTION

4. "No longer can areas exist . . ." Gen. Giulio Douhet, transl. Dino Ferrari, *The Command of the Air* (New York: Coward-McCann, 1942, orig. Italian Ministry of War, 1921), 10.

5. "The efforts of terrorist networks to recruit . . ." Admiral Giampaolo di Paola, Chairman of the Military Committee: North Atlantic Treaty Organization, Speech to the Officers' Association's 50th Annual Symposium, NATO (Mons, Belgium: October 16, 2010), www.nato.int/cps/en/natohq/opinions_69910.htm?selectedLocale=en, accessed December 5, 2015.

II. SCENARIOS

Scenario 1: The Post-NATO War

9. "In Europe, we remain steadfast in our commitment to our NATO allies." US Department of Defense, "The United States Military's Contribution to National Security," June 2015, www.defense.gov/news/newsarticle.aspx?id=121220, accessed July 12, 2015.

11. "At its origin, the organization's goal . . ." Admiral Giampaolo di Paola, Speech to the Officers' Association 50th Annual Symposium, NATO.

11. "There will be pressure from the United States . . ." Steven Erlanger, "NATO Nations No Longer Question Need for Alliance," *New York Times*, December 15, 2015.

13. "Long live free Flanders . . ." Ian Traynor, "The Language Divide at the Heart of a Split That Is Tearing Belgium Apart," *Guardian* (Brussels), May 8, 2010.

13. "Dutch-speaking Flemings and the French-speaking Walloons . . ." Chams Eddine Zaouguin, "Molenbeek, Belgium's 'Jihad Central,'" *New York Times*, November 19, 2015.

16. "Suppose that there were a way to end this depression." Paul Krugman, "Does Greece Need More Austerity?" *New York Times*, June 19, 2015.

16. "Greece, with just 11 million people . . ." George Will, "So What If Greece Leaves the European Union?" *Washington Post*, June 19, 2015.

17. "The European Union strode forward . . ." Richard N. Rosencrance and Steven E. Miller, eds., *The Next Great War? The Roots of World War I and the Risk of U.S.-China Conflict* (Cambridge, MA: MIT Press, © 2014 Belfer Center for Science and International Affairs), 215.

18. "The EU has a flag . . ." Will, "So What If Greece Leaves the European Union?"

22. "The Parties agree that an armed attack . . ." The North Atlantic Treaty (Washington, April 4, 1949), www.nato.int/cps/en/natolive/official_texts_17120.htm, accessed May 6, 2015.

23. "One [Russian] exercise in March . . ." Erlanger, "NATO Nations No Longer Question Need for Alliance."

25. "After the Treaty has been in force for twenty years . . ." The North Atlantic Treaty.

26. "The Chinese-Albanian relations are developing . . ." "China-Albania to Further Develop Military Relations," *Albanian Daily News,* July 29, 2015, www.albaniannews .com/index.php?idm=2313&mod=2, accessed December 5, 2015.

29. "Why has Poland, the poster child of post-Communist success . . ." Ivan Krastev, "Why Poland Is Turning Away from the West," *New York Times,* December 11, 2015.

37. "When the U.S. military tries to explain . . ." Barbara Demick, "Seoul's Vulnerability Is Key to War Scenarios," *Los Angeles Times,* May 27, 2003.

Scenario 2: The Great Russian War

41. "While Russia has contributed in select security areas . . ." US Department of Defense, "The United States Military's Contribution to National Security."

41. "I cannot forecast to you the action of Russia . . ." Winston Churchill, *The Gathering Storm* (Boston: Houghton Mifflin Company, 1948), 448–49.

45. "The White Man's Burden . . ." Rudyard Kipling, Thomas James Wise, Poem: "The White Man's Burden." New York: Doubleday and McClure Company, *McClure's* magazine, February 12, 1899.

47. "The continuing expansion of NATO . . ." Steven Erlanger, "NATO Unveils Plans to Grow, Drawing Fury and Threats from Russia," *New York Times,* December 2, 2015.

48. "Putin's Russia, in contrast . . ." Alexander John Moytl, "Ukraine: Merkel and Putin Go Nose to Nose," *Newsweek,* May 30, 2015.

50. ". . . forward-deployed forces," US Department of Defense, "The United States Military's Contribution to National Security."

53. "In October 2014 the Russian defense budget . . ." "Russian Defense Budget to Hit Record $81 Billion in 2015," *Moscow Times,* October 16, 2014, www.themoscowtimes .com/business/article/russian-defense-budget-to-hit-record-81bln-in-2015/509536 .html, accessed April 24, 2015, and "US Military Spending Falls, Increases in Eastern Europe, Middle East, Africa and Asia says SIPRI," Stockholm International Peace Research Institute, April 13, 2015, www.sipri.org/media/pressreleases/2015/milex -april-2015, accessed April 24, 2015.

60. "Russia's Baltic Fleet consists of . . ." Gerald O'Dwyer, "Nations Respond to Russian Buildup in Baltics," *Defense News,* April 12, 2015.

Scenario 3: The Great China War

64. "We support China's rise and encourage it to become a partner . . ." US Department of Defense, "The United States Military's Contribution to National Security."

64. "[Fascists] demand free enterprise . . ." Russell Lord, ed., *Democracy Reborn* (New York: Reynal & Hitchcock, 1944), 259.

64. "These conditions gave rise to Fascism . . ." Chris Butler, "Benito Mussolini and the Rise of Fascism in Italy (1919–25)," The Flow of History, 2007, www.flowofhistory .com/units/etc/20/FC133, accessed June 5, 2015.

65. "China really is the Middle Kingdom . . ." Stephen Chen, "Scientists Confirm That China Really Is the Middle Kingdom," *South China Morning Post* (Beijing), September 23, 2015.

65. "In modern Chinese, the term for China is Zhongguo . . ." Joseph Esherick, Hasan Kayali, Eric Van Young, eds., *Empire to Nation: Historical Perspectives on the Making of the Modern World* (Lanham, MD: Rowman & Littlefield, 2006), 232.

65. "We all need to work together . . ." Graham Allison, "The Thucydides Trap," in *The Next Great War?* eds. Rosencrance and Miller, 74.

66. ". . . the perpetual alternation of a Yin state . . ." "Barbarism and Civilization— China's Yin-Yang Polarities," *Science Encyclopedia*, http://science.jrank.org/pages/8441/ Barbarism-Civilization-China-s-Yin-Yang-Polarities.html, accessed December 5, 2015.

Scenario 4: The Chinese Civil War

82. "The presence of U.S. military forces in key locations . . ." US Department of Defense, "The United States Military's Contribution to National Security."

83. "Extend the sphere . . ." James Madison, *The Federalist: A Collection of Essays Written in Favour of the Constitution, As Agreed Upon by the Federal Convention, September 17, 1787* (New York: J. and A. McLean, 1788), 76–77.

84. "The CCP convenes its National Party Congress . . ." Beina Xu and Eleanor Albert, "The Chinese Communist Party," Council on Foreign Relations, August 27, 2015, www.cfr.org/china/chinese-communist-party/p29443, accessed November 27, 2015.

85. "Use any means." Andrew J. Nathan, "The Tiananmen Papers," in *Tiananmen and After*, ed. Gideon Rose (Tampa, FL: *Foreign Affairs*, June 11, 2014), 37.

85. ". . . the Chinese People's Liberation Army . . ." Steven Van Evera, "European Militaries and the Origins of World War I," in *The Next Great War?* eds. Rosencrance and Miller, 172.

86. ". . . individual outside China who . . ." Ezra Vogel, *Deng Xiaoping and the Transformation of China* (Cambridge, MA: Belknap, 2011) quoted in Rosencrance and Miller, eds., *The Next Great War?*, 75.

86. ". . . the legitimacy of the Chinese government . . ." Joseph S. Nye Jr., "Inevitability and War," in *The Next Great War?* eds. Rosencrance and Miller, 192.

87. "Ultimately, however, China's leaders must realize . . ." *New York Times* Editorial Board, "China's Obsolete Economic Strategy," January 9, 2016.

87. "Under President Xi, China is rapidly retreating . . ." "China: Political Repression at a High Mark," Human Rights Watch, January 29, 2015, www.hrw.org/ news/2015/01/29/china-political-repression-high-mark, accessed August 18, 2015.

Scenario 5: The Polar War

98. "While we prefer to act . . ." US Department of Defense, "The United States Military's Contribution to National Security."

100. "The world does not doubt that Russia's interest . . ." Alexander Gabuev, "Cold War Goes North," *Kommersant*, August 4, 2007, www.kommersant.com/p792832/Arctic_ocean_bed_causes_upsurge_of_Russia-West_competiton, accessed April 3, 2015.

101. "The Russian Arctic contains significant reserves of hydrocarbons . . ." Duncan Depledge, "Russia and the Arctic: Crunch Call on Moscow's Territory Claim Is Fast Approaching," The Conversation, March 17, 2015, http://theconversation.com/russia-and-the-arctic-crunch-call-on-moscows-territory-claim-is-fast-approaching-38625, accessed April 3, 2015.

102. "This is posturing. . . ." "North Pole: A Hotbed of Competing Claims," *Telegraph*, May 18, 2011, www.telegraph.co.uk/news/worldnews/europe/denmark/8520081/North-Pole-a-hotbed-of-competing-claims.html, accessed November 30, 2015.

102. "Article 76 of UNCLOS defines the conditions . . ." "Defining Canada's Continental Shelf," Fisheries and Oceans Canada, www.dfo-mpo.gc.ca/science/hydrography-hydrographie/unclos-eng.html, accessed April 10, 2015.

103. "I read reports of the statements made by my Canadian colleague . . ." The Ministry of Foreign Affairs of the Russian Federation, Transcript of Remarks . . . by Russian Minister of Foreign Affairs Sergey Lavrov . . . August 3, 2007, http://archive.mid.ru//brp_4.nsf/e78a48070f128a7b43256999005bcbb3/d70a7ab-f573e5873c325733200428884?OpenDocument, accessed February 26, 2016.

103. "President Putin assured me . . ." Allan Woods, "Relations Thaw after Flag 'Stunt,'" *Star News*, September 26, 2007, www.thestar.com/news/2007/09/26/relations_thaw_after_flag_stunt.html, accessed March 30, 2015.

104. ". . . eight Arctic patrol ships . . ." "Harper Announces Northern Deep-Sea Port, Training Site," *CBC News*, August 10, 2007, www.cbc.ca/news/canada/harper-announces-northern-deep-sea-port-training-site-1.644982, accessed March 31, 2015.

104. "This potential conflict . . ." Alicia Zorzetto, "Canadian Sovereignty at the Northwest Passage," ICE Case Study No. 185, May 2006, www1.american.edu/ted/ice/northwest-passage.htm, accessed April 2, 2015.

104. "Denmark Challenges Russia and Canada over North Pole," *BBC News*, December 15, 2014, www.bbc.com/news/world-europe-30481309, accessed April 2, 2015.

106. "Tensions have increased a notch . . ." Depledge, "Russia and the Arctic."

106. "Rock samples retrieved last month . . ." Richard A. Lovett, "Russia's Arctic Claim Backed by Rocks, Officials Say," *National Geographic News*, September 21, 2007, http://news.nationalgeographic.com/news/2007/09/070921-arctic-russia.html, accessed April 5, 2015.

106. "With a high degree of likelihood . . ." *Russian News Room*, April 14, 2015, http://news.russiannewsroom.com/details.aspx?item=12584, accessed April 14, 2015.

106. "[S]hould Russia fail to gain . . ." Todd L. Sharp, "The Implications of Ice Melt on Arctic Security," *Defence Studies* 11, no. 2 (June 2011), 304.

Scenario 6: The Blue Gold War to Nowhere

111. "Youth populations are rapidly growing in Africa and the Middle East . . ." US Department of Defense, "The United States Military's Contribution to National Security."

112. "Demand in our key rivers . . ." Jennifer Medina, "California Cuts Farmers' Share of Scant Water," *New York Times*, June 12, 2015.

112. "As California guzzles groundwater . . ." Victoria Burnett, "Mennonite Farmers Prepare to Leave Mexico, and Competition for Water," *New York Times*, November 16, 2015.

112. "We live in a time when demand for fresh water . . ." Aaron Schwabach, "Diverting the Danube: The Gabcikovo-Nagymaros Dispute and International Freshwater Law," *Berkeley Journal of International Law* 14, no. 2 (1996), http://scholarship.law.berkeley.edu/bjil/vol14/iss2/2, accessed June 7, 2015.

115. "It appears that in addition to the issue . . ." Alicia Zorzetto, "Canadian Sovereignty at the Northwest Passage, and Alanna Mitchell, "The Northwest Passage Thawed," *Globe and Mail* (Toronto), February 5, 2000.

116. ". . . 220 gallons per person per day?" Paul Rogers, "California Drought," *San Jose Mercury News*, May 5, 2015.

116 "Production capacity of all of Israel's desalination plants . . ." Zafrir Rinat, "Water, Water, Everywhere: Desalination Trumps Drought in Israel," Jerusalem: *Haaretz Daily*, June 8, 2015.

116. "Water Authority director Alex Kushnir . . ." Ibid.

Scenario 7: The Lunar War

129. "Of particular concern are the proliferation of ballistic missiles . . ." US Department of Defense, "The United States Military's Contribution to National Security."

129. "China is beginning to develop . . ." Lt. Gen. Ronald L. Burgess Jr., *Annual Threat Assessment: Statement Before the Senate Armed Services Committee*, United States Senate, February 16, 2012 (Washington, DC: National Archives, 2012).

130. "China's growing capabilities translate into military . . ." Anthony H. Cordesman, *Chinese Strategy and Military Power in 2014: Chinese, Japanese, Korean, Taiwanese, and US Perspectives* (Washington, DC: Center for Strategic & International Studies, 2014, and Lanham, MD: Rowman & Littlefield, 2014), 332.

131. "Low earth orbit satellites . . ." Dr. Thomas Finn, retired US Department of Energy physicist, author interview, December 31, 2015.

132. "There is no blast from a nuclear weapon . . ." Ibid.

Scenario 8: The Nuclear Terrorist War

135. "Iran also poses strategic challenges to the international community." US Department of Defense, "The United States Military's Contribution to National Security."

136. "We live in a world where threats . . ." Admiral Giampaolo di Paola, Speech to the Officers' Association 50th Annual Symposium, NATO.

136. "The rogue military danger . . ." Steven Van Evera, "European Militaries and the Origins of World War I," in *The Next Great War?*, eds. Rosencrance and Miller, 172.

136. "With as many as 120 warheads . . ." *New York Times* Editorial Board, "The Pakistan Nuclear Nightmare," November 8, 2015.

137. "The madrasas are a cover, a camouflage . . ." Carlotta Gall, "What Pakistan Knew about Bin Laden," *New York Times*, March 29, 2014.

138. "Because states throughout our region know that the deal paves Iran's path to the bomb . . ." Ron Dermer, "The Four Major Problems with the Iran Deal," *Washington Post*, July 15, 2015.

141. ". . . detect nuclear or radioactive material." Mohana Ravindranath, "Your Next Fitbit Should Detect Nuclear Bombs, DHS Hopes," *Defense One*, November 9, 2015, www .defenseone.com/technology/2015/11/your-next-fitbit-should-detect-nuclear-bombs -dhs-hopes/123512/?oref=d-river, accessed November 10, 2015.

141. ". . . small, wearable radiation detector devices . . ." Huban Gowadia, "Equipping Frontline Personnel with New, Portable Radiological & Nuclear Threat Detection Capabilities," US Department of Homeland Security blog, November 5, 2015, www.dhs.gov/blog/2015/11/05/equipping-frontline-personnel-new-portable -radiological-nuclear-threat-detection, accessed December 27, 2015.

Scenario 9: The Commerce, Currency, and Cyber War

150. "The presence of U.S. military forces . . ." US Department of Defense, "The United States Military's Contribution to National Security."

152. "China's nearly $4 trillion in reserves . . ." Kwasi Kwarteng, "A Chinese Gold Standard?" *International New York Times*, July 25, 2014.

153. ". . . recognition of the progress . . ." Keith Bradsher, "China's Renminbi Is Approved by I.M.F. as a Main World Currency," *New York Times*, November 30, 2015.

153. "China was forced to give up . . ." Ibid.

155. "On a wall facing dozens of cubicles at the FBI office in Pittsburgh . . ." David Talbot, "Cyber-Espionage Nightmare," *MIT Technology Review*, June 10, 2015.

158. "The fate of our empire depends upon this fight." Ronald H. Carpenter, *Rhetoric in Martial Deliberations and Decision Making* (Columbia: University of South Carolina Press, 2004), 124.

158. "England expects every man to do his duty." Carpenter, 125.

III. HISTORICAL PERSPECTIVE

The Atomic Bomb—Weapon of War, Deterrent of War, or Limiter of War

170. "A kind of bureaucratic momentum. . ." Andrew J. Rotter, *Hiroshima: The World's Bomb* (New York: Oxford University Press, 2008), 236.

171. ". . . that the Secretary of War should be advised that . . ." "Notes of Meeting of the Interim Committee, June 1, 1945," The Harry S. Truman Library and Museum, 8–9, www.trumanlibrary.org/whistlestop/study_collections/bomb/large/documents/pdfs/40 .pdf, accessed August 30, 2015.

171. "Recommendations on the Immediate Use . . ." US National Archives, Record Group 77, Records of the Office of the Chief of Engineers, Manhattan Engineer District, Harrison-Bundy File, Folder No. 76.

172. "A PETITION TO THE PRESIDENT . . ." Ibid.

174. "Once it had been tested . . ." William Leahy, *I Was There* (New York: Whittlesey House, 1950), 441.

174. ". . . said he thought these weapons might first be used . . ." William Burr, ed., "Memorandum of Conversation with General Marshall, May 29, 1945," *The Atomic Bomb and the End of World War II*, National Security Archive Electronic Briefing Book No. 162, Top Secret Documents, Safe File, Folder No. 100, accessed August 31, 2015.

178. "In [July] 1945 . . . Secretary of War Stimson . . ." Dwight D. Eisenhower, *Mandate for Change* (New York: Doubleday & Company, 1963), 380.

178. "It wasn't necessary to hit them . . ." Dwight D. Eisenhower, "Ike on Ike," *Newsweek*, November 11, 1963.

178. "When I asked General MacArthur . . ." Norman Cousins, *The Pathology of Power* (New York: W. W. Norton & Company, 1988), 70–71.

178. "MacArthur was appalled." William Manchester, *American Caesar* (New York: Back Bay Books, Little, Brown and Company, 1978), 512.

179. "The Japanese had, in fact, already sued for peace . . ." Adm. Chester W. Nimitz, speech quoted in *New York Times*, October 6, 1945.

179. "We felt that our incendiary bombings . . ." Alfonso A. Narvaez, Obituary in *New York Times*, October 2, 1990.

179. "The first atomic bomb . . ." Gerard J. Degroot, "Killing Is Easy: The Atomic Bomb and the Temptation of Terror." Hew Strachan and Sibylle Scheipers, eds. *The Changing Character of War* (Oxford: Oxford University Press, 2011), 99.

179. "Based on a detailed investigation . . ." United States Strategic Bombing Survey, 1 July 1946, Harry S. Truman Library and Museum.

187. "Hiroshima is the largest untouched target . . ." William Burr, ed., "Notes on the Initial Meeting of the Target Committee, April 27, 1945," *The Atomic Bomb and the End of World War II*, National Security Archive Electronic Briefing Book No. 162, Top Secret Documents, File No. 5d, accessed August 31, 2015.

189. "Truman said he had given orders to stop atomic bombing." William Burr, ed., "Papers of Henry A. Wallace," *The Atomic Bomb and the End of World War II*, Special Collections Department, University of Iowa Libraries, Iowa City, Iowa, National Security Archive Electronic Briefing Book No. 162, accessed August 31, 2015.

189. "Seventy years on . . ." Sergey Radchenko, "Did Hiroshima Save Japan from Soviet Occupation?" *Foreign Policy*, August 5, 2015.

IV. CONCLUSION

World War 4

193. "1. Were you aware the nuclear war-heads were in Cuba?" Robert S. McNamara, "Forty Years after 13 Days," Arms Control Association, 2002, www.armscontrol.org/act/2002_11/cubanmissile#mcnamara, accessed December 9, 2015.

Selected Bibliography

Albanian Daily News. "China-Albania to Further Develop Military Relations." July 29, 2015.

BBC News. "Denmark Challenges Russia and Canada over North Pole." December 15, 2014.

"Barbarism and Civilization—China's Yin-Yang Polarities." *Science Encyclopedia*. http://science.jrank.org/pages/8441/Barbarism-Civilization-China-s-Yin-Yang-Polarities.html, accessed December 5, 2015.

Betros, Lance. *Carved in Granite*. College Station, TX: Texas A&M University Press, 2012.

Bradsher, Keith. "China's Renminbi Is Approved by I.M.F. as a Main World Currency." *New York Times*, November 30, 2015.

Bradley, Gen. Omar N. *A General's Life*. New York: Simon and Schuster, 1983.

Burgess Jr., Lt. Gen. Ronald L. *Annual Threat Assessment: Statement Before the Senate Armed Services Committee*. United States Senate, February 16, 2012. Washington, DC: National Archives, 2012.

Burnett, Victoria, "Mennonite Farmers Prepare to Leave Mexico, and Competition for Water." *New York Times*, November 16, 2015.

Burr, William, ed. "Memorandum of Conversation with General Marshall, May 29, 1945." *The Atomic Bomb and the End of World War II*, National Security Archive Electronic Briefing Book No. 162, Top Secret Documents, Safe File, Folder No. 100.

Burr, William, ed. "Papers of Henry A. Wallace." *The Atomic Bomb and the End of World War II*, Special Collections Department, University of Iowa Libraries, Iowa City, Iowa. National Security Archive Electronic Briefing Book No. 162, accessed August 31, 2015.

Burr, William, ed. "Notes on the Initial Meeting of the Target Committee, April 27, 1945." *The Atomic Bomb and the End of World War II*, National Security Archive Electronic Briefing Book No. 162, Top Secret Documents, File No. 5d, accessed August 31, 2015.

Butler, Chris. "Benito Mussolini and the Rise of Fascism in Italy (1919–25)." The Flow of History, 2007. www.flowofhistory.com/units/etc/20/FC133, accessed June 5, 2015.

CBC News. "Harper Announces Northern Deep-Sea Port, Training Site." August 10, 2007. www.cbc.ca/news/canada/harper-announces-northern-deep-sea-port-training-site-1.644982, accessed March 31, 2015.

Carpenter, Ronald H. *Rhetoric in Martial Deliberations and Decision Making*. Columbia: University of South Carolina Press, 2004.

Chen, Stephen. "Scientists Confirm That China Really Is the Middle Kingdom." *South China Morning Post* (Beijing), September 23, 2015.

Churchill, Winston. *The Gathering Storm.* Boston: Houghton Mifflin Company, 1948.

Cohn, Douglas Alan. *The President's First Year.* Guilford, CT: Rowman & Littlefield, 2016.

Cordesman, Anthony H. *Chinese Strategy and Military Power in 2014: Chinese, Japanese, Korean, Taiwanese, and US Perspectives.* Washington, DC: Center for Strategic & International Studies, 2014, and Lanham, MD: Rowman & Littlefield, 2014.

Cousins, Norman. *The Pathology of Power.* New York: W. W. Norton & Company, 1988.

Degroot, Gerard J. "Killing Is Easy: The Atomic Bomb and the Temptation of Terror." Hew Strachan and Sibylle Scheipers, eds., *The Changing Character of War*, Oxford: Oxford University Press, 2011.

Demick, Barbara. "Seoul's Vulnerability Is Key to War Scenarios." *Los Angeles Times*, May 27, 2003.

Depledge, Duncan. "Russia and the Arctic: Crunch Call on Moscow's Territory Claim Is Fast Approaching." The Conversation, March 17, 2015. http://theconversation .com/russia-and-the-arctic-crunch-call-on-moscows-territory-claim-is-fast -approaching-38625, accessed April 3, 2015.

Dermer, Ron. "The Four Major Problems with the Iran Deal." *Washington Post*, July 15, 2015.

Douhet, Gen. Giulio. *The Command of the Air.* Translated by Dino Ferrari. New York: Coward-McCann,1942, orig. Italian Ministry of War, 1921.

Eisenhower, Dwight D. *Mandate for Change.* New York: Doubleday & Company, 1963.

Eisenhower, Dwight D. "Ike on Ike." *Newsweek*, November 11, 1963.

Erlanger, Steven. "NATO Nations No Longer Question Need for Alliance." *New York Times*, December 15, 2015.

Erlanger, Steven. "NATO Unveils Plans to Grow, Drawing Fury and Threats from Russia." *New York Times*, December 2, 2015.

Esherick, Joseph, Hasan Kayahi, and Eric Van Young, eds. *Empire to Nation: Historical Perspectives on the Making of the Modern World.* Lanham, MD: Rowman & Littlefield, 2006.

Finn, Thomas. Author interview, December 31, 2015.

Fisheries and Oceans Canada. www.dfo-mpo.gc.ca/science/hydrography-hydrographie/ unclos-eng.html, accessed April 10, 2015.

Gabuev, Alexander. "Cold War Goes North." *Kommersant*, August 4, 2007. www .kommersant.com/p792832/Arctic_ocean_bed_causes_upsurge_of_Russia-West_ competiton, accessed April 3, 2015.

Gall, Carlotta. "What Pakistan Knew about Bin Laden." *New York Times*, March 29, 2014.

Gowadia, Huban. "Equipping Frontline Personnel with New, Portable Radiological & Nuclear Threat Detection Capabilities." US Department of Homeland Security blog, November 5, 2015. www.dhs.gov/blog/2015/11/05/equipping-frontline -personnel-new-portable-radiological-nuclear-threat-detection, accessed December 27, 2015.

Human Rights Watch. "China Repression at a High Mark." January 29, 2015. www
.hrw.org/news/2015/01/29/china-political-repression-high-mark, accessed August
18, 2015.

Kipling, Rudyard, and Thomas James Wise. Poem: "The White Man's Burden." New
York: Doubleday and McClure Company, *McClure's*, February 12, 1899.

Krastev, Ivan. "Why Poland Is Turning Away from the West." *New York Times*, December 11, 2015.

Krugman, Paul. "Does Greece Need More Austerity?" *New York Times*, June 19, 2015.

Kwarteng, Kwasi. "A Chinese Gold Standard?" *International New York Times*, July 25, 2014.

Leahy, William. *I Was There*. New York: Whittlesey House, 1950.

Lord, Russell, ed. *Democracy Reborn*. New York: Reynal & Hitchcock, 1944.

Lovett, Richard A. "Russia's Arctic Claim Backed by Rocks, Officials Say." *National
Geographic News*, September 21, 2007. http://news.nationalgeographic.com/
news/2007/09/070921-arctic-russia.html, accessed April 5, 2015.

McNamara, Robert S. "Forty Years after 13 Days." Arms Control Association, 2002.
www.armscontrol.org/act/2002_11/cubanmissile#mcnamara, accessed December 9, 2015.

Madison, James. *The Federalist: A Collection of Essays Written in Favour of the Constitution, As Agreed Upon by the Federal Convention, September 17, 1787*. New York:
J. and A. McLean, 1788.

Maier, Charles. *The Economics of Fascism and Nazism: In Search of Stability*. Cambridge:
Cambridge University Press, 1987.

Manchester, William. *American Caesar*. New York: Back Bay Books, Little, Brown and
Company, 1978.

Medina, Jennifer. "California Cuts Farmers' Share of Scant Water." *New York Times*,
June 12, 2015.

Mitchell, Alanna. "The Northwest Passage Thawed." *Globe and Mail* (Toronto), February 5, 2000.

Montgomery, Bernard. *A History of Warfare*. New York: The World Publishing Company, 1968.

Moscow Times. "Russian Defense Budget to Hit Record $81 Billion in 2015." October
16, 2014. www.themoscowtimes.com/business/article/russian-defense-budget-to
-hit-record-81bln-in-2015/509536.html, accessed April 24, 2015.

Moytl, Alexander John. "Ukraine: Merkel and Putin Go Nose to Nose." *Newsweek*, May
30, 2015.

Nathan, Andrew J. "The Tiananmen Papers." In *Tiananmen and After*, ed. Gideon Rose.
Tampa, FL: *Foreign Affairs*, June 11, 2014.

New York Times Editorial Board. "China's Obsolete Economic Strategy." January 9,
2016.

New York Times Editorial Board. "The Pakistan Nuclear Nightmare." November 8, 2015.

North Atlantic Treaty Organization. The North Atlantic Treaty. Washington, DC, April
4, 1949. www.nato.int/cps/en/natolive/official_texts_17120.htm, accessed May 6,
2015.

"Notes of Meeting of the Interim Committee, June 1, 1945." Harry S. Truman Library and Museum. www.trumanlibrary.org/whistlestop/study_collections/bomb/large/documents/pdfs/40.pdf,accessed August 30, 2015.

O'Dwyer, Gerald. "Nations Respond to Russian Buildup in Baltics." *Defense News*, April 12, 2015.

Paola, Admiral Giampaolo di. Speech to the Officers' Association's 50th Annual Symposium, NATO (Mons, Belgium: October 16, 2010). www.nato.int/cps/en/natohq/opinions_69910.htm?selectedLocale=en, accessed December 5, 2015.

Potter, E. B., ed. *Sea Power*. Annapolis, MD: Naval Institute Press, 1981.

Powell, Colin. *My American Journey*. New York: Ballantine Books, 1995.

Radchenko, Sergey. "Did Hiroshima Save Japan From Soviet Occupation?" *Foreign Policy*, August 5, 2015.

Ravindranath, Mohana. "Your Next Fitbit Should Detect Nuclear Bombs, DHS Hopes." *Defense One,* November 9, 2015. www.defenseone.com/technology/2015/11/your-next-fitbit-should-detect-nuclear-bombs-dhs-hopes/123512/?oref=d-river, accessed November 10, 2015.

Rinat, Zafrir. "Water, Water, Everywhere: Desalination Trumps Drought in Israel." *Haaretz* (Jerusalem), June 8, 2015.

Robinson, Andrew, ed. *The Scientists*. New York: Thames & Hudson, 2012.

Rogers, Paul. "California Drought." *San Jose Mercury News*, May 5, 2015.

Rosencrance, Richard N., and Steven E. Miller, eds. *The Next Great War?: The Roots of World War I and the Risk of U.S.-China Conflict*. Cambridge, MA: MIT Press, © 2014 Belfer Center for Science and International Affairs.

Rotter, Andrew J. *Hiroshima: The World's Bomb*. New York: Oxford University Press, 2008.

Russian News Room, April 14, 2015, http://news.russiannewsroom.com/details.aspx?item=12584, accessed April 14, 2015.

Scientific Panel of the Interim Committee on Nuclear Power. "Recommendations on the Immediate Use of Nuclear Weapons," June 16, 1945. US National Archives, Record Group 77, Records of the Office of the Chief of Engineers, Manhattan Engineer District, Harrison-Bundy File, Folder No. 76.

Stockholm International Peace Research Institute. "US Military Spending Falls, Increases in Eastern Europe, Middle East, Africa and Asia says SIPRI." April 13, 2015. www.sipri.org/media/pressreleases/2015/milex-april-2015, accessed April 24, 2015.

Schwabach, Aaron. "Diverting the Danube: The Gabcikovo-Nagymaros Dispute and International Freshwater Law." *Berkeley Journal of International Law* 14, no. 2 (1996). http://scholarship.law.berkeley.edu/bjil/vol14/iss2/2, accessed June 7, 2015.

Sharp, Todd L. "The Implications of Ice Melt on Arctic Security." *Defence Studies* 11, no. 2 (June 2011).

Sorely, Lewis. *A Better War*. New York: Harcourt Books, 1999.

Summers, Col. Harry G. Jr. *On Strategy*. Novato, CA: Presidio Press, 1982.

Szilard, Leo, et al. "A Petition to the President of the United States." July 17, 1945. US National Archives, Record Group 77, Records of the Chief of Engineers, Manhattan Engineer District, Harrison-Bundy File, folder No. 76.

Talbot, David. "Cyber-Espionage Nightmare." *MIT Technology Review*, June 10, 2015.

Telegraph. "North Pole: A Hotbed of Competing Claims." May 18, 2011. www .telegraph.co.uk/news/worldnews/europe/denmark/8520081/North-Pole-a -hotbed-of-competing-claims.html, accessed November 30, 2015.

Thomas, Evan. *Ike's Bluff.* New York: Little, Brown and Company, 2012.

Thucydides. *History of the Peloponnesian War.* Richard Crowley, trans., and M. I. Finley, ed. Baltimore: Penguin Classics, 1972.

Traynor, Ian. "The Language Divide at the Heart of a Split That Is Tearing Belgium Apart." *Guardian* (Brussels), May 8, 2010.

Truman, Harry S. Correspondence between Harry S. Truman and Samuel Cavert, August 11, 1945. "The Decision to Drop the Bomb, Official File," *Truman Papers,* Harry S. Truman Library and Museum, 1945.

United States Strategic Bombing Survey, 1 July 1946, Harry S. Truman Library and Museum.

US Department of Commerce, Bureau of the Census, Historical Statistics of the United States, Colonial Times to 1970, Part 2.

US Department of Defense. "The United States Military's Contribution to National Security." June 2015. www.defense.gov/news/newsarticle.aspx?id=121220, accessed July 12, 2015.

Will, George. "So What If Greece Leaves the European Union?" *Washington Post,* June 19, 2015.

Woods, Allan. "Relations Thaw after Flag 'Stunt.'" *Star News,* September 26, 2007. www.thestar.com/news/2007/09/26/relations_thaw_after_flag_stunt.html, accessed March 30, 2015.

Xu, Beina, and Eleanor Albert. "The Chinese Communist Party." Council on Foreign Relations, August 27, 2015. www.cfr.org/china/chinese-communist-party/p29443, accessed November 27, 2015.

Zaouguin, Chams Eddine. "Molenbeek, Belgium's 'Jihad Central.'" *New York Times,* November 19, 2015.

Zorzetto, Alicia. "Canadian Sovereignty at the Northwest Passage." Case Study No. 185. Washington, DC: Inventory of Conflict and Environment, American University, 2006. www1.american.edu/ted/ice/northwest-passage.htm, accessed May 15, 2015.

INDEX